Advance Uncorrected Proof

Author _____ Nicholas Daniloff _____

Title _____ TWO LIVES, ONE RUSSIA _____

_____

Probable Publication Date: Sept. 30, 1988

Probable Price: _____ $19.95 _____

☐ Illustrations
☐ Index
☐ Bibliography
☐ Appendix
☐ Glossary
☐ Other front or back matter

Sent by _____
☐ Publicity Department   ☐ Sales Department

Houghton Mifflin Co.

YESTERDAY'S RUSSIA, TODAY'S SOVIET UNION: in his long-awaited book, Nicholas Daniloff weaves a double narrative that vividly brings both worlds to life. One story describes the author's five-year search for his Russian heritage, a search inspired by an old family ring and a passionate curiosity about his great-great-grandfather's long prison sentence for revolutionary activities. Part treasure hunt, part odyssey, Daniloff's investigation into the life of Alexander Frolov paints a fascinating portrait of nineteenth-century Russia. The other story is as chilling as it is contemporary, for it provides a detailed account of Daniloff's arrest and imprisonment by the KGB in the fall of 1986. At the center of this dramatic, often harrowing story is Colonel Sergadeyev, the interrogator who was determined to prove that Daniloff was an American spy. Told in alternating chapters, the two stories come together in surprising ways, each illuminating and enriching the other.

At a time when Americans are especially curious about Gorbachev's Soviet Union, Nicholas Daniloff offers a unique and deeply personal book about his long experience with that still-mysterious nation. *Two Lives, One Russia* reads like a novel, but its twin stories are true, revealing, and always compelling.

Nicholas Daniloff is a contributing editor of *U.S. News & World Report* and a resident fellow at the Joan Shorenstein Barone Center on Press, Politics and Public Policy at the John F. Kennedy School of Government at Harvard University. He and his wife, Ruth, live in Cambridge, Massachusetts.

Two Lives, One Russia

Books by the Author

The Kremlin and the Cosmos
Two Lives, One Russia

Nicholas Daniloff

Two Lives, One Russia

Houghton Mifflin Company   Boston   1988

For my friends in Moscow, Soviet and American,
diggers of truth, preservers of memory,

and, most of all,

for Ruth

The diplomatic corps and Westerners in general have always been considered by this government, with its Byzantine spirit, and by Russia as a whole, as malevolent and jealous spies.

— The Marquis de Custine,
Russia, 1854

⌁ Acknowledgments

Without the help of friends, acquaintances, and officials in both the Soviet Union and the United States, this book would not have been written. Unfortunately, as a result of my arrest by the KGB, I was never able to say good-bye to many people in Moscow, let alone offer them my thanks. I hope they will understand.

I owe a great debt to all those Soviet citizens who are fighting to preserve an accurate record of their nation's history and who were willing to share information with me. They include historians, architects, archaeologists, and writers. In particular, I want to thank the descendants of Decembrists Nikolai Bestuzhev, Nikita Muravyov, Colonel Ivan Pavlo-Shveikovsky, and Dmitrii Zavalishin, who live in Leningrad, Moscow, and New York. Sergei Petrov, a photographer, and Alexander Kalugin, and engraver, both of Moscow, provided me with unique artistic help.

I would like to acknowledge the cooperation of the press department of the Soviet Foreign Ministry, without which my activities in the Soviet Union would have been impossible. Some of the officials who encouraged me were Valentin Kamenev, now Soviet consul-general in San Francisco but then deputy chief of the Foreign Ministry press department, Vladimir Mikoyan, Sergei Pechernikov, Yevgeny Petrusievich, and Alexander Voznikov. My appreciation goes, too, to Ludmilla B. Belova, director of the Museum of the History of the City of Leningrad; Yuri A. Ivanov, director of the Lenin Memorial Park at Shushenskoye; M. Kapran and his colleagues at the Chief Administration of the State Archives in Moscow; Vladimir A. Kovalev, director of the Martyanov Museum at Minusinsk; Ilya S. Zilbershtein, the discoverer of the Bestuzhev watercolors; and the personnel at the Pushkin Museum and the State Historical Museum.

In the United States, I took advantage of help from the Widener, Houghton, and Russian Research Center libraries at Harvard University, Cambridge, Massachusetts; the Hoover Institution library and archives, Stanford, California; and the Library of Congress, Washington, D.C. I would especially like to thank Hilja Kukk of the Hoover Library for her immense enthusiasm and help in digging out historial materials relating to both the Frolovs and the Danilovs. Special thanks, too, to Rober Stoddard of the Houghton Library at Harvard.

Needless to say, this book is much different from the one I started writing before my arrest in Moscow on August 30, 1986. It has acquired new dimensions, and I would like to thank scores of officials in Washington and friends and colleagues in the United States for helping during our family crisis and in the succeeding months. My thanks go especially to President Reagan and Secretary of State Shultz; to the members of the U.S. Senate and House of Representatives; to all the officials in the White House, National Security Council, State Department, and Justice Department who were involved in my case. In particular, I would like to express my gratitude to Armand Hammer for always being there in times of Soviet-American crises. My thanks also go to Senator Edward M. Kennedy as well as to Ray Benson, Phil Brown, Richard Combs, Greg Craig, Roger Daley, John Evans, Bill Freeman, Gregory Guroff, Bernadine Jocelyn, Bernard Kalb, Curt Kamman, Arthur Hartman, Elizabeth Keefer, David Major,

John Martin, Jack Matlock, Mark Palmer, Mark Parris, Stephen Rhinesmith, Rozanne Ridgway, Tom Simon, Abraham Sofaer, John Whitehead, Stanley Wolfe, and Warren Zimmermann.

My colleagues and many professional associations played a key role in focusing attention on the Zakharov-Daniloff affair and afterward shared with me many valuable insights. I wish to thank them all for their support. All the editorial employees of *U.S. News & World Report* signed a long telegram, which I read in Lefortovo prison. My considerable thanks to Mort Zuckerman and Dave Gergen, who understood the importance of "screaming," and to Carey English, Mary Ann Lowenstein, Douglas Stanglin, Henry Trewhitt, Jeff and Gretchen Trimble, Paul Vizza, and all the hard-working foreign correspondents in Moscow — American, European, and Japanese.

I especially want to thank family members: my children, Mandy and Caleb, for handling a difficult situation with grace; also thanks to my sister-in-law, Prinky Roberts, and her husband, Adam; to all of the Dykema family, to Jere and Annette most particularly; my sister, Aya; her husband, Walter, and my cousins Bill and Dick Burke.

Friends and relatives were unswervingly supportive, among them: Bill Beecher, Hal Berman, Bob Gillette, David Goldfarb and his family, Marshall Goldman, Rick Jacobs, Kevin Klose, Mort Kondracke, Marvin Lyons, Bill McSweeney, Evie and Mac Musser, Guy de Muyser, Esther Newburg, Al Remson, Norm Runnion, Bernie Shaw, Marshall Shulman, Howard Simons, Cathy and Jim Stone, Strobe Talbott, Phil Taubman and Felicity Barringer, Bob Toth, the Reverend Richard Unsworth and the Northfield–Mount Hermon School, Cyrus Vance, Jimmy Walker, John Wallach, and Paul Wheeler.

My editor at Houghton Mifflin, John Sterling, brought to this effort an architectural sense and an unbound enthusiasm that helped me weave past and present into what I hope is a cohesive whole. To Luise Erdmann, my thanks for her good humor and meticulous editing of every paragraph, line, and word. Thanks to Marvin Kalb, director of the Joan Shorenstein Barone Center for Press, Politics and Public Policy at the John F. Kennedy School of Government, Harvard University, for the book's title. the toughest editor of all turned out to be Ruth, who saved the enterprise more than once. How can I ever thank her enough?

To all my unnamed friends in Moscow whom I think of often but silently, I hope the day will come when I shall be able to recognize you with joy rather than trepidation.

Nicholas Daniloff
Vermont, Spring 1988

∽ *Illustrations*

✎ One

IT ALL BEGAN quietly enough. On Sunday morning, August 24, 1986, my wife, Ruth, and I were sitting at the kitchen table in our apartment in Moscow, drinking coffee, listening to the eight o'clock broadcast of the BBC. It looked like a fine day, and we had opened the door to the balcony, letting in the warming air and the sound of traffic on Leninsky Prospekt, six floors below.

I fiddled with the dial on the short-wave radio, trying to get the clipped British voice to come in more clearly. A moment later, I heard the announcer say something about the arrest, in New York, of a Soviet employee of the United Nations on charges of espionage. He gave the man's name, but I missed it because Zeus, our brown and white fox terrier, was barking.

The report from New York did set off a small alarm. I recalled that when the United States had arrested Soviet citizens before, the Soviet Union had quickly retaliated by arresting U.S. citizens. I also knew the KGB's practice of moving against a correspondent, scholar, or businessman in the last days of an assignment, usually once the successor was in place. That way the KGB could strike without precipitating a round of reprisals. Diplomat fallout was kept to a minimum, and the new man in Moscow was suitably intimidated.

I knew all this, but the story of the arrest and its possible implications quickly receded; there were so many last-minute matters to deal with. After five years in Moscow as bureau chief of *U.S. News and World Report,* I was finally returning home. In another week — once I could pack everything and help get my replacement, Jeff Trimble, settled — Ruth and I would leave for three weeks of travel through the Soviet Union. I was doing research on the life of my great-great-grandfather, and we wanted to see for ourselves some of the places where he had lived so many years earlier. After the trip, we would return to Moscow, take the overnight train to Finland, and fly from there to the States. In the fall we would move to Vermont, where I planned to take a year off and write a book about my ancestor.

We were looking forward to our return to America, yet we hated to leave the Soviet Union. Moscow had been home for Ruth and me and for our two children, twenty-three-year-old Miranda — Mandy — and sixteen-year-old Caleb, who were both about to fly back directly after spending the summer with us. We had made many Soviet friends, and I wondered whether we would ever see them again. I would also miss the excitement of working in the capital of the other great superpower, and I doubted that I would ever find another assignment as rewarding — or as tough. The years in Moscow had also been good professionally for Ruth, a free-lance journalist, who had written many articles for American magazines.

I spent that day at the office, just one floor up from our apartment, clearing out my desk, doing my final expense account, and explaining to Jeff the ins and outs of running a one-man news operation in a country where everything takes twice as long to do as elsewhere. Finally, around 9:00 P.M., I went back down to the apartment and collapsed on my bed, exhausted from the long day.

A few minutes later the telephone rang. Caleb answered and then handed me the receiver.

"Hello, this is Frunze." The voice was familiar: it was Misha. At home, we called him "Misha from Frunze," to distinguish him from half a dozen other Mishas we knew. Few Soviets identify themselves on the telephone by their family names, as that would make it too easy for the KGB's eavesdropping devices. In fact, Soviet acquaintances rarely identify themselves at all, leaving you to guess who is at the other end of the line.

"Where are you?" I asked. I was pleased to hear from Misha, for I wanted to say good-bye and give him some books he had asked for.

"I'm at the airport, on my way back to Frunze. But I'll be back next weekend and I'd like to see you."

"Fine," I replied, relieved that I did not have to go out that evening. "Give me a call. I've got something for you."

As it turned out, Misha had something for me, too.

๛ ๛ ๛

I had first met Misha — Mikhail Luzin — more than four years earlier, in March 1982, in a restaurant in Frunze. I was on assignment to the Muslim republic of Kirghizia, in Soviet Central Asia, with my colleague Jim Gallagher of the *Chicago Tribune*. The region was of particular interest to journalists because of its high birth rate; its population threatened to outnumber that of European Russia by the year 2000. Also, Kirghizia was close to Afghanistan, and we hoped to discover how the Muslim population in the Soviet Union viewed the guerrilla war, then in its third year.

We were staying at the Ala-Too Hotel, a pretentious, unimaginative place. The evening of our arrival, we went down for a late dinner. The dining room was like most Soviet restaurants that cater to foreigners. First to be seated in the cavernous room were the overseas visitors, with their hard currency. The rest of

the diners that evening appeared to be townspeople, and I was
sure they had waited in line for hours for the chance to eat a
better- than-average meal, dance to the deafening band, and watch
or perhaps even talk to foreigners.

As we were finishing our meal, a tall young man at the next
table left his companions and approached us. His features were
unmistakably Russian: the high, broad cheekbones, the slightly
ruddy complexion, the blond hair. His teeth were unusually white
and straight; Soviet dentistry is decades behind that in the United
States.

"May I join you? I heard you speaking English." Offering his
hand, he introduced himself: "My name is Misha."

He was not dressed in the flashy clothes preferred by black
marketeers. Nor did he have the overconfident furtiveness typical
of the KGB types who hang around hotels frequented by foreigners. Still, Jim and I were cautious, because in the Soviet Union
chance meetings with strangers are always suspect. At the American embassy in Moscow, in fact, suspicion becomes outright
paranoia. The embassy's security officers automatically assume
that every Soviet who associates with a foreigner is a potential
KGB agent; diplomats are instructed to venture out only in pairs
and to report each contact with a citizen. But correspondents are
in a different position. To cover the Soviet Union they must take
risks; they cannot rely solely on official briefings and newspaper
reports. They must dig below the surface, develop their own,
unoffocial sources wherever possible, and immerse themselves in
Soviet life.

Jim and I exchanged a glance and a nod. Misha looked okay,
so we invited him to sit down. We ordered a bottle of champagne — a regular part of Soviet social life, along with cognac
and vodka. As we sipped our drinks, Misha told us he was a
fourth-year student in the philological department of Frunze University. Like so many young Soviets who are deprived of information about the West, he was immensely curious about the
United States, and American literature in particular. He longed

for books and magazines, and listened to the Voice of America for rock music and news of the latest Western fads. Our conversation ranged over a host of politcal issues, from the troubles in Poland to the Soviet Union's relations with China, which in Kirghizia lies to the south, just beyond the Tien Shan mountains.

Since we were particularly interested in Afghanistan, and since Misha was a young man of military age, he was an ideal person to question. Only recently, Marshal Nikolai Ogarkov, chief of the Soviet General Staff, had publicly complained that many young men were developing pacifist tendencies. Misha acknowledged a certain restlessness and boredom among his university friends, and said that some students he knew were taking drugs. He described poppy-growing near Kirghizia's Lake Issyk-Kul and the black market trade in pot with Moscow. A joint, he said, would bring one ruble on the streets of the capital.

"Our life is so boring that some people try to make it more interesting with narcotics. They aren't exactly imitating Western ways, but they think they're giving meaning to their lives."

But when discussing the Afghan war itself, Misha's views were more orthodox. He gave us the party line: "The Afghan government invited us in to help them. Our military is very strong, and that's what counts. In Afghanistan we will win. We will crush them. Our people are very patriotic and we believe in our government."

Despite his clear acceptance of the Soviet position, there was something very likable about Misha, and I found him a refreshing change from Moscow's jaded intellectuals. He still believed in the Soviet system, yet he was critical: he did not seem to accept the propaganda blindly. He had tried to be honest with two American newsmen who bombarded him with questions. If the Soviet Union was to change for the better, I thought, it needed more Mishas.

Misha got up to leave, and Jim and I agreed to meet him and his friends the following day for a tour of the city. Later, as Jim and I walked back to our rooms, we asked the obvious question:

Was Misha KGB? We were sure our presence in Frunze had been noted; it was more than possible that the KGB would try to discover our purpose there. But our instinct said that Misha wasn't a plant. KGB agents were usually glib and self-assured, whereas Misha seemed naive and a bit uncertain. He simply wasn't the type.

During our three days in Frunze, we saw Misha and his pals several times. They were well-informed guides, explaining that Frunze was once a Russian imperial outpost called Pishpek. It was renamed Frunze after the local Red commander who succeeded Leon Trotsky as defense minister in 1925. The central promenade, lined with tall trees on either side, was called Brodwei, or Broadway, by the citizens.

After our visit in Frunze, Misha disappeared from my life for quite some time. Then, in March 1984, he surprised me with a telephone call: he was passing through Moscow, he said, pursuing his hope of getting into the university. Ruth and I invited him over for dinner. Fortunately, we did not live in a diplomatic ghetto — one of those dreary neighborhoods that is inhabited only by foreigners and is protected by Soviet police guards — so our Societ friends could visit us more or less freely.

Within a few minutes of our greeting, I saw that Misha had changed. He was no longer the excitable young man Jim and I had met two years earlier. He seemed very ill at ease, as if unsure of my continued interest in him. He presented Ruth with a native hat from Kirghizia and insisted on taking his shoes off in order to protect our carpets. Sitting at our kitchen table, he told us that he was currently working at the Institute for Automatic Devices in Frunze. He said his job was in the unclassified section, dealing with mining equipment. He explained that he had finished his university studies in June 1983 and had spent three months on active duty as a reserve lieutenant. "I really wanted to come to Moscow University to continue my work in philology," he said, "but the point was made to me that I had better get a job. I'm worried that I could be called up for Afghanistan. I really want to avoid that."

Misha poked at the pepperoni pizza we served him, barely eating anything. He seemed intimidated and suddenly shy. That didn't surprise me: Ruth and I had often seen such a reaction among Caleb's Russian friends. By American standards, our apartment was far from luxurious — we had a living room, a kitchen, and two bedrooms — but compared to the cramped living conditions of most Soviets, it was almost palatial. A visit to a foreigner's apartment and the offer of foreign food so inhibited some Russians that they sometimes refused to eat at all.

When our conversation returned to the subject of Afghanistan, Misha shook his head and appeared genuinely disturbed.

"In Frunze," he said, "you can see the coffins come in weekly, often on Saturdays. And the military has its own special cemeteries where the young men are buried."

He fell silent. Then, with obvious emotion, he told us what was really bothering him: he had recently attended the funeral of a school friend. "It was terrible. He was only twenty-two and left a wife and a small child. He had been in Afghanistan for just one week before he was killed. It was lack of experience — he was shot from ambush."

As soon as he finished eating, Misha went to the entrance hall, where he had left his briefcase. Without saying a word, he opened it and drew out a cheap, blue photograph album. He silently turned the pages, and soon I became intrigued. A crude scrapbook put together by recruits in Afghanistan, it contained a number of poems and black-and-white snapshots of raw-faced Soviet soldiers posing with antitank guns and armored personnel carriers. These were simple Ru-sian boys whose parents didn't have enough pull to keep their sons out of the military. I knew of families in Moscow who took up a collection among friends and relatives, hoping to put together the 800 rubles (about $1,100) needed to bribe the army doctor to certify their son unfit for service.

More interesting than the album's pictures, however, were the poems interspersed among the thick pages. The verses began amusingly enough, but as they progressed, a sad note crept in. They spoke of longing for girlfriends and home; they grieved for teenage comrades already lost to the war. It occurred to me that these poems might well be published as part of a magazine article. How better to illustrate the similarities between Afghanistan and Vietnam than with the simple words of these young Soviet recruits? But the article would need pictures, and the quality of the photographs was so poor that they would probably not be acceptable to my magazine's picture department.

I drove Misha back to his hotel that night through a light snow. During the ride, I had an idea. If Misha could obtain a better selection of pictures, the article might be feasible. I asked him if there was any chance he could get me some good photographs of the graves of soldiers killed in Afghanistan — perhaps even one of his friend's grave. Misha nodded. "I'll see what I can do."

I cautioned him as we parted: "Be careful. Don't do anything to get yourself into trouble."

Driving home that night, I worried for Misha. Soviets are sometimes so eager to please foreigners — either out of friendship or in hopes of obtaining foreign goods — that they take risks, not realizing that one suspicious action could land them in trouble. But I worried for myself a bit, too. It was one thing to accept information passed to my by Soviet citizens; it was riskier, however, to actively solicit their help. Again I wondered if Misha could be working for the KGB. Had he been sent to see me? Was that why he'd been so edgy? No, it wasn't possible. His distress was genuine; the war in Afghanistan deeply upset him. I was certain he had come on his own.

Six months later, Misha called again. He was passing through Moscow on his way to Leningrad. This time we invited him to see *One Flew over the Cuckoo's Nest* on our VCR. Milos Forman's film about the inmates of a mental hopsital striking for freedom left him silent and subdued. Before he left, Misha gave me an envelope of photographs. Later that evening, I opened the envelope: Instead of the soldiers' graves I had requested, there were about six black-and-white shots of soldiers in Afghanistan. Again their quality and composition were poor. Disappointed, I placed them in my Afghan file; there was no point in even bothering to send them to the States.

Another year passed, and it was a warm summer day in June 1985 when Misha called again. We mat at the Leninsky Prospekt metro station, about a ten-minute walk from our apartment. Even the old grandmothers, or *babushki*, had shed their winter coats. We decided to go for a walk by the river in Lenin Hills. As we passed under a railway bridge, Misha said that he had brought some more photographs and handed me a sealed envelope. "Take a look at them and see if they are of any use to you."

As we said good-bye a few minutes later, Misha asked if I could get him some of Stephen King's books. He said he wanted to write an academic paper on the horror story writer which would prove that American publishing is crassly commercial and exploitative. Although he professed to be shocked by King's writing, I suspect he secretly enjoyed the horror and the sex. Misha specifically asked me not to mail the books to him, since he did not want the authorities to know he was receiving packages from a foreigner.

Back at the office, I opened Misha's package. It contained a few black-and-white photographs, including a shot of a mustachioed soldier driving an open Red Cross jeep. There were also several rolls of 35-millimeter negatives. I examined them on our light table under a loupe. Like those in the scrapbook, the pictures were amateur snapshots that soldiers might send home: poses of the men next to various pieces of military equipment. One picture showed a group of officers looking through large binoculars on a tripod, as if observing maneuvers of some kind. There was also a series of wall maps showing large swaths of Afghan territory around Kabul and Herat, extending to the Pakistan border and beyond to Peshawar. Some of the negatives were light-struck, others were out of focus. And there was no clear indication of when they had been taken; the film carried the dates 1981 and 1983. I judged that the shots were probably a year and a half old, certainly no more recent than early 1984.

The maps made me a little nervous. At one time they might have been classified, though they were now probably too old to be of any military importance. I was concerned that Misha — whom I had come to trust as a friend — might be taking too great a risk in passing the maps to me. And they put me in a ticklish position, too: if the KGB ever searched my office (not at all imposible), they could use the maps against me in whatever way they pleased. In July, just to be safe, I found a diplomatic traveler going to the West and dispatched the collection to my office in Washington. I might have been able to take the pictures out myself, but since I didn't have diplomatic immunity, I wanted to avoid the risk of a customs search.

On October 17, 1985, a few weeks after we returned from a vacation in the States, Misha came back to Moscow. Again, we went for a long walk along the Moskva River, trudging up to the spot in the Lenin Hills park where two famous nineteenth-century dissidents, Alexander Herzen and Nikolai Ogaryov, pledged to wage a lifelong struggle against the czarist autocracy.

Misha said that his institute had sent him to Moscow to get a Xerox machine mended. This was not unusual: in a country plagued by widespread shortages, it was often necessary to dispatch an employee thousands of miles to the capital to get something fixed or find a spare part. Misha again expressed his frustration that he was not able to get into Moscow University. "But at least I get regular trips here with my job," he said.

Misha then asked about the Stephen King novels, and I told him that several were coming from the States by mail. "I could mail them on to you," I said, ignoring his earlier injunction.

"No, don't do that. It might look fishy. I'll be coming back to Moscow soon, anyway. I'll get them then."

Before we parted, I asked Misha if he could clip some of the Frunze newspapers, which our office did not receive. I was especially interested in articles concerning Mikhail Gorbachev's new policies. How were they being implemented in the provinces? How much approval was there? How much resistance? I had asked several other Soviet friends to do the same in three or four other provincial cities.

Misha and I walked out of the park, agreeing to meet the next evening by the subway station at 6:00 P.M. I would bring him some English magazines and paperbacks, and we would continue our conversation. But Misha never appeared, nor did he telephone. Several weeks later I received the novels. By then I knew I wouldn't be in the Soviet Union much longer; what would I do with the books if I didn't see Misha again?

✺ ✺ ✺

The days following Misha's call of August 24 were so busy that I almost forgot his promise to return. The whole week had been thrown out of joint by a ridiculous confrontation with Soviet customs. The Finnish moving company that was shipping our belongings had driven our goods out to the customs' southeast checkpoint at Butovo for inspection. Usually the Finnish driver would slip the inspector a bottle of vodka, and the goods would clear easily. Not this time.

We were not living in Gorbachev's anticorruption era. The customs inspector, working *po-novomu,* in the new style, insisted on inspecting all but one of our eighty-six cases of household goods, my personal diaries and notes, thousands of photographic slides, and several cartons of Soviet books. In the course of two and a half days of scrutiny, all done in our presence, the conscientious official dug out several items — my father's gold fob watch, some pieces of junk jewelry — that we had neglected to declare when we entered the country, and a number of other small gifts from Soviet friends. A special commission from the Ministry of Culture was convened to assess the value of these items. By the end of three days of bureaucratic nitpicking, I longed for the good old corrupt days of Leonid Brezhnev.

Misha — this time true to his word — called me on Friday. He asked to see me that evening, but I put him off. That afternoon I had to drive Mandy to the airport to catch a plane to Paris and I was still far behind in my work. I suggested that we meet the following day, August 30, at 11:00 A.M.

"Fine," he said. "Our usual place."

Shortly after breakfast the next morning, I left the apartment for my meeting with Misha. First, I stopped by the office and went out on the balcony with Jeff Trimble. We all assumed the office itself was bugged, and I wanted to tell Jeff about Misha. I said that I would try to bring Misha back to the office for lunch, for I hoped he would become a good source for Jeff, just as he had been for me.

Heading toward the Leninsky Prospekt metro station, I felt a touch of fall in the air. The leaves were yellowing, and since it was the weekend, shoppers crowded the streets. The line at the shoe store stretched around the corner of the apartment building and into the next block. Outside the metro, a group of teenagers jostled one another in front of the ice cream kiosk while the large, white-coated saleswoman yelled at them.

Misha was about ten minutes late. He waved cheerfully as he emerged through the doors of the station.

"You're getting unreliable," I quipped as we shook hands. "Today you're late. Last time you didn't show up at all!"

He must have sensed my irritation, for he apologized profusely. "Excuse me. I know I should've been there last time. But, you know, I got involved with friends, we drank a little, and everything got away from me."

We decided to take our usual route along the river. As we walked, I told Misha that this would probably be our last meeting, because I was returning to the States.

"You're leaving?" Misha seemed surprised.

"I'm afraid so. I've been here for five years, longer than most correspondents. If you remain in one place too long, you begin to take all sorts of things for granted, which does not make for good reporting. You need a fresh eye."

Misha was silent.

"By the way, would you like to meet my successor? He's a good guy, about your age."

Misha hesitated and then said, "Let me think it over. We'll talk about it later."

His reluctance to meet Jeff did not surprise me. Meeting foreign correspondents can bring trouble, and of course personal relationships are not easily transferred, anyway.

I glanced at the muddy river as it flowed under the two-tier metro bridge. Several people were in the water, despite the No Swinning signs. The swimmers seemed unconcerned as a militiaman looked on, making no attempt to stop them. This was typical: the Soviet Union is a nation of complicated rules and regulations that no one keeps if he can possibly get away with it.

I turned our conversation to drug abuse, explaining to Misha that Jeff and I had to produce an article on the subject for the next week's magazine. As always, Misha responded volubly. Drugs, he said, were becoming more and more of a problem in the Soviet Union, for Gorbachev's campaign to eradicate alcoholism was driving many people to experiment with other substances.

Then he asked abruptly, "What did you do with those pictures I gave you the last time?"

"I sent them all to my office. Why do you ask? Do you want them back?" I didn't want to tell him that due to their indifferent quality they remained, unpublished, in the magazine's photo archives in Washington. Later, of course, I realized the significance of his remark.

"Oh, no. I was just wondering." He paused, then tapped his coat pocket. "By the way, you asked if I could clip the Frunze newspapers. I've brought you a present. I included some photographs, too."

We approached a clapboard A-frame shelter on one of the grassy slopes and sat down on the bench inside. I removed the King novels from the white plastic bag and handed them to Misha. He seemed pleased. Then he pulled a small brown bag from his inner pocket and drew out a package about the size of a book. It was made out of black photographic wrapping paper, and was stapled at each end.

Misha's bag was a little small for the seven novels. I offered him mine, but he refused it. "That's all right. It'll be better if I squeeze them all into this bag." Misha looked at his watch and got up. He explained that he was late and had to rush off.

I said that I might return the following March to finish some research for a book I was writing. "I'll send you a postcard signed Nik." Remembering his caution about the mail, I added, "Maybe I'll sign it Nik Ogaryov," referring to the dissident whose monument we had visited, but I thought better of it almost immediately. "Hell, no! Why be so secretive and use a false name? After all, I've got nothing to hide."

Misha shrugged his shoulders and checked his watch again. "I'm philosophical," he said. "I do what I have to do to survive. Now I must run." At the time, I thought it a sad comment.

"You don't want to come by the office and meet the new man?" I asked.

"No," he replied, holding out his hand. "I don't have much time and I really must go. I have to leave Moscow tomorrow."

"Then I'll take you to the metro," I said.

"I'm going to walk along the embankment and over the bridge to the Sportivnaya station. It's a longish way, and I'm in a hurry now."

I wondered why he was going to such a distant metro stop instead of Leninsky Prospekt, which he always used on his visits.

"Then I'll walk with you along the embankment."

"No, really, there's no need," Misha said, shaking off my gesture and holding out his hand once again.

I did not press further, and Misha strode off toward the river.

I took the exit road that begins at the embankment and leads up and out of the park, bending to the right. In seconds, Misha was out of sight.

I walked slowly along the narrow road toward Ulitsa Kosygina, once known as Sparrow Boulevard. I was sorry to say good-bye to Misha and wished he hadn't been in such a rush. Would I ever see him again? Almost certainly not.

I passed the covered escalator on my right, which went up the hill from the Lenin Hills subway to the boulevard. I very nearly decided to take the escalator but wasn't sure whether it was working. I walked slowly, enjoying the pleasant day. In my right hand, I carried the white plastic bag containing the unopened package from Misha.

Halfway up the hill, the exit road divides. The right fork curves steadily toward the boulevard; the left fork continues straight for about a hundred yards before it, too, divides. The second, leftmost branch doubles back to the embankment where Misha was presumably striding along. I would not follow Misha; instead, I would continue along the middle branch, which narrows to an uneven path marred by potholes and puddles. To the left of the path was the spot where an old woman who lived in our apartment block had buried her dog under a bush and planted flowers on its grave. She had also turned several milk cartons into bird feeders and hung them from the branches overhead. At the end, I would climb up an iron and wooden staircase that comes out near the prime minister's mansion on the boulevard. It was all very familiar to me because of my morning walks with Zeus — indeed, we had been there that very morning.

As I approached the first split in the road, I noticed two vehicles descending toward me. One was a large white autombile with red diplomatic license plates. The other was a nondescript white van.

It struck me as odd to see cars in the park. This road was rarely used by private vehicles, although dump trucks frequently rumbled over it on their way to the construction site at the Lenin

Hills Metro station, which was under repair. I was especially puzzled by the diplomatic car. It reached the point where the road divides, made a U-turn into the left branch, and disappeared in the direction Misha had taken.

This looks suspicious, I thought. I wonder how many "vigilant" Soviet citizens are going to rush to their phones to report the presence of a strange car in their midst?

I watched as the white van, too, approached the divide and began making the same turn as the first car. At this point, I was standing exactly where the road splits. I glanced at my watch. It was 12:20 P.M.; I had been walking a little more than five minutes since leaving Misha. I would be home in a quarter of an hour for lunch with Jeff. Ruth and I would spend the afternoon packing, and — suddenly, my thoughts came to a halt. The van was pulling over right next to me. Startled, I stepped to one side.

The van stopped, and its sliding door opened abruptly. Some half a dozen men, wearing ordinary street clothes, emerged and seemed to glide toward me. To my right, a heavyset man in a windbreaker eyed me warily. He advanced slowly, as if pulled by some hidden force, his face paralyzed by tension. To my left, another figure approached silently. Across from me, a third man began filming the scene with a videocamera. Next to him, a fourth man took photographs.

Clearly, these men were about to kidnap someone. Yet I, the apparent victim, felt for a moment like a disembodied presence observing the operation from afar. It seemed like a dream: it couldn't really be happening to me. But the heavyset man on my right was already throwing me forward against the van, pinning me down. He pulled my arms behind my back and snapped handcuffs on my wrists. No one spoke a word. It was over so fast that I never dropped the white plastic bag. And the men had moved so quickly, with such precision, that it took me a moment to understand what had happened: I had just been arrested by the KGB.

∾ Two

I WENT LIMP. I made a split-second decision not to resist — and not to say anything. It was more an emotional response than an intellectual one. The men surrounding me said nothing; they offered no explanation, produced no identification. They waved no arrest warrant because they had none and needed none.

As the men hustled me into the van and slammed the door shut, I glimpsed the two other agents outside.

"There was a second man," one shouted to the other. "Quick! He went that way!"

What an odd remark, I thought, for Misha had been out of sight for at least five minutes. Were they going to arrest Misha? Or did they simply want me to think that? Or was Misha part of a carefully orchestrated plan? Had he carrying a radio transmitter to guide the KGB squad?

The van was moving quickly along the exit road toward the boulevard. The driver gunned the engine as we sped past the mansion being built for General Secretary Gorbachev, next to the prime minister's house.

The driver made a fast U-turn to point the van down the hill past my apartment building, through the tunnel by the immense titanium monument to Yuri Gagarin, the first man in space, onto Leninsky Prospekt and, right, onto the southern section of the Garden Ring.

I felt totally helpless. Wedged between two guards on the middle seat, I was held rigidly upright. In the front seat, the cameraman kept his Panasonic minicam churning away. The still photographer sat in the back, occasionally snapping pictures.

The man on my right patted my trouser legs for weapons. Really, this was absurd! He asked if the plastic bag behind me was digging into my back — the first indication that he had any feelings. On my left, the man was fishing in my trouser pocket. He found my brown leather wallet and extracted a laminated Foreign Ministry press card.

"My God!" he exclaimed. "A foreigner!" His surprise was understandable. Foreigners in the USSR are usually treated with greater respect than Soviet citizens. To bungle the arrest of a foreigner would be trouble. But they did not seem to be bungling mine.

I struggled to gather my thoughts. Sunday's BBC broadcast came into focus, and I realized my arrest was in retaliation for the incident in New York. But I couldn't recall the facts of that case, not even the name of the man who had been arrested. And something didn't make sense: Why would the United States arrest a Soviet spy and spoil the atmosphere just when the two superpowers were edging toward a summit meeting?

I tried to think of parallels to my predicament, and at once I recalled the arrest of Frederick Barghoorn, in 1963, which I had covered for U.P.I. The Yale professor had been standing outside the Metropole Hotel in Moscow the night before he was to leave the Soviet Union. Someone thrust a roll of newspapers containing secret documents into his hand, and the KGB seized him moments later. He became a hostage for Igor Ivanov, a Soviet chauffeur without diplomatic immunity, who had been arrested in New York earlier as a spy. Barghoorn was thrown into Lubyanka prison and held incommunicado until, two weeks later, President Kennedy made it clear that he had no connection with U.S. intelligence.

The case of Robert Toth of the *Los Angeles Times* was somewhat different and perhaps more like mine. In June 1977, the KGB was preparing an espionage case against Anatoly (Nathan) Shcharansky and wanted to incriminate him. They lured Toth, who was a close friend of Shcharansky's, onto a street to meet a scientist. This man, whom Toth already knew, passed him some secret materials. Toth, who was also at the end of his assignment in Moscow, was instantly arrested. He was ordered to report to Lefortovo prison for interrogation about Shcharansky every day for five days and then was released. A more recent case concerned Allison Smale, of the Associated Press. In 1983, she was questioned by the KGB for three days as a prosecution witness in the case of a would-be Soviet defector. None of these three Americans had been held very long; how soon would I be set free?

The van swung onto Radio Street, and I noticed through the front window that a black Volga sedan, the kind often used the the KGB, was immediately ahead of us. Its blue dome was not flashing, so I guessed that it might be a radio car, signaling ahead that we were coming.

Working in Moscow, a foreign correspondent is always aware of the KGB security police. The Second Chief Directorate — KGB counterintelligence — routinely monitors diplomats, journalists, businessmen, and students. That's their job; the FBI does the same to Soviet residents in the United States.

I had to assume that the KGB knew more about me than most of my colleagues did. They, of all people, should know I was not a spy. They bugged our apartment; they listened in on our telephone conversations. If necessary, they could monitor a table in a restaurant or a train in which I was traveling. A small device hidden on my car could tell them where I was at any time. When I journeyed about the Soviet Union, they checked me in and out of hotels, airports, and train stations. Ruth and I accepted their attention as a part of being journalists in Moscow. Occasionally, however, it was more than a simple nuisance.

One of the most blatant KGB intrusions into our life occurred when we were on vacation in New Hampshire in the summer of 1982. Two Soviet friends, who were looking after Zeus and our plants, were summoned to the 114th police station. At the same time, KGB officers entered and searched our apartment with the help of the maid, who was sworn to secrecy. As they sometimes do, the KGB men purposely left their signature: they took fourteen cans of beer from the refrigerator and left the toilets unflushed. So while the KGB was never far from our consciousness, this little excursion was already more serious than any I had previously experienced.

As the van bumped over the cobbles, I became more and more apprehensive. Was I going to be held and questioned for hours? Was I going to be released at night, like Toth? Was I going to be drugged?

There had been several instances of drugging. Two of my own predecessors had been drugged by the KGB in separate incidents eighteen years apart. The first one happened in the summer of 1961 to Aline Mosby, the correspondent for United Press International, whom I was replacing. She went to lunch with a Soviet friend in a downtown restaurant, and her companion pressed a glass of champagne on her. Although it tasted strange, she emptied the glass. Within minutes she was incapacitated: her eyes rolled spasmodically, and her limbs wobbled uncontrollably. A photographer appeared from nowhere to capture her in this state. And in 1979 Robin Knight, the Moscow correspondent for *U.S. News and World Report,* was drugged by the KGB just as he, too, was nearing the end of his assignment. He had made himself unpopular with Soviet officialdom because of his hard-hitting articles about Soviet life. Visiting Tashkent, he and his wife, Jean, were invited to an Uzbek teahouse by one of their Soviet guides. After several glasses of vodka, Robin passed out and remained unconscious for fifteen hours. Again, a photographer appeared and snapped his picture. But both Mosby and Knight refused to be intimidated; they insisted on completing their Moscow assignments to the very last day.

The van veered into Energy Street and stopped before number 3A. I was ordered out and repeatedly photographed to show the handcuffs and the bag in my hands behind my back. I had no idea what was going on; in fact, we had arrived at Lefortovo prison, where many well-known dissidents like Alexander Solzhenitsyn and Yuri Orlov had been held.

My captors ordered me back into the van, and we drove around the corner to the vehicle entrance, marked by a circular, red and white No Entry sign. The van drove through an outer gate toward a yellow stucco wall. A large brown metal door opened, and we proceeded into a kind of sluice gate.Once the street door was closed, a second, inner door slid open. The van moved into a courtyard and stopped.

The men pushed me out, then marched me at a fast clip into the building. Like most Soviet office buildings, it was sparsely furnished and smelled slightly of cheap floor polish and disinfectant. We climbed a flight of stairs to the second floor and hustled down a corridor covered by a red runner. We passed a large bulletin board decorated with photographs of outstanding KGB men, turned left around a corner, and didn't stop until we reached Room 215.

My heart was pounding, my head ached with tension. What next? I had heard many frightening stories of Soviet prisons and their unsanitary conditions, terrible overcrowding, and minimal food. Former prisoners had told me that the worst moment was being transferred from one prison to another in overheated boxcars with no toilet facilities. I remembered, too, that Newcomb Mott, a young American who crossed illegally into the Soviet Union from Norway in 1965, had died mysteriously on a prison train.

The door opened. Room 215 was a plain office, with windows giving out onto the inner court. It seemed especially spartan: there were no deocrations on the grayish-brown walls save a Soviet emblem and a clock. There wasn't even a portrait of Lenin, which is usually mandatory in any Soviet office.

Two men stood in the middle of the room. One was a young man with a sallow complexion, apparently an assistant. His superior was a tall, imposing figure in his late fifties or early sixties, wearing a well-cut dark gray suit. He had rather refined features, high cheekbones, and black, bushy eyebrows. His black hair, flecked with a few strands of gray, was combed straight back with no part. He walked stiffly toward me, pinning me with his dark eyes.

Ordering the handcuffs removed, he then spoke to his team of kidnappers: "*Vy svobodnye.* You are free." The words sent a shiver through me because I was anything but free. My one thought was: control. Don't show how scared you are; control yourself. But I knew only too well how completely vulnerable I was. I caught sight of the clock, on the wall between the two windows; it read 12:50 P.M.

Turning to me, this senior KGB officer said solemnly in Russian, "You have been arrested on suspicion of espionage. I am the person who ordered your arrest."

I indicated that I understood, but remained silent.

After a pause, the officer ordered, "Bring in the witnesses." Another KGB officer in am imitation leather jacket led two Soviet citizens into the room. They sat down at a long table that extended halfway across the room from the investigator's desk, which was on the left. The KGB often uses their trainees as witnesses, but these people looked as if they had been summoned off the street. One was a middle-aged woman who might have been doing her Saturday shopping. The other was an athletic-looking young man, about thirty-five, wearing a sports jacket.

They sat silently at the table as the investigator grasped my white plastic bag and drew out Misha's black package. The photographer, who was recording the scene, stood facing me from behind the two witnesses.

The officer described the package to the witnesses, noting its size, color, and staple closures. Then he carefully opened one end and shook out the contents: the clippings from the Frunze newspapers, dated November 1985; some negatives; and two charts.

"And what have we here?" he exclaimed dramatically, as though trying to impress the witnesses. "Negatives, black-and-white photographs, maps!" He placed one photograph before me which showed a mustachioed soldier driving a Red Cross jeep. "I daresay you've seen that one before!"

I cringed inwardly but said nothing. The picture was identical to the one Misha had given me a year earlier. The officer's remark meant that the KGB knew all about Misha's relations with me, going way back, and it was unlikely that they had learned it all in the last hour.

The officer acted as if he already knew everything about the package. So Misha must have been working with the KGB. Had that been true? From the very beginning? Or had he been recruited later on? I could imagine how it might have happened. One day a KGB agent approaches him and says, "We know that you have been seeing a foreign correspondent in Moscow. We have reason to believe that he is not what you think he is. We would be grateful if you would help us." As a young man just starting out, Misha would know that to refuse would be to invite the KGB to block his plans for a career: massive police power can force decent individuals into indecent actions. Misha was a decent man, but above all he was a realist.

"And what are these?" The officer held several negatives up to the light which showed charts thumbtacked to a wall. I looked at them, too, but they were overexposed, and without a magnifying glass it was impossible to determine their contents.

Finally, he turned to the folded maps, which I had never seen before. "Two military maps, marked Secret." He began his description of the negatives. "The first one shows part of Afghanistan and has handwritten markings on it, symbols noting the deployment of troop formations. And the second is a hand-drawn diagram of a region indicating where military equipment is located. The map contains a code with a variety of names — Abakan, Shushenskoye . . ."

Shushenskoye! I couldn't believe my ears; even today, it seems incredible that I heard that name in Lefortovo. Every Soviet citizen knows that it is the Siberian village where Vladimir Lenin, the father of the Russian Revolution, was exiled in 1897 as a dangerous revolutionary. Shuskenskoye also had a special significance for me: my great-great-grandfather Alexander Frolov had been exiled there in 1836. I had just been there in June, looking for traces of his life and hoping to find the stone house he'd built for his family. What were they implying? Did they believe I had gone there on a spying mission?

The photographer was busily shooting pictures of the incriminating evidence, which lay spread out on the table in front of me. Not knowing if and when I might be able to contact my family and friends again, I placed my right hand next to the evidence and extended my middle finger in a gesture known to all Americans. If these pictures were published, I hoped my gesture would signal that I had recognized the frame-up from the start. I remembered that the crew of the U.S.S. *Pueblo*, which was captured by North Korea in 1968, had given a similar signal to tip off the U.S. Navy that they were acting under duress.

Next, the contents of my pockets were examined. Thankfully, I was not carrying my address book, which contained telephone numbers of all my Soviet friends and contacts. My wallet yielded 43 rubles in cash, a slip of paper with the phone number of an acquaintance I had called on my way to the metro station, my expired District of Columbia driver's license, my 1952 social security card, a variety of credit cards, a blue 1-ruble tax stamp, and a color slide of a grossly overweight Soviet woman bending over two puppies at a pet market. This tasteless picture had been given to me a few days earlier as a joke by a Soviet friend.

"What is this?" the officer said, frowning at the slide. I tried to explain, but he looked skeptical.

"And these?" he asked, pointing to the plastic cards.

"Credit cards."

"Credit cards? What are they? How do they work?"

The Soviet Union does not have credit cards and is conservative about loans and advances. Salaries and bills are usually paid in cash. Individual checking accounts do not exist — not even the old-fashioned kind, before computers. And the idea that you can insert a plastic card into a machine in the wall of a bank and receive cash is dismissed as American boasting. A male secretary drew up the official record of the search and wrote "19 credit cards." He could not differentiate among the various cards, and I did not bother to enlighten him.

When this initial protocol was completed, the witnesses were dismissed, and I was left alone with the investigator and his assistant, an interpreter probably fresh out of language school who seemed none too happy to be there. The senior officer introduced himself civilly, in Russian: "I am Colonel Sergadeyev, Valery Dmitriyevich, of the Committee of State Security, investigative section."

Was Sergadeyev his real name or just his KGB name? It was an unusual name; perhaps he was a Tartar of came from some Russified Caucasian nationality. It was certainly not Russian.

"Valery Dmitriyevich," I began, "I don't know why I have been brought here." I replied in Russian, for I speak the language fluently, althouth it is not my mother tongue. I felt that if I spoke Russian, it would be easier to converse and explain. As it turned out, that was a mistake. I should have insisted on speaking through the interpreter, thus complicating the questioning and placing a buffer between me and my inquisitor.

I continued, "My arrest very much resembles that of my friend Robert Toth a few years ago."

The colonel frowned. "I would say your case is quite different." His reply was ominous; I trembled at the implied warning.

I added, "I have a request. I was expected home at one o'clock. I would be grateful if you would call my wife and tell her that I will not be there on time. Tell her I am in reliable hands. Also, if I remember correctly, I have the right under the U.S.-Soviet consular convention to telephone my embassy immediately and inform them I have been detained."

"All agreements will be observed," the colonel replied coolly.

I could feel panic creeping in. I searched my mind wildly for my rights. What should I do? How should I handle the situation? Unlike diplomats, American journalists going off to Moscow get no security briefings other than the conventional wisdom passed on by their predecessors. For many years, correspondents have assumed that expulsion is the stiffest penalty they are likely to suffer. I wondered what worse fate lay in store for me.

I was clearly in deep trouble, despite my efforts over the years to abide by Soviet regulations. When I received my press card at the Foreign Ministry in April 1981, for example, I specifically inquired about what restrictions I should observe. I even asked for a map óf "closed zones," where foreigners are not allowed, so that I would not wander into one by mistake. To my surprise, the official said that there were no special rules and that I should behave as I would anywhere else. He replied further that the ministry's own supply of maps was exhausted and he referred me to the American embassy, which gives maps to anyone who asks for them. The thought that the Soviet government relies on the American embassy to distribute maps to show the location of Moscow's "closed zones" struck me as ludicrous — the CIA prepares these maps from satellite photographs!

Contemplating my situation, I recognized that a lengthy period questioning by the KGB was be inevitable. I tried to dredge up the guidelines developed by a Soviet dissident, Vladimir Albrecht, and published in an underground pamphlet on coping with interrogation. Albrecht's research, based on Soviet law and common sense, was considered anti-Soviet because it strengthened the hand of the defendant; his thanks was a hefty prison sentence. As far as I could recall, Albrecht's advice was to answer questions relating only to the case at hand, to avoid comment on third parties, and not to deny the undeniable. It was good advice, and I would try to live by it.

૭ ૭ ૭

"Well, then." Sergadeyev broke the silence. The colonel was beginning what grew into some thirty hours of questioning over the next thirteen days. His taciturn translator sat beside him.

"I would like to inform you of your rights. You have the right to legal counsel after the preliminary examination. You may take notes, you may even use a tape recorder. You may present your own affidavits and explanations. The subject of your intimate family relations is not relevant to this investigation."

I took this to mean that the KGB had obtained no useful information from our pillow talk through their hidden microphones near the bed.

The colonel walked around the desk to hand me a copy of the procedural code and motioned me to a small desk at the far end of the room and urged me to study the code. By then I was completely shaken and could barely concentrate. Asking for a pen and paper seemed pointless; I didn't know what I should take down. I felt utterly powerless. The KGB had shot me in the chest and was offering me a Band-Aid. The real nature of the colonel's introduction became clear only much later, when I learned that he had omitted my most important rights under the Russian Republic Procedural Code: the right to remain silent (Article 46) and the right to withhold signature from any papers (142).

"Now then," Colonel Sergadeyev began, "tell me about your relationship with Misha. I should tell you that he has been arrested on suspicion of treason under Article 64 of the criminal code and is being interrogated at the same time as you. I would urge you to be honest and sincere. I think you will find that cooperation will be to your ultimate benefit."

This information put me in a difficult spot, for I had to make an immediate decision about how to handle the investigation. I remembered that both Toth and Smale had answered questions and signed statements, and I couldn't recall any American in this situation who had refused to cooperate, at least initially. I am not very adept at lying; it is always simpler to tell the truth. As a journalist, I have never covered the courts, and I have no legal training. I never served in the military and was never instructed on how to resist if captured by the enemy. Common sense would have to serve. It seemed to me that refusing to answer Sergadeyev's questions would imply that I was trying to hide something. I also felt that if my testimony was entirely credible in the beginning, it would be easier later on to mislead my investigator if it was necessary to protect friends.

So the interrogation began with the story of my meeting Misha at the hotel in Frunze with Jim Gallagher. Sergadeyev wanted to know everything about Misha, starting with his last name and patronymic (his middle name; for Russians, it is always derived from the father's first name). Every detail of our meetings seemed important: when Misha came to Moscow, how he contacted me, where we met, what we did, what we said. I felt increasingly uncomfortable; every question was designed to make our relationship look suspicious. And even though the arrest had clearly been set up, I kept wondering if I owed Misha any protection.

After two hours of sitting on a hard chair, I asked the colonel if I could relieve myself.

"Of course," he replied. "I will call a guard to take you to the toilet."

A few minutes later, a KGB noncom in a khaki uniform marched me, hands behind my back, to the washroom at the end of the corridor. It was a small room, about six by eight feet, containing a toilet and a washbasin, divided by a partition. Unlike most washrooms in the Soviet Union, this one was spotless, although a few wall tiles were missing here and there.

My guard was a young man about my height, with closely cropped hair. We entered the room together. Since childhood I have suffered from a bashful bladder, and on this occasion I couldn't open the stream. Feeling awkward, I explained to the guard that his presence inhibited me. He moved off to a corner, out of sight.

"Don't worry," he said in a friendly tone. "You're just frightened. It will be fine." He was right. A few minutes later, we were marching back to Room 215.

The colonel handed me a glass of water and resumed his questioning. Where did Misha live in Frunze? Who joined him for dinner with Gallagher and me? What did we talk about? What was I most interested in? I explained that Misha had taken us on a tour of Frunze the morning after we met, that he introduced us to some of his friends at dinner that night, and that we talked about drug problems among Soviet university students, about China, and about the unpopular war in Afghanistan. At 5:00 P.M., after four hours of exhausting questions, Sergadeyev called a halt.

"You may make your call now," he informed me. "Here, use this phone," he said, pointing to one of three on a small table beside the desk.

I first thought of calling the American embassy, but by then it was nearly five-thirty. At the embassy I would get a marine, who would eventually connect me with a duty officer. The most I could do then would be simply to communicate the fact of my detention. I decided to call my office instead.

Jeff Trimble answered. I told him what had happened, but he did not seem shocked. TASS, the Soviet news agency, had already announced that an American correspondent had been arrested.

"Where are you?" Jeff asked.

"I'm not sure. Somewhere in the northeast section of Moscow. I've been arrested on suspicion of espionage and have been interrogated all afternoon."

"It's in retaliation for the arrest of Gennadi Zakharov in New York," he said. "He was refused bail . . ."

I wasn't sure of the verb. Refused? Granted? Was he still in jail or had he been released? Somehow, with the translator and Sergadeyev staring at me, I was reluctant to ask Jeff to repeat his words. I didn't want them to know how vitally interested I had suddenly become in Zakharov's case.

"Where's Ruth?" I asked.

"She's coming just now."

Ruth came on the line, and I repeated the basic facts in short, clear sentences: the meeting with Misha at the metro station, the novels I had given him, the package he had given me, my arrest after his departure. Staring at the phone as I spoke, an idea took shape. "Ruth, have you got a pencil?" I said. "Write down this number: 361–6556. That's where I am."

"Got it," she said. I was right to have called the office, for Jeff and Ruth would know what to do. They would give the number to colleagues, who in turn would call Sergadeyev. That would bring my case out in the open and undermine the official Soviet contention that I was a spy and that my case had no connection with Zakharov's.

I glanced at the colonel and the translator. They were totally expressionless, observing me as if nothing in particular had happened.

"How long do you think you're going to be held?" Ruth asked.

"I would guess weeks, at this rate," I said. "And by the way — I'm concerned about all the research on my family in case they go through the apartment."

"Don't worry." Ruth was reassuring. "The place is already surrounded by correspondents. As long as they're here, I doubt the KGB will make a search. I'm putting your papers in a safe place."

We talked for a few more minutes. Ruth promised to call Sergadeyev the next day, when she would ask to see me and meet with him. Just before hanging up, I said, "They want me to stop talking now. But remember: I love you, and I will deal with this with as much dignity as possible."

Ruth's warmth and support stayed with me for a moment, then quickly evaporated. Again I felt desperately alone. As I eyed Sergadeyev, I found myself thinking of my father, Serge. In 1917, as a junior military officer in Russia, he was posted to Rome two weeks before the Russian Revolution. He always warned me against venturing onto Soviet territory. Two years earlier, I had buried Serge in Paris. Now, as I sat in a Moscow prison, his words floated back to me:

"Stay away from Russia. The Bolsheviks won't give a damn about your American passport. If you go to Moscow, you'll get yourself arrested and end up in the salt mines!"

∽ Three

MY KGB INTERROGATOR put down his pen and straightened his notes, signaling the end of our first encounter. I noticed his hands: his fingers were slim and tapered. He had an air of refinement despite his teeth, which were stained by nicotine and capped with gold. As he squinted over his glasses, I tried to read his eyes; they revealed nothing. The colonel was no low-level KGB thug. He was a sophisticated professional with a veneer of civility, and he made me extremely apprehensive.

"The guards will take you to the place where you will spend the night." Colonal Sergadeyev spoke calmly, as if describing a comfortable room in a country inn. Any hopes I had of going home that night, as Robert Toth had done, were shattered. Instead, I was to be the first American journalist locked up in a Soviet prison since 1949, when Stalin threw Anna Louise Strong, an American Communist, into Lubyanka. It was a terrifying prospect.

Within minutes, two young officers in khaki uniforms with KGB shoulderboards entered the room to take me to the cellblock.

"Hands behind your back," the senior lieutenant snapped. He produced no handcuffs, but I complied.

"*Khorosho.* Good," he said. "You will walk smartly, look straight ahead. Do not talk. *Vperyod!* Move ahead. One, two; one, two . . ." We headed out the door.

This KGB prison was notorious. Since the nineteenth century, Lefortovo has held thousand of prisoners whose only crime was to speak too freely. Because it was run by the KGB, it was said to be more efficient. I wondered: more efficient at what? Eliciting false confessions? Under Stalin, people were beaten and tortured. Some were given drugs to break them down. Many were never seen again.

My mind was in turmoil. How far would the KGB go? First, they framed me. Then they claimed to be civilized, telling me my rights would be observed. But I knew from long experience that Russian civility is often only skin deep.

Russian history is very different from ours. The Russians were not part of the age of chivalry, when the knights of Europe promoted a code of courage, honor, and noblesse oblige. Under the Mongol occupation, from the thirteenth to the sixteenth century, Russian culture was tragically repressed by foreign overlords. In succeeding generations, the Renaissance and the Enlightenment did not have the same influence in Russia as they did in Europe. By the early nineteenth century, however, Russian science, literature, and art at last began to blossom, producing some of the world's greatest masterpieces. Then, as so often happens in Russia, this flowering was cut short in the late 1920s by another barbarian, Joseph Stalin.

Decency and goodness do exist in Russian, but they live cheek by jowl with barbarity. It was the barbarity I feared now. The KGB is capable of doing anything to suit their purposes, and they answer to nobody, save possibly the office of the general secretary or strong condemnation from abroad.

I tried to combat my rising anxiety with political logic. Just when Gorbachev was trying to present a human Soviet face to the world, promoting openness and disarmament, he would not authorize the torture or drugging of an American correspondent. When there was the likelihood of a superpower summit, when a meeting between Secretary of State Geroge Shultz and Foreign Minister Edward Shevardnadze was expected, Gorbachev was unlikely to send an American reporter to Siberia. My arrest didn't make sense, of course, but the Kremlin is often unpredictable, occasionally acting against its own best interests.

Marching through Lefortovo prison is not conducive to clear thinking. But the questions kept coming: How the hell did I get into this mess? Who was to blame? Misha? Me? The KGB? Should I have met Misha? Should I have accepted his package? No. I should have opened the package and thrown it in the river. I should have refused to take it at all. I should have taken the long way home, up the escalator. I should have . . . The recriminations echoed in my head, picking up the rhythm of my steps as we marched along. I should have . . . I should have . . . I should have . . .

ᔓ ᔓ ᔓ

Had I been able to reflect clearly, I would have realized that my problems with the Soviet authorities had not begun that day, or even the week before. They began on a granite boulder in New Hampshire, at the end of Route 101D, overlooking the Atlantic Ocean and the Isles of Shoals. My troubles flowed from my Russian grandmother and from an antique iron ring, lined with gold, which my father wore on the fourth finger of his left hand.

My sister, Aya, and I nicknamed our grandmother Baboota, a corruption of the Russian *babushka*. She was born in Moscow into a military family on December 31, 1874. Baboota — more properly, Anna Nikolayevna Danilova, née Frolova — was sixty years older than I. A short, stout woman, she usually wore black or floral prints. A coif of flowing gray hair was swept back from her moon face, and around her neck on a gold chain she wore a

small, eighteen-karat gold watch, made by Moser brothers of
Geneva at the turn of the century. Her initials were affixed to
the back in raised letters of green gold.

Baboota and I would sit on that gray boulder for hours during
the summers of the Second World War; the townspeople called
it Baboota's Rock. While I held a colored parasol over her head,
Baboota would regale me, in Russian and French, with tales of
life in St. Petersburg and Moscow — the harvests in the Ukraine,
the Russo-Japanese War, and the horrors of the civil war —
stories about the dogs that barked in the night as the Red Guards
approached and the families who hid jewelry under the floors
only to forget later where they had put them.

Our neighbors in New Hampshire viewed Baboota as an ec-
centric grande dame who invariably took liberties with the truth.
She had a feminine charm that appealed to all ages: young boys
and older men gravitated to her. Much later, when I dug into the
history books and documents in the archives in Moscow, I was
surprised to discover that most of what she had told me was true
(with one or two blatant exceptions).

Russia, Baboota always insisted, was very, very special. It was
not just a state, but a state of mind. It was, she acknowledged,
a country of irreconcilable contradictions: generosity, hospitality,
and kindness were mixed with slovenliness, cruelty, and stupidity.
Russians had many faults, and laziness was high among them.
Tyap-lyap was an expression she used, and it is still used today,
to describe the "slip-slop" attitude of the ordinary *muzhik* toward
his work. But, Baboota would say again and again, "Russians
are the world's most talented people and have something important to tell the world. Look at the great writers of the last
century, like Pushkin, Gogol, Tolstoy. Or the great scientists, like
Mendeleyev and Lobachevsky." Russian aircraft designers, she
confided to me when my attention flagged, had developed a new
bomber of radical design that was made entirely of rubber. Enemy
shells bounced off it harmlessly.

Considering that Baboota had lost everything during the Revolution, her liberal views were hard to understand. She never tired of explaining to me the origins of serfdom, oppression, and revolution. She made me draw a picture of a house in which the masters upstairs enjoyed all the possible pleasures of life while the servants downstairs toiled in the kitchen.

"You know," she would say, "I've often wondered what would have happened if Lenin had not succumbed so young. He was only fifty-four when he died, in 1924. He was a more reasonable man than Stalin and the others who came after him." I was to recall Baboota's words many years later. "If only Lenin had lived" was a sentiment I heard often as a correspondent in the Soviet Union. If only Lenin had lived, there would have been no Stalin, no purges, no labor camps. The belief that Lenin's ideas were perfect, but their execution flawed, lies at the heart of Gorbachev's efforts to reform Soviet society.

Even as a young boy, I sensed Baboota's homesickness. The Atlantic Ocean, she would say, reminded her of the Black Sea; the New Hampshire coast, of Yalta. She made me learn verses that captured her yearning for Russia, especially Alexei Tolstoy's lines, written in 1856, comparing a lover's passion to the flood tide.

> Believe not, my friend, when in a fit of bitterness
> I say that I have stopped loving you.
> At ebb tide, believe not that the sea has betrayed you.
> The waters will flow lovingly back to the shore.

Like many émigrés of her generation, Baboota harbored secret hopes of returning to Russia, or at least visiting again. Many refugees and sympathizers did go back in the 1930s as well as after the First World War. Most were misinformed or naive; many disappeared in the purges. Baboota's nostalgia for Russia, which washed over her like the waves below our rock, found a captive audience in me. Like two conspirators, we traveled into the past. The stories I enjoyed most were about the family, life in St. Petersburg before the Revolution.

"I was so well connected," Baboota would say dramatically, pausing for effect, "I was born in the Kremlin!" The American side of the family, of New England stock going back to the seventeenth century, took this boast good-naturedly, but considered it a flight of fancy.

"My husband — your grandfather," she used to tell me, "was a very famous general. Everybody decorated him — the British, the French, the Russians. There is a coffer in Moscow filled to overflowing with his decorations. The St. George's Cross, the Order of St. Vladimir, of St. Anna, of St. Stanislav, the French Legion d'honneur, the British Order of St. Michael and St. George. One day you will go to Russia and find that coffer." I believed everything Baboota said; I was ready to leave the next day.

At home, we called my grandfather Le Général, for he had been the chief of staff of the northern armies. French was the lingua franca of the family: the American side could not speak Russian, and the Russian side had difficulty with English. Le Général had advised the czar to abdicate in March 1917, Baboota claimed. The czar was returning to St. Petersburg when suddenly a crowd of Communist railroad workers swarmed onto the track, and the imperial train had to stop and pull into Pskov. Then Le Général arrived, followed by two members of the Duma, and gave the czar their advice. They thought if Nicholas stepped down in favor of his son, that would stop the Reds. But the czarevitch was only ten years old, and he was ailing. "Poor little Alexei," Baboota would say. "He was about your age, and every time he fell over he couldn't stop bleeding."

Le Général was so influential, according to Baboota, that the czarina sent spies to follow him. Alexandra thought he might be plotting with the supreme commander, Grand Duke Nikolai Nikolayevich, to overthrow her husband. Poor Alexandra! So many people disliked her because of her German origins. Actually, Baboota explained, the czarina was a bit unbalanced and had got herself all entangled with the mad monk Rasputin. The court was filled with rumors. Some people said Rasputin really helped stop the czarevitch's bleeding; others said he was a sex maniac. With such a sick child, no wonder the czar couldn't concentrate on governing the country.

According to Baboota, even Lenin recognized Le Général's great strategic mind. After he resigned his commission and retired, he was asked to join the Red Army. Imagine! Lenin offered him three top posts, including the position of chief of staff. But Le Général had no use for the Bolsheviks and refused them all. Still, in February 1918, the War Ministry pleaded with him to join the Soviet delegation leaving for Brest-Litovsk. Lenin wanted to sign a separate peace with the Germans so that he could get on with his revolution. Le Général thought that making peace with the Germans was a bad idea. Russia owed loyalty to France and England. He urged guerrilla warfare. Trotsky, the commissar of war, wanted the same thing as Le Général, but for different reasons, for Trotsky believed that revolution was about to break out all over the world. Germany was ripe for it, he argued, so Russia should continue to fight the kaiser.

It was only because Le Général loved Russia so much that he finally agreed to join the Soviets at Brest-Litovsk, Baboota said. He thought he could influence the outcome. Of course, the Bolsheviks were so stupid, they didn't take his advice. Lenin pushed through his peace with the Germans — and what happened? The Germans seized huge pieces of Russian territory, inluding the Ukraine and the Baltic states. Le Général was disgusted. He and Baboota gathered a few possessions and left for his home of Kiev. "But," announced Baboota, "your grandfather did not give up. He had given his life to Russia. He joined the White Russian forces, first in the Ukraine, then in Siberia and the Crimea."

The counterrevolution failed. Baboota and Le Général left Yalta in the great seaborne evacuation organized by Britain and France in 1920. They traveled to Serbia and finally settled in Paris, where my grandfather taught at the French Military Academy and tried to help the White Army until he died. It was all very sad for him,

Baboota insisted, because he had dedicated himself to army and country. "You can't imagine how upset he was after the Revolution when he walked past the barracks in St. Petersburg. Imagine! The guard was actually lounging on a cot outside the gate — in bed on duty! And he refused to get up and salute Le Général!"

The murder of Baboota's uncle Peter was also a spellbinder. Another famous general, he had been the commander of the Petersburg military district and an aide to the minister of war, Vladimir Sukhomlinov, Baboota told me proudly. He retired in 1918 to grow roses in his country house at Issar, south of Yalta. The Crimea was in chaos in those days: controlled by the Whites, it was under attack from the Reds. There were also sailors from the Black Sea fleet who used to go on rampages.

"One day in the fall of 1919," Baboota explained, "two strangers arrived at Uncle Peter's gate. " 'Are you General Frolov?' they asked. All he had to say was, 'No, I am just the gardener.' Instead, he drew himself to attention and said, 'I am General Frolov.' They stabbed him to death on the spot."

Another favorite story concerned Baboota's cousin, Sasha Manganari, the son of Uncle Peter's sister, Nadejda (Hope). She had married a Russian naval officer of Greek descent. Sasha and Baboota were about the same age, and they often got into mischief together. "One day he had this crazy idea that he was a bird and could fly. He made himself a pair of wings and jumped off a tall bookcase, crashing and breaking his hip. He always walked with a limp after that. His mother was furious with him, but he never lost his sense of humor."

All these stories made an enormous impression on me, and from an early age I was deeply curious about my Russian origins. I did not recognize it then, but Baboota was turning me into a Slavophile. Years later, when I came across a poem by Fyodor Tyutchev, the words seemed to capture perfectly my grandmother's passion for Russia, a passion she was determined to bequeath to me.

You cannot measure Russia with your mind.
No common yardstick can encompass her.
For Russia's of a very special kind.
You may only believe in her.

Baboota had one story that stood above all the others in my
boyhood imagination. It was the tale of her own grandfather,
Alexander Frolov. He was supposedly a revolutionary who was
sent to Siberia for thirty years for trying to overthrow Nicholas I
in 1825. There the story pretty much stopped, leaving plenty of
room for my imagination. To my frustration, questions about
Frolov received few answers from Baboota, and our conversations
about him went round in unsatisfying circles. But my curiosity
did uncover one astonishing bit of treasure, and inevitably I would
return to it. According to family legend, Alexander Frolov had
forged a ring from his prison chains.

ᔕ ᔕ ᔕ

Ever since I first noticed that gray band on my father's hand, I
felt compelled to uncover its history. My father — whom we
always addressed as Serge — wasn't much help. He arrived in
New York in the fall of 1918 from Bordeaux, aboard the French
liner *Chicago*, determined to become an American and forget the
past. When I plucked up enough courage to ask him about the
ring, he would only say that it was Russian and had belonged to
some ancestor who got into trouble.

"But how was it make?" I would ask. "And why is it iron on
the outside and gold on the inside?" Irritated, he would twist it
off his finger and thrust it at me. "Here, you look at it. Your
guess is as good as mine."

Then I would take a magnifying glass and scrutinize the ring.
It looked rather ordinary: slightly more than a quarter of an inch
wide on top and narrowing a bit toward the bottom. To the
naked eye, the gray metal seemed smooth, but under the glass it
appeared porous and uneven and I noticed a tiny fault in the gold

lining the inside. When I first studied the mysterious letters on the level ellipse that surmounts the ring, I became excited. These markings could be a vital clue that would unlock the story or, at least, lead to the next clue.

"You know Russian. What does it mean?" I once shouted at my father, who was reading the *Boston Herald* by the fire. I knew that he hated to read or speak Russian, but my curiosity about the history of the ring overcame my fear of upsetting him.

"One looks like a Russian D, the otherlike a Roman I, and I don't know what the squiggle above them means," he replied indifferently. I learned soon enough that questions only annoyed him, and I finally stopped asking.

When I turned twenty-one, my father gave me the ring, hoping it would appease my curiosity. I asked art experts in the United States about it, but they had no answers. "If it's so old and made of iron, why hasn't it rusted?" asked one dealer, doubting its authenticity. The ring was loose on my finger, and once I nearly lost it. Apparently my ancestor had the hands of a laborer, not an intellectual. Eventually, I took the ring off and consigned it to the darkness of a bank vault.

I suppose my father's reluctance to discuss Russia and the ring was understandable. Overnight, a bloody revolution had disinherited him, depriving him of both status and future. In August 1917, Le Général, seeing the Revolution ahead, arranged for his sons — twenty-year-old Mikhail (known in the family as Mish) and nineteen-year-old Serioja — to go abroad. Mish went to Paris as the secretary to a Russian aircraft procurement mission. Serge, a recent graduateof the Corps of Imperial Pages, was sent as a second lieutenant to the Russian embassy in Rome. When the October Revolution exploded two months later, Serge and the other officers divided up the embassy account and went their separate ways. Serge arrived in New York with $900 in his pocket and, with the assistance of the Carnegie Foundation, made his way to Cambridge, Massachusetts, where he entered Harvard

College. There he joined Mish, who had preceded his brother to the States by several months.

Although Serge and Mish both graduated with the class of 1921, they never felt American. Instead of going to football matches, Serge walked around Harvard Yard wearing pearl gray spats and swinging a cane. After college, he became a mechanical engineer and worked in a textile factory, the Saco-Lowell Shops, where he met my mother, Ellen Crosby Burke of Lowell, Massachusetts. But marrying her did not help, for her old New England family never fully accepted him. He was too urbane, too suave, too polyglot: he spoke English, French, German, and Russian. He was also an accomplished horseman, and he loved powerful cars, witty men, beautiful women, and tailored suits with four real buttonholes on the sleeves. Americans, he believed, were untutored and unworldy.

My father felt most at home in France. Like most educated Russians of his generation, he spoke French easily and with a far better accent than his Slavic English. The French had style, he said, something Americans knew little about. For many years, Serge worked for the Packard Motor Car Company, and he managed to arrange it so that most of the time he could live overseas, first in Paris, then in Argentina, and again in Paris after the Second World War.

Needless to say, Serge found it hard to forgive his mother for filling my head with Russia, not to mention her kind words for Lenin. He was trying to build his life in the New World, and even if he didn't fully make the transition, Aya and I, in his view, should grow up as full-blooded Americans. We should succeed where he had failed.

Looking back on it, I believe my father wanted to be an American but also to enjoy the things he might have had if Lenin hadn't appeared. He wanted the best for me. He wanted me to mix with the wealthy and powerful, and he was delighted when I joined one of the secret clubs at Harvard, had a flirtation with a debutante, and expressed a fleeting interest in the Morgan Guaranty Trust Company. He wanted me to be a good horseman and take an interest in racing cars. Poor Serge! With Baboota as my ally, the cards were stacked against him in the father-son conflicts of my adolescence. I was indifferent to horses and refused to mount one. Horsepower, whether under a saddle or in an engine, bored me. I began dressing in sloppy tweeds, developed an interest in French existentialism, and insisted on studying philosophy in England, a country he despised because of its lack of cuisine.

The subject of the Soviet Union provoked our greatest quarrels, and in the end, politics became taboo. For Serge, the Soviet Union was a menace to civilization; he would have approved Ronald Reagan's characterizing it as "the Evil Empire." To the end of his life, Serge never understood that for me, the Soviet Union was a fact of life. He seemed to believe that the USSR would one day disappear, that somehow it would revert to the good old days of benign czarism. But I knew that if change was to come in the empire, it would have to come from Moscow, from within.

Serge would always make two remarks about our family and its approach to life. The Daniloff side had reason and discipline, something that, on the whole, Russians lacked. The Frolovs had something else; emotion. "On my mother's side," he'd say, "everything was subordinated to natural inclinations. I daresay my mother's side was more Russian."

Baboota's influence on me grew as I matured, especially after my mother died suddenly when I was fifteen. There was no stopping Baboota then; my father was no match for her. She manipulated her two sons, just as she manipulated me, right up until her death, in 1954.

I remember the summer she took ill in Paris. She became increasingly irritable and finally retired to bed in our apartment with severe high blood pressure. She lapsed into a coma after I returned to Harvard for the fall term, and she died soon after, attended by Serge and his new wife. When I received the news by cable, I cried all night, to the distress of my roommate on the bunk below. I felt a grievous loss — as great as that at my mother's death. Baboota had loved me unconditionally until the very end.

At last, when she could no longer defend herself, my father took his revenge — consciously or unconsciously, I do not know. He consigned her ashes to a five-year niche at Pére Lachaise Cemetery and forgot to renew the contract. With no notice to the family, the cemetery unceremoniously took Baboota's remains from the columbarium and scattered them in a common grave.

But this dispersal did not eradicate her power. When Serge became infirm in his late eighties, he still prattled on about his mother, referring contemptuously to her "ludicrous" opinions and prejudices. When I visited him just before he died, he was mumbling, "*Ma pauvre mère disait . . . Ma pauvre mère disait . . .* My poor mother used to say . . ." Mish was affected no less. While being transported to a nursing home in Lexington, Massachusetts, as a frail old man of eighty-eight, he turned to my stepsister and asked, "Do you think my mother would approve of the place you're taking me to?"

Mish's obsessional relationship with his mother was illustrated by a story his mind kept returning to in the last years of his life — although I sometimes thought it a figment of the imagination. "The incident," as Mish called it, occurred in the early summer of 1916, when Le Général was at the front, fighting the Germans. Mish and his friends had taken the day off from their studies at the Petrograd Institute of Technology to go to the public gardens of Pavlovsk, north of the capital. The young men sang and danced the night away and missed the last train home, so they took the milk train in the early morning hours.

It was the season of the White Nights, when the sun barely sets, and the whole city was bathed in an eerie light. "Suddenly," Mish recalled, "I saw this woman walking toward me in a white dress carrying a parasol. As she came closer, I couldn't believe my eyes. It was Mams!" His mother stopped for a split second, looked straight through her son, and continued walking. "She recognized me, but she never said a word." A few hours later, when mother and son met at the breakfast table in the family's apartment at 4 Nevsky Prospekt, nothing was said. It was as though it had never happened.

"What do you think your mother was doing?" I asked him after hearing the story several times.

"How should I know? I never asked her." He chuckled wickedly, shrugging his bony shoulders.

After Mish died, in 1986, I took his ashes to sea and scattered them in full view of Baboota's rock.

かか かか かか

There had always been vague rumors in the family about Baboota's affairs. For me, a teenage boy, the idea of my grandmother's carrying on thirty years earlier in the imperial Russian capital was as close as you could get to the absurd. Shortly after I arrived in Moscow on my latest assignment, however, I had an experience that allowed me to reconcile my gray-haired *babushka* with her Petersburg adventures. One Friday afternoon in 1982, I went to the American embassy for the ambassador's regular briefing. Every two weeks or so, Arthur Hartman would discuss the latest twists in superpower relations with the two dozen American correspondents based in Moscow. That afternoon, the questions centered on President Reagan's hard line toward the Kremlin. Would the White House rupture all contacts? Would the efforts toward arms control be curtailed? Were we heading into an era of unremitting distrust?

After about an hour the meeting broke up, and I left the library where we had gathered and went downstairs to check my mail. I could hear the trucks rumbling by on Tchaikovsky Boulevard as I sifted through my pigeonhole. Suddenly, a woman's voice called my name. I turned to see Roza, a Russian secretary at the embassy; she was blond, statuesque, and wearing a bit too much makeup, as Soviet women often do.

"Nikolai Sergeyevich," she asked, "are you related by chance to General Danilov?"

"As it happens," I replied, "I am his grandson."

"Then I have a surprise for you," Roza said mysteriously.

A few days later, when I was again at the embassy, Roza was standing in the mailroom. She spotted me and, darting into her office, returned with a large brown envelope.

"My husband is a collector," she explained, carefully taking several prerevolutionary magazines from the package. "Take a look. I think you will find something of interest."

She placed one magazine on her desk: *Stolitsa i Usadby,* a glossy, illustrated journal roughly equivalent to *House and Garden.* Dated 1915, it had a large, Russian double-headed eagle on the cover. I turned the pages slowly. As far as I could tell, the whole issue was devoted to the war efforts of the Russian elite. There was one section on Grand Duke Nikolai Nikolayevich, the supreme commander. I turned another page. Staring out at me was a portrait of a full-faced, dark-haired woman, wearing a dress with a high white collar fastened by two studs. I recognized the small gold watch on the gold chain, with its raised initials turned outward. Her hair was darker and thicker, but the style was the same, swept up around her head.

There she was, the wife of the deputy chief of the Russian General Staff Anna Nikolayevna Danilova, — Baboota — smiling at me ever so slightly like a Russian Gioconda.

✺ *Four*

ONE, TWO. One, two. The guards, one on each side, marched me out of Room 215, down the corridor, past the other interrogation chambers, past the washroom I had used earlier, to an oak door at the end of the hall. One of the guards pressed a few buttons on an electronic lock; the door swung open, and we entered the old part of the prison.

I found myself on a balcony that girdled the cavernous interior like a belt. I could see four or five tiers of cells, each giving out on higher balconies. The open space in the middle was intersected at several levels by metal netting, apparently to catch any prisoner who might jump over the edge.

The guards said not a word. They led me along the walk and down an iron staircase at the midsection of the building. As we descended, the guard on my right snapped his fingers sharply to warn the other guards that a prisoner was being conveyed. Lefortovo is an isolation prison; except with a cellmate, no prisoner is supposed to meet or even make eye contact with another.

The farther we proceeded through the bowels of the prison, the more vulnerable I felt. We reached the basement, where several guards were sitting at an old-fashioned wooden desk under a wall clock, and walked down another long corridor, past windows covered with bars. At last we reached an antiseptic tiled hall with numerous doors, the place was empty, leading off it. Apart from a few wooden benches, and it smelled like a locker room. One of the guards unlocked a door and motioned us to follow him. We entered a small cubicle, about six by eight feet. Inside was an examination table and a chair or two. The door swung closed. No one spoke.

"What are we waiting for?" I ventured, dreading the reply. There was silence. I tried to humor the guards, asking them about their rank. One of them, a lieutenant, had two small stars on his shoulderboards; the other, a senior lieutenant, had three. Their relatively high rank attested to the importance of my case. They stared through me, pretending not to hear. Finally, raising my voice, I pressed them: "Come on. What are we waiting for?"

"*Vrach*. The doctor," one of them grunted. He fell silent again.

It is probably customary in all countries to have a medical examination on entering prison. I tried to put the stories of Soviet psychiatric abuse out of my mind, although, as a journalist, I knew those reports only too well. In the eyes of Soviet ideologues, anyone who repeatedly criticizes the regime is medically unbalanced and a candidate for "reforming." In 1983, the Soviet Union was forced to resign from the World Psychiatric Association for using drugs to treat dissidents. Did the KGB have special potions that would turn my will to jelly?

I didn't keep track of how long we waited. It seemed like ages, but it probably wasn't more than fifteen or twenty minutes. Finally, the door opened to admit a middle-aged, waspish woman in a white coat: the doctor. I wasn't particularly surprised, for some seventy-five percent of Soviet physicians are women, although the top specialists are usually men.

My doctor seemed harassed; her gray hair was awry. Without a word of greeting, she clamped a blood pressure cuff on my right arm and squeezed the rubber bulb. The cuff swelled slowly, gulping the air in hurried breaths, then wheezed as she released the valve. She listened through her stethoscope for the telltale change of tone as blood rushed through the main artery again.

"One hundred and fifty over eighty," she announced. I was relieved. I have suffered from labile hypertension since adolescence and was afraid that my arterial pressure had gone through the roof from the stress. Normally, I took a mild medication every morning to control it. Doctors once advised me to seek a quiet career, to be an archivist or librarian. Instead, I became a journalist — as it happens, a career sure to test your blood pressure.

"Get completely undressed," the doctor commanded. "I am going to check for veneral disease."

I felt completely defenseless as I removed my clothes and stood naked before this unpleasant woman.

"Bend over and spread your buttocks!" she ordered. She scrutinized the large, exterior hemorrhoid that had developed in the past few hours, during my arrest.

The guards viewed the scene with indifference, as though an American prisoner were placed in this position every day. But for me the indignity was unbearable. I felt an overwhelming need to make human contact with these people. I stood up and turned to her.

"What is your name?"

"What does it matter?" she snapped.

"You're also a human being," I replied. She turned her back to me and started filling out the forms.

"May I go to the toilet?" I inquired.

"You'll get your chance," she answered. "Off to the shower with him," she said to the guards. Then she walked out, slamming the door.

One of the guards explained that he was obliged by regulations to confiscate certain of my possessions. My watch and belt were the first to go. I knew, of course, that belts could be used for suicide, though the thought was unsettling. Was it really going to be that bad?

Next, the guards examined my shoes. They were of soft leather, rather like moccasins, with thick crepe soles. The junior officer undid the shoelaces and slipped them out. Each one was about twenty-four inches long.

"Allow us to cut your shoelaces in half," he said with exquisite politeness.

"*Pozhaluista.* Go ahead," I replied. The idea of committing suicide with two shoelaces seemed farcical, but rules are rules.

The senior guard twisted his key in the lock, opening the cubicle. We stepped back into the large hall with the benches. I asked again for the toilet; the call was becoming more and more urgent. They brushed my request aside, motioning me toward the showers.

The bathhouse had several ceiling showerheads with lead plumbing that looked as time-worn as the building itself. The cement floor, sloping gently toward a drain, was cold and damp. I stepped onto the dark, wooden slats, slimy from constant drenching, and turned on the hot water. I found a bar of white laundry soap and, at last, enjoyed a brief respite from tension under the warm spray.

When I had dried myself, an orderly in a white coat matter-of-factly laid out a set of prison underwear: loose-fitting dark blue cotton shorts and a pale blue sleeveless, ribbed undershirt. I refused the offer and put my own clothes back on — it was a way of reassuring myself that Nick Daniloff was still all there. Later, when I discovered how infrequently Soviet prisoners get to wash, I changed my mind. I would muddy their clothing, not mine. The orderly instructed me to grab a *komplekt* of bedding — a mattress about two inches thick, a sheet, and a light blanket.

Again, I asked the guard for the toilet; the desire was now very urgent. Being unable to relieve myself was taking on enormous psychological importance. Twenty years earlier, a urinary infection had caused my bladder to block completely, requiring repeated catheterization. For years thereafter, I dreaded any kind of air travel because, inevitably, I would develop an urgent need to urinate on takeoff, then be unable to go once I reached the head. I recalled one nightmarish occasion in a military helicopter, with no access to a toilet and parachute straps digging into my groin. When we finally landed, I was in excruciating pain. The KGB would never have to pull my fingernails. All they needed to do was resort to one of the oldest tricks of the interrogator's trade: make it difficult for a prisoner to perform natural functions. From the beginning, I knew that this was my most vulnerable area.

"Don't worry, you'll go to the toilet," one of the guards replied as we marched out of the hall into the long corridor leading back to the old-fashioned desk and the wall clock. Here we took a left turn and entered a wing, perhaps two hundred feet long, which went off at an angle and contained cell after cell. We walked a few steps down this corridor and halted in front of a metal door painted the same dirty rust brown as the gate through which the white van had brought me some five hours earlier. The number on the door was 26.

"Name?" A third guard, evidently the duty officer on the wing, glanced at his papers and looked me in the eye.

"Danilov, Nikolai Sergeyevich," I replied in Russian and in the Russian manner: last name first, then first name and patronymic.

The guard inserted a key and turned the lock. The door opened. I hesitated, but as the guards closed in around me, I found myself pushed over the threshold. The door instantly slammed shut. For the first time since my arrest, a wave of claustrophobia hit me: it was difficult to breathe; my knees went weak; my throat felt plugged with sand. I took a step toward the door. I wanted to strike it with my fists, to scream, to shout "Open up, you *svolochi*, you bastards, let me out!"

Suddenly I stopped. I was not alone. There was another man

in the cell. He sat on the edge of a cot in a dark blue sweat suit, scribbling something on a piece of paper. He raised his head; a surprised look crossed his face.

"Welcome to the firm's hotel! Let me introduce myself. I'm Stanislav Zenin — Stas to you," he said cheerily.

When I introduced myself as an American, he seemed astounded. I said that my greatest need was to urinate; I believed my bladder had seized up.

He immediately reassured me, pointing to a primitive cast-iron toilet that rose like a cone from a five-inch sewer pipe running along the base of one wall. A wooden cover, with a handle screwed to the top, lay across the top of the cone. On one side of this receptacle stood the inevitable metal wastebasket, rusty at the edges, filled with used toilet paper. Russians never drop paper down the toilet for fear of blocking it. On the other side was a small basin set into the side of the cell.

"Turn on the faucet to keep the smell down when you use the toilet," Stas said, pointing to the small copper water pipe protruding into the cone, just below the top. "The rule here is, by the way, not to use the toilet when the other prisoner is eating." Then, almost as an afterthought, he said, "Make yourself comfortable. Standing. Sitting. Don't mind me."

I followed Stas's instructions, but it didn't work. It was the airplane nightmare all over again.

"Look," I pleaded, increasingly panicked, "the trouble is you. Either I have to rig up a screen and get some privacy or you've got to go away."

Stas chuckled and agreed to drape one of the thin blankets over his head and sit facing away fror me. What a sight! But it brought results.

At that moment, the feed window in the metal door — what prisoners call the *kormushka* — banged open. A stern face appeared in the opening and bellowed at us: "What in the name of the devil's mother are you doing in there? You're not allowed to hide from the guards!"

Stas threw the blanket on the floor. I didn't care anymore. I had squeaked over my first hurdle.

I slumped down on a cot and glanced around. We were in a basement *kamera*, which measured about fifteen feet long and nine feet wide. I judged the vaulted ceiling to be about ten feet high, maybe a bit more. At the far end of the cell, opposite the metal door, was a single window. I guessed it gave out onto an interior courtyard. The base of the window was well over my head, about seven feet from the floor. It was hinged at the bottom and opened into the room. Through the translucent panes I could make out that constant of prison life: seven vertical iron bars and two horizontal ones.

The cell was sparsely furnished. Three cots, painted a dirty robin's egg blue, were arrayed along the three solid stone walls. The same light blue ran shoulder high on the walls. The rest of the walls and the vaulted ceiling were painted a dull beige; no pinup girls, no slogans, not even a picture of Lenin graced the cell. The cement floor, badly scuffed at the entrance, was painted Lefortovo brown, like the cell door and the vehicle entrance. A revolting, sodden rag lay at the threshold like a mat. Each bed had a small night table about a foot and a half square. Over the two beds on the long walls was a set of wooden shelves for the prisoners' meager belongings.

Stas said that his previous mate, who had been charged with anti-Soviet agitation, had been carted off to a psychiatric hospital. This young man, he said, had sex on the mind. He had written a lascivious sex manual of three hundred pages and had sent some materials abroad to be published.

Stas told me that prisoners at Lefortovo were fed three times a day, but that relatives could bring supplementary food packages. He handed me a white enamel bowl with four delicately painted red roses on the lip, an aluminum cup, and a soup spoon from one of the shelves — all identical to the utensils he kept for himself. Like shoelaces, knives and forks were considered potential weapons and were banned.

The *kormushka* flopped open and a woman's voice called out roughly, *"Misku daite*. Pass out your bowl." Through the feed window, which was about eighteen inches wide, I could make out the figure of a hefty woman in a stained white coat that barely closed over her ample bosom. She was ladling buckwheat gruel out of a large aluminum cauldron, which she pushed along on a trolley. An assistant passed in a pot of black tea.

Sitting on the edge of our beds, Stas and I arranged our food on the night tables and spooned in the kasha. Almost against my better judgment, I found I liked the gruel: it was oddly reminiscent of the buckwheat groats Baboota used to serve.

Stas reached up to his shelf, seized three lumps of Cuban sugar, and dropped them into his teacup.

"Sugar for you?" he asked.

"No thanks."

"No? Really? We Russians always take three cubes with our tea. You'll find the sugar gives you a bit of a lift," he remarked.

"Thanks, but no thanks," I repeated. "For me, the sugar leaves an unpleasant aftertaste."

"Well, do eat slowly. Around here, you try to draw out anything remotely pleasurable for as long as possible. I know it's hard. It will take you at least a couple of days to get used to things."

For the first time, I fixed my attention on my cellmate. He was in his mid-forties, a little younger than I, with dark hair receding at the temples. He said he had entered Moscow University in 1959 and graduated in physics five years later. He struck me as a pleasant, straightforward person, and I was grateful for his kindness when I was thrown into the cell. However, what he told me next — the reason for his imprisonment — made my blood run cold: he had left classified documents in a friend's apartment. He had worked in a "post office box" (the Russian euphemism for a secret institute) and had been arrested on April 11. Here I was, being held on suspicion of espionage, and they put me in a cell with a secret scientist. Soviet citizens who do classified work are not allowed to talk to foreigners, let alone share a room with them. It was unbelievable. Was this another setup? In prison? Were they going to say that I was such an inveterate agent that I tried to extract secrets from my cellmate? If the situation hadn't been so grave, it would have been ridiculous.

I couldn't wait for the lights to be turned off that first night. I wanted desperately to escape into sleep. At ten o'clock, the *kormushka* opened again. "*Otboi! Otboi!* Lights out! Turn in!" came the call. Stas signaled to me that it was time to hand over our eyeglasses. We passed them through the feed window to a guard who placed them, with great care, in individual cloth cases. There would be no suicides that night.

To my disappointment, the guard extinguished only one of the two naked bulbs in the ceiling fixture, leaving enough light so that the guards could see you clearly through the peephole. "They must be able to see your face and hands at all times," Stas said. "You should not hide them under the covers. The best way to deal with the light," he added, removing a rag from his pocket, "is to fold your handkerchief lengthwise four times, like this." It was a time-tested device among Soviet prisoners. He placed the handkerchief over his eyes and lay back on his cot. I could tell by his breathing that he was asleep within minutes.

Though I was exhausted, I slept badly. Every ten or fifteen minutes, the guards would look in through the peephole, rotating the metal hatch that covered it with a loud, rasping noise. I was also aware of noises in the corridor. Soon I noticed that the temperature in the cell was dropping and that the cold air from the partly open windows was hitting my shoulders. I had been wearing light summer clothes when I was arrested, and now I began to shiver under my thin blanket. After several hours, the small of my back began to ache horribly, for the horsehair mattress offered little respite from the steel slats. I dozed fitfully.

As I passed in and out of sleep, I became aware of an eerie sense of déjà vu. It was all strangely familiar, yet I had never been imprisoned before. Then I remembered: yes, I had been in a Russian cell — a brick-lined, vaulted dungeon, where the cold and damp penetrated its walls from an icy river outside.

In 1985, Ruth and I had gone to Leningrad to visit the Peter and Paul Fortress, which sits on an island across from the Winter Palace. We hoped to find the place that Alexander Frolov had been taken in 1826 after his arrest. The director of the Leningrad History Museum had been wonderfully helpful, placing her research department at our disposal. Our guide, a young woman, was studying the treatment of political prisoners under the czars. All the cells, she explained, were being restored so that visitors would understand the inhuman conditions prisoners suffered before the Revolution.

Cell 15, where Frolov had been held, no longer existed: it had been remodeled into a museum office. But, said our guide, there were other cells exactly like it. She led us across the cobbled confines of the fortress to the massive outer walls, which overlooked the Neva River and the Kronwerk slip.

The tiny cells were built like honeycombs, one above the other. As I stepped across the threshold of the first one, I felt I was stepping into a nether realm. Outside in the sun lay one of the world's most beautiful cities, full of excited tourists scurrying about with cameras, exclaiming over the eighteenth-century Italianate architecture. Across the Neva you could see the green-washed façade of the winter Palace. But inside the cell, darkness and dampness reigned. I could almost reach out and touch the river's cold, and it chilled me to the bone.

I asked Ruth and the guide to leave me alone for a short while. I wanted to experience, just for a few fleeting moments, what my ancestor must have felt when the door slammed shut: darkness, silence, chill, and, finally, panic. I felt all those things and more, for the cell was just about the loneliest place I had ever been. I was relieved when Ruth returned; she had a flash on her camera and insisted on taking a few pictures.

And now I was imprisoned in a cell of my own. There in Lefortovo, the recollection of Frolov's imprisonment disconcerted me. But it also calmed me down. I had a gnawing premonition that history was repeating itself, that I was destined to follow Frolov to Siberia. At the same time, I felt better knowing that he had survived against terrible odds. If he could, I must.

᷈ ᷈ ᷈

"*Podyom! Podyom!* Get up! Get up!" The guards were shouting in the corridors. It was still dark at 6:00 A.M. on Sunday, August 31, and I was exhausted. The night had come and gone, but had brought no relief. Stas said that the guards would let us lie prone on our cots till eight.

"But first we have to get up, make our beds, and clean up the cell," he added.

I longed for a hot shower and a shave. In Moscow, I usually took two showers a day: after walking Zeus in the morning and after jogging six miles at night.

"You get a shower here once a week, a shave twice," Stas explained.

After splashing cold water on my face at the grimy basin and dabbing it on my chest and under my arms, I still felt grubby. I had no toothbrush, of course, and irritating little pieces of buckwheat husks had lodged between my molars. I had slept in my street clothes, so they were now hopelessly rumpled. Without a belt, I had to hitch my trousers constantly.

"You'll feel better in a few days, I promise," Stas told me as he collected the basket of dirty toilet paper. This "tissue" had been cut in small sheets from a coarse, light brown paper, about the consistency of the cheapest European scratch paper and glazed lightly on one side. It was excellent for writing, but it had to be soaked thoroughly in water to serve its intended purpose.

"Being brought in is always a shock," Stas continued, "no doubt about it. You'll find there is some order in this madness, though. I have been here for months, and I'm surviving. Look at this time as a *tvorcheski otpusk*, a creative holiday, and get on with some constructive work."

"Like what?"

"Well, I'm working on a number of projects. For example, I'm convinced there are other itelligences in outer space. That's something I want to explore. Also, I want to demonstrate that some birds can fly backward. When I get out, I'm going to design a man-powered flying machine."

During the thirteen days I lived with Stas, I believed he was a bona fide prisoner, not just a KGB plant. But could I ever be sure? No doubt, in exchange for promises of easy treatment, he had agreed to inform on me. Occasionally, he would try to influence my thinking, and he never gave me tips on how to resist my interrogator. He seemed like a genuine Russian intellectual with a wide range of interests, from the mundane to the bizarre. And he loved to talk. I concluded that Stas was like Misha, a decent man pressured into running indecent errands for the KGB. He certainly couldn't tell the KGB to go to hell. Clearly, no one in the Soviet Union could.

Breakfast on that first morning was tea and a mixture of tiny vermicelli sprinkled with sugar. I found the combination unpalatable and could hardly get it down. I braced myself for further interrogation, but there was no call. I tried to read one of the books Stas had taken out of the prison library, a Soviet edition of Victor Hugo's *The Little Napoleon*. But it was hard to take anything in. Finally, at 2:30 A.P., the *kormushka* opened.

"You." A guard pointed a finger at me. "Name?"

"Danilov, Nikolai Sergeyevich."

"Danilov! *Gotovte na vyzov!* Prepare to be summoned!" The window slammed shut.

Soon I was climbing the stairs to the balcony with a single guard. I strode along, hands behind my back, until we reached the thick oak door that led to the offices. The guard executed the code on the electronic lock, and we moved into the long corridor, past the toilet, past the interrogation chambers, to Room 215. The journey took about five minutes.

Colonel Sergadeyev, who had taken off his suit jacket and put on a dark gray cardigan, sat behind his desk, smoking. When he rose to greet me, he carried himself erect but moved somewhat stiffly, as though he suffered from arthritis.

"Well, it's nice to see you," he began as we sat down. He stopped to sign the prisoner receipt, which he then handed back to the guard. "You will be having a visit shortly from your wife," he said, "but first we must attend to a few details."

The colonel was all politeness on this Sunday afternoon. In his dark, well-cut suit, he would not have looked out of place at a diplomatic reception. He spoke faultless Russian, but I continued to sense another nationality hidden somewhere.

"By the way," Sergadeyev continued, "how shall I address you? Mr. Daniloff? Gospodin Danilov?" He varied the pronunciation to make it sound more Western or more Russian.

I suggested the polite Russian form — Nikolai Sergeyevich. *Gospodin,* mister, is a prerevolutionary appellation used only with foreigners today. Psychologically, the choice of address was important. I always preferred speaking Russian to officials, a courtesy that was usually appreciated. The Russians have a saying: "Don't go into another monk's monastery with your own rules," which means the same as "When in Rome . . ." Somewhere in the back of my mind was the notion that if I could establish a direct channel of communication with the colonel, I might convince him I was not a spy — a very misguided idea, as I would soon discover.

At about three o'clock, Sergadeyev left the room, consigning me to another officer. After waiting for a few minutes, we followed him to the visitors room, which was around the corner. Ruth and Roger Daley, the American consul, were already there with Sergadeyev.

Ruth and I rushed to each other and embraced emotionally. She whispered in my ear so that Sergadeyev could not hear: "You can't imagine the uproar your arrest is causing. It's the number one story everywhere." This news cheered me up no end. If the media could keep the pressure on, I might actually get out of here.

"I've brought you some things," she said, opening a small brown suitcase. It contained pajamas, a sweat suit, clean underwear, and my toilet articles, as well as some packages of cookies, cheese, coffee, and chocolate (some of which were later confiscated; stimulants were forbidden) and four books about the Decembrists.

"From the look of it, you expect your husband to be here for a long time," Sergadeyev said with a wintry smile. "Leave the things. We will have to inspect them," he continued, motioning us toward the couch.

We stepped back and sat down on a sofa at the left-hand side of the room. This reception room was very pretentious, furnished in reproduction French furniture. In front of the couch, upholstered in brocade, stood a coffee table, with two small armchairs on either side. An oil painting of a pastoral scene, done in rather crude colors, hung on the wall. White net Victorian curtains, gathered at regular intervals, covered the windows, barely disguising the iron bars. The whole tableau seemed to have been designed to impress foreigners.

Knowing that the meeting could be cut short at any moment, I turned to Roger Daley, who sat in one of the armchairs. He had arrived in Moscow several months earlier and I had not met him before. This soft-spoken, gentle man looked strangely out of place in his light gray suit and full red beard. I quickly filled him in on my arrest and took the opportunity to deny categorically the charges against me; he repeated the U.S. assertions that I was innocent.

Sergadeyev sat at a large writing desk opposite us, the interpreter at his side. The colonel listened intently to our exchange, occasionally making notes on a pad, and made no effort to dispute my professions of innocence. In response to a question from Daley, he explained that I would be arraigned or released within ten days. If formally charged, I would have the right to a Soviet lawyer, but only after the preliminary investigation was complete — and that could take six months or more.

"Does bail exist under the Soviet system?" the consul asked. Daley was still unfamiliar with the Soviet procedural code.

"Yes," Sergadeyev replied dispassionately, "but it applies to less serious cases."

Ruth took advantage of the breaks for translation to whisper to me without being overheard. "This whole thing is a farce," she said. "They set you up, and then they talk about legal procedures and lawyers. It's an outrage!"

I recognized the anger in her voice and tried to calm her down, reasoning, "It's no good getting mad. This is what we are dealing with."

"But how can they accuse you of being a spy, you of all people?"

I wanted to change the subject, knowing that we had little time.

"The only reason you are here is because the FBI arrested a Soviet without diplomatic immunity," Ruth continued. "They haven't even searched our apartment. You would think that if they seriously thought you were a spy, they would have turned the place upside down. Why didn't they stop our baggage leaving if they thought you were a spy?"

"Tell me about Caleb," I said. "Is everything ready for his return to the States on Wednesday?" Ruth said he was fine. She did not tell me that she had brought Caleb to the prison on the off-chance he might be allowed to see me. Sergadeyev had refused permission on this occasion, so Caleb remained outside with the journalists who had accompanied them.

"Everyone is fine," Ruth went on. "You must not worry about anything. I have told the Soviet office staff not to come in tomorrow — all this will be too upsetting for them."

Any doubts I might have had about Ruth's ability to cope were fast disappearing. Once she had expressed her outrage, she would concentrate on the matters on hand. Given her long experience in Moscow, she knew that the thing to do was to keep the case in the public eye. I noticed her glancing with irritation at Daley as, a little nervously, he took a legal form from his briefcase. Through the translator, he explained to Sergadeyev something about the form. The colonel looked puzzled.

"Oh God," Ruth muttered. "We have only a few precious minutes and we've got to waste time with American bureaucracy."

"Please explain what this is about," said Sergadeyev, turning to me. "The translator does not understand it, and neither do I."

The form was a release under the U.S. Privacy Act when signed by me, it would allow the American embassy to comment on my case. The problem was that there is no clear concept of privacy in Russian and no exact translation for the word *privacy*. In a country where each individual is alloted about nine square yards of living space and many still share bathrooms and kitchens, the problem is called overcrowding, not lack of privacy.

With some irritation, I attempted to explain to Sergadeyev the Freedom of Information Act and the companion Privacy Act. He had trouble absorbing the notion that a private citizen could petition the government for internal memoranda and other documents, subject to considerations of individual privacy. I finally finessed the issue by saying that the paper was essentially a *formalnost*, a formality, which my government insisted on. Since the Soviet Union is bogged down with formalities, he finally understood. He shrugged his shoulders and said I could do as I wished. I signed the form on the coffee table, handed it to Daley, and turned back to Ruth.

"The thing that worries me most is what this arrest does to our Soviet friends," I said. "I can't bear the thought that they will be pressured to testify against me. The ones who don't know me well might really think I'm a spy."

"Don't worry," she said. "They recognize the hand of the KGB better than anyone. We'll soon find out if friends are being questioned.

After more than an hour, Sergadeyev indicated that the meeting should end. Ruth put her notebook back in her bag and approached the colonel, who had risen from his desk.

"Colonel Sergadeyev, we know very well what you are up to," she declared. From the expression on her face, I knew she was about to give Sergadeyev a tongue-lashing. "My husband has been arrested in retaliation for the arrest of your man in New York. You set him up with false evidence. The whole thing is a farce and you know it."

The expression on the colonel's face did not change. But after a brief silence, he said, "The whole thing came as a surprise to me as well."

Ruth's outburst made me nervous. I feared that telling Sergadeyev his investigation was a farce would anger him and jeopardize future visits. To be firm with Soviet officials was important; they respected that. To insult them was unwise. I knew only too well that deep in the Soviet psyche resides a feeling of inferiority before the Western world. Officials are quick to sense condescension from foreigners and, when pushed, can strike back in petty ways.

"How many times do I have the right to see my husband?" Ruth asked, softening her tone considerably.

"Under Soviet law, once a month," the colonel replied. "More depends on the investigator."

"My son is leaving for America to go back to school. He is terribly upset by the arrest of his father and thinks he will never see him again. Would it be possible for him to visit before he leaves?" she asked.

I recognized her ploy. She was appealing to Sergadeyev's emotions, hoping to touch the core of goodness that Baboota always claimed was in the Slavic soul.

"You have my telephone number," Sergadeyev replied coldly. "You may call me on Monday. I will give you an answer then."

I hugged Ruth once more before she left.

"Remember," she said in a very low voice. "I will stay here

as long as they have you in jail. If they want to expel me, they will have to drag me to the airport in handcuffs with the press in tow."

She was close to tears. So was I.

As the door closed, I wondered when I would see Ruth again. After five years in Moscow, we were both exhausted; we longed for some peace together. But when would we find it? In a month? In a year? In a decade?

ꙩ *Five*

ON THE SECOND NIGHT the tapping on the cell wall began. From then on, this mysterious signaling recurred intermittently, always at night, throughout my stay at Lefortovo. A few minutes after the guards had sounded the call to turn in, I would hear it: *tap, tap; tap, tap-tap*.

I lay on the cot under the window with my head toward the northeast wall, my feet pointing at Stas. I turned over and edged toward the wall to listen more closely. There seemed to be a pattern: one tap followed by a short pause and another tap. Then one tap followed by a pause and two quick taps. The sound was distinct — as if someone on the other side was aware that a new prisoner had been brought into Cell 26 and was trying to make contact by beating on the stone with an aluminum spoon.

I looked at Stas. He lay on his back with his handkerchief over his eyes, not making a sound. I couldn't tell whether he was asleep. If he had noticed anything, he didn't show it.

I had read about communications by "prison Morse" in Soviet camps and prisons. The taps usually corresponded to letters of the Russian alphabet, but I couldn't remember exactly how the system worked. To decipher it, I would have to tap back. I looked over at Stas again, almost tempted to give it a try. But was the tapping designed to provoke me into deeper trouble? If I was caught tapping back, I would probably be thrown into an isolation cell, or perhaps Sergadeyev would use the incident to incriminate me further. I decided then and there to assume it was a trap, so I never responded.

But the tapping did set me thinking about Frolov again. How had he survived the long days and nights in his cell. How had be weathered the horrible loneliness? Had he succeeded in communicating through the walls of his dungeon. That night I began making notes about him on pieces of toilet paper. I was more determined than ever to write a book about Frolov.

ᔔ ᔔ ᔔ

My search for Frolov began with a chance discovery of a newspaper article. I was working in my office on a late November afternoon in 1981. Snow had begun to fall, and I walked over to the window to watch the flakes descend in lazy whorls, transforming Moscow before my eyes. The ugly corners, the gaping potholes, the monotony of gray, formless apartment blocks and strident red banners — all were sinking under a blanket of pristine whiteness.

In the courtyard below I could see Sasha, the *dvornik*, janitor, heaving snow with his handmade shovel. The quiet that had descended over the city was broken periodically by the whirring of angry wheels as a driver tried to gun his car off the ice. The annual battle with winter had begun.

Bitter weather has made the Russian people patient and long-suffering; some would say that it inures the Russian soul to obedience and resignation. But if winter is an enemy, it can also be a friend, and at critical moments it had intervened to rescue the nation. Winter scattered Napoleon's army, forcing his frostbitten soldiers to withdraw in humiliation across the frozen steppes. A century later, winter thwarted Hitler's invincible war machine, and once again Moscow was saved. Winter may now have found a match in strategic missiles that can skim over the North Pole and rain destruction across the Russian heartland, but I wouldn't count on it.

Reluctantly, I sat down at my desk to continue reading the day's newspapers. Foreign correspondents lived in a closed society and, like medieval diviners, we would read between the lines for any evidence of a change in Soviet politics. It had been a depressing year. President Reagan, determined to rebuild American military strength, was talking tough to "the Evil Empire." Leonid Brezhnev, the Soviet leader, was dying slowly and hardly able to walk, let alone govern. The Soviet skipper of a Whiskey class submarine had run aground in Swedish waters, causing an international scandal that was dubbed "whiskey on the rocks." And word had circulated among diplomats that the Kremlin was considering a token withdrawal of troops from Afghanistan, yet nothing seemed to happen.

One more newspaper, I thought, and I, too, would succumb to winter by picking up my cross-country skis and taking off along the Moskva River at the foot of the Lenin Hills. Halfheartedly, I began skimming through the smudgy pages of *Sovietskaya Rossiya*, the official organ of the Russian Soviet Federated Socialist Republic. A headline suddenly caught my eye: "From the Chains of the Decembrists."

The writer described how secret societies in the North and South had tried to overthrow Czar Nicholas I in 1825, at the start of his thirty-year reign. These radical groups had grown out of the wave of nationalism that followed the defeat of Napoleon in 1812, when the Russian forces chased the Grande Armée all the way back to Paris and occupied the French capital for more than a year. There, the Russians had the opportunity to absorb many of the political ideas of the French Revolution — free speech, free assembly, and government by the people, not by the king.

But if their ideals were admirable, their planning was amateurish, and the uprising of December 14, 1825, failed. The rebels, who have come down in history as "the Decembrists," were beaten back by loyal troops, shackled in iron, and sentenced to hard labor in Siberia. When they were freed, they beat their chains into rings, crosses, and bracelets — probably a hundred pieces or more. The article described how some pieces had surfaced as far away as France, even in the United States, and asked anyone who knew of others to come forward.

Childhood memories of my father's iron ring with its curious inscription flooded back, leaving me enormously excited. Could it be that the mysterious ring was part of this Decembrist legacy? Had Frolov really been a Decembrist? I wondered whether I should contact the writer. Would he see me? And if he did, would he pressure to return the ring to the Soviet Union?

Twenty years earlier, when I had worked in Moscow as a correspondent for UPI, Soviet citizens were distinctly nervous about meeting Americans. And for a long time after the Revolution, people burned any document or photograph that connected them, their prents, or their grandparents to the old regime, and many priceless papers were lost. The new society was supposed to be a workers' and farmers' paradise; people with an educated background were suspect. My own grandfather had been branded an enemy of the people. I wondered if it was wise to reveal my connections. In the 1960s, I purposely kept them quiet. Could that family secret be dangerous for me now?

After several days of indecison, however, I decided to contact the paper. There had been many changes in Russia in twenty years, not so much in people's material well-being as in their psychology. In 1981, a destructive cynicism permeated Soviet society. People no longer believed that socialism would improve their lives. Before, Soviets would boast, "*U nas luche*. Everything is better in our country." Now they would say with a resigned shrug, "*U nas nye khuje*. It's no worse here than elsewhere." The people knew the rest of the world was leaving Russia behind.

Along with disillusionment, nostalgia for the past was growing. Gone were the days of the tabula rasa, when the commissars tried to expunge the past to build a more perfect future. Now there was a demonstrable interest in the period before the Revolution: archives were being opened, museums established, and churches restored. Blue blood in one's veins was becoming more a source of pride than embarrassment. I counted, too, on the writer's curiosity about my Russian-American background; that ought to help overcome any nervousness about meeting a foreigner.

My first step was to write a letter. In Moscow, everything begins with a letter. You can't simply pick up the telephone as you would in the United States. But I had a problem, too: my written Russian was imperfect, and I had recently fired my Soviet secretary. Like many Soviet women who work for foreigners, she had become more interested in fancy Western clothing than in doing a good day's work. Months of trying to obtain a replacement through the official Diplomatic Service Bureau had led nowhere.

Finally, I called Lyuba, a friend, who came from a privileged but repressed Soviet political family. (Her father was a Central Committee member who was executed in 1937 in Stalin's purges.) I had known her ever since I first worked in Moscow.

"May I come over this evening?" I asked when she picked up the telephone. "I have something important to discuss." One of the reasons that everything takes to long to accomplish in Moscow is that no one wants to discuss private business over the phone, especially with a foreign correspondent.

"Come on over," she answered warmly. "We'll drink tea."

I knew that Lyuba did not like me to use the car, with its yellow correspondent number plates — it was too visible. Instead, I took the metro. After taking the escalator up from the station, I walked left along the badly lit street toward Lyuba's apartment building. It had been built by German prisoners during the Second World War and stands in a small wooded park. Large banks of snow were piled along the road, and I almost slipped on the ice in the courtyard before reaching the door. As I tried to open it, I cursed myself for forgetting the door code. Electronic locks were just beginning to be installed in Moscow apartment buildings to combat the rising number of robberies. I pushed the buttons of the lock at random. Suddenly for no very good reason the door swung open, and the odor of putrefying garbage wafted out from the dank, unlit vestibule. I took the rickety elevator to the fifth floor.

I rang the bell and Lyuba opened the door. Glancing suspiciously behind me across the landing, she pulled me silently over the threshold into the small foyer of her modest two-bedroom apartment, which she shared with her husband, a writer, and her grown son. Once we were inside, she gave me a big hug and chided me about not coming to see her more often.

"I know you," she said, laughing. "You only come when you want something."

"But you always greet me in that old housecoat," I teased. On the street, Lyuba was one of the most elegant Muscovites I knew. At home, like so many Soviet women, she wore sweat pants or a robe.

"Come into the kitchen and I will make you a cup of tea, and you can tell me why I deserve this honor," she said, leading me to the place where all important business is conducted in Soviet households. Sitting at the small table, we drank tea and munched on chocolates, which Lyuba had received from a friend who had access to the special store of the Central Committee.

"Such chocolates you can't find anywhere else," she told me proudly. In the Soviet Union, much of life revolves around whom you know — what they can get for you, what you can get for them. As we chatted, I told Lyuba about the article and Frolov's ring.

"Why didn't you tell me about this before?" She scolded me with mock anger. "Where have you been hiding your Russian roots? And Revolutionary roots, no less? Come on, let's dash off a letter to the newspaper."

Lyuba had an intuitive sense for how to craft a persuasive appeal to Soviet officials. She took out her typewriter and swiftly composed the following letter: "Your article has unfolded for me, an American correspondent, a whole new perspective on the Decembrist uprising. I have a ring that may be connected to the mutiny. I would like you to look at it. Perhaps you can help me find out its history and even something of my Russian past." We talked a good deal more that evening about the effect of the failed uprising. Finally, at about midnight, I went home across town.

The next day I retyped the letter with our Russian-language Royal on magazine stationery and asked Pavel, our driver, to take it to the newspaper's office. Weeks went by with no response. Had it ever arrived? I began to regret having asked Pavel to deliver the letter. At the time, we were in the middle of a power struggle. Conditions in Moscow make a driver virtually essential. Without one, most of the day would be spent running errands, which in Moscow invariably includes standing in long lines, going to the airport to ship film, paying bills, picking up mail, obtaining theater tickets, and making travel arrangements. Practically nothing can be ordered over the telephone. Important letters must be sent by registered mail or delivered by hand. Bills must be paid in cash.

I knew that Pavel reported to the KGB when called upon, informing them about my views, my habits, the stories I was working on. This I understood as a fact of life for a resident correspondent. My main complaint against him was that he worked for himself, not that he monitored me. He was driven by an insatiable appetite for Western goods, which he expected me to produce. The trouble was that Pavel equated *U.S. News and World Report* with the Soviet government, which Russian workers considered miserly and withholding; therefore it deserved to be cheated. Pavel thought there was nothing wrong with siphoning gas out of the office car to sell on the black market, visiting a mistress on the way back from the bank, or telling me that he had taken four hours at customs when he only took two. He wouldn't have dreamed of stealing from me personally, but he had no qualms about bilking an amorphous institution in Washington to which he owed no loyalty. Months later, Pavel went to Helsinki to have the car serviced, he bought a VCR and a sheepskin coat on my account. Of course, he would pay for the goods out of his salary, he protested. But it was too late: I finally decided he had to go. By this time, the whole family was spending too much energy trying to stay one step ahead of Pavel's latest trick.

In February 1982, just as I was preparing to write a new letter, I received a call from the assistant editor of the paper. My letter had reached its destination, and the editor invited me to the office for a talk about the ring.

It was an unusually crisp winter day when I drove the blue Volvo down Komsomolskii Prospekt, past the orange and green church of St. Nicholas the Weaver onto the Garden Ring, which-circles central Moscow. The golden cupolas of the Russian Orthodox churches glittered brightly against the dreary apartment blocks, a reminder that for centuries Moscow had prided itself on being the Third Rome. On Gorkii Street, near the green and white Belorussian railroad station, grandmothers in shapeless overcoats and brown shawls of fluffy Orenburg wool formed lines for Chinese cabbage. Women street sweepers, wearing orange vests, dusted the flakes from the sidewalks with twig brooms. The wheels of the car pounded over the cobblestones as I turned right on Truth Street, Ulitsa Pravda. This unprepossessing road off the Leningrad Highway is Moscow's Fleet Street, where the party newspaper, *Pravda*, is printed along with the youth paper, *Komsomolskaya Pravda*, and *Sovietskaya Rossiya*. I maneuvered the car between the banks of snow, looking for an empty space. It is sometimes hard to find a parking space in Moscow since there is little turnover during the day: the city has yet to introduce parking meters. I finally found a spot near *Pravda* and pulled next to several black Central Committee sedans, parked with their motors running and their drivers dozing.

I found the Bureau of Passes and, armed with a cardboard *propusk*, entered the building and approached a policeman in a gray and red uniform. He was pulling furtively on a cigarette, which he hid under his desk when he saw me coming. He glanced at my pass and waved me on. Inside, only a few bored-looking people came and went along *Sovietskaya Rossiya*'s dreary corridors. Soviet newspaper offices, unlike American ones, are as quiet as a tomb. There is no hum of activity — no message center, no phones ringing constantly, no word processors or luminescent video screens. Many leading commentators, defensive about their computer illiteracy, still write their stories in longhand, although a few have accepted typewriters as a useful tool.

I took a creaky elevator to the fourth floor and walked along a ragged red and black runner. At Room 411, I knocked twice. A woman's voice answered, "Da." I pushed open the blond wood door, revealing two rather nervous citizens. One was a plump, middle-aged woman wearing a skirt and heavy sweater. She was editing copy as I entered, stuffing a sticky brush back into a paste pot. The other was a dark-haired, older man of average height who seemed to cower inside his brown raincoat.

"Gospodin Danilov?" The woman editor greeted me tentatively.

"Yes," I replied, "I am Gospodin Danilov. But please call me by my Russian name . . . Nikolai Sergeyevich."

"*Khorosho*. Very well," she replied. "I am Svetlana Stepunia, and I want to introduce you to Svyatoslav Alexandrovich, the author of the Decembrist article."

I shook hands with the dark-haired man, who on closer inspection seemed more shy than nervous. Without pausing for small talk, Svyatoslav Alexandrovich immediately began describing his search for Decembrist memorabilia: "You know, every year, new bits and pieces from the Decembrists show up, even one hundred and fifty years later. Not so very long ago, one of our collectors happened on a batch of water colors that the Decembrist Nikolai Bestuzhev painted around 1832. They had been lost for over a century."

Turning to the subject of my ancestor, he continued: "You say in your letter that you might be related to Frolov."

"Yes. My grandmother was Anna Frolova," I replied.

He started. "What a coincidence! I was just working in the archives on material related to the Frolovs. But, you know, six different Frolovs were arrested after the uprising. Which one was yours?"

"I really don't know, Svyatoslav Alexandrovich," I said. "I'm not even a hundred percent certain that my Frolov was a Decembrist. All I can say is that my grandmother's father was Nikolai Frolov, and his father was Alexander. My own father sometimes said that our Frolov was a young officer who happened to be ambling through St. Petersburg at the time of the uprising. Apparently he was arrested for walking through the square and was banished to Siberia by the czar himself."

"Yes," the writer replied, pausing for a moment, "Czar Nicholas did insist on meeting each of the arrested men, and we have some good records of those occasions. But which Frolov your ancestor might have been . . . that I don't know. Not a famous one, I'm sure of that. By the way, do you have ny relatives here?"

"I don't know. Probably not," I answered, amazed and pleased that Svyatoslav Alexandrovich was willing to delve into this area. "My uncle says the last contact our family had with any relatives in Russia was during the war, in about 1942. I think we got a letter from Moscow at that time, then all communications stopped. Would you be able to check further for me?"

Svyatoslav Alexandrovich seemed interested; as we talked, he became increasingly relaxed, "I'll do what I can," he said. "It will take me some research, but I may be able to come up with something. But I do have a favor to ask." He hesitated for a moment, giving me time to wonder what I could possibly do for him. "Your letter mentioned a ring. I'm trying to catalogue all the known pieces of Decembrist jewelry, so I would very much like to see your ring and examine it. If that is impossible, I would like a good, clear photograph and exact measurements to the nearest tenth of a centimeter. I would like to scrape a bit of the iron to determine if it is the same iron used in the Decembrists' chains."

He made this request as if it were the most natural one in the world. So there it was: I was being asked to bring the ring back to Russia, exactly as I had feared. In recent years, the Soviet government had been trying to recover many of its art treasures that had found their way abroad after the Revolution, when people would swap a Fabergé Easter egg for a crust of bread. The cultural authorities believed that Western collectors had taken advantage of the poverty after the Revolution to rob the country of its masterpieces. The Soviets wanted them back; they were even willing to pay high prices at international auction houses whenever such pieces came on the market.

Suddenly I became very suspicious. Was the KGB at work here. I could imagine how: by listening to Ruth and me in the apartment, they had learned about the ring. They had pressured Svyatoslav Alexandrovich to entice me to bring it back to Moscow. Then they would pounce on it and find some pretext for not returning it to me. Worse still, they would accuse me of trying to smuggle it out of the country. I knew of several Soviet dissidents who had been falsely accused of dealing in icons and sent to prison; I didn't want any such trouble.

I equivocated; Svyatoslav Alexandrovich pleaded. Sensing my fears, he assured me that Soviet law protects the personal property of individuals. But how could I be certain? The protection offered by Soviet law did not fill me with confidence. Our first meeting ended on this indecisive note. I promised to consider his request, and Svyatoslav Alexandrovich agreed to find out more about Frolov.

ᔕ ᔕ ᔕ

In the next few days, I wrote to my few remaining relatives for more information about my Danilov and Frolov forebears. Letters went off to my elderly cousins, Olga and Vladimir Matousievitch in France, who were in the cognac business, and, of course, to my father and Uncle Mish. Soon they all wrote back with little tidbits of information.

Once, as a teenager, I had drawn up a family tree. Now I started sketchng it out again, and this draft became the first of many of the Frolov tree. Eventually, the tree went back eight generations to Fyodor Frolov, who lived in the middle of the eighteenth century.

In April, armed with this information, I called Svetlana Stepunina. Pleased to be of help, she said she would arrange a second meeting at her office. A few days later, she called and invited me back to Truth Street. As he had promised, Svyatoslav Alexandrovich had drawn up his own Frolov tree. We compared the two versions: his was based solely on archival materials: mine, on family recollections. They turned out to be strikingly similar; he had missed two of my grandmother's sisters, but the central lines were identical.

Then Svyatoslav Alexandrovich delivered astonishing news. He had discovered that only one of the six Frolovs involved in the uprising had been sent into exile. That Frolov was indeed my great-great-grandfather, Lieutenant Alexander Filippovich Frolov, to be exact. The five others had been released or given minor punishments. To my great excitement, Svyatoslav Alexandrovich now began to reel off details I had never heard before and which I was sure neither Serge nor Baboota knew. He talked with such confidence, as though the events had happened only recently and that he had known some of the participants. Lieutenant Frolov had been assigned to the Penza Regiment of the second Army in the Ukraine during the summer of 1825. A month after the mutiny in January 1826, he was arrested in the Ukrainian grain town of Zhitomir and sent to Siberia for life. There was no indication at all that he had been in St. Petersburg at the time of the uprising, as Serge sometimes claimed at cocktail parties.

Why, then, did Frolov receive such a terrible sentence? Why banish a man to Siberia for life if he didn't even particpate in the mutiny? Nothing I had learned so far had shed any light on the question that intrigued me most. It was a mystery I was determined to unravel, and my conversation with Svyatoslav Alexandrovich provided a powerful shot of adrenaline. Like an athlete at the start of a race, I was keyed up and ready to go. In two short meetings with Svyatoslav Alexandrovich, I had already learned more about Frolov than Baboota had known. And how much more awaited me?

"By the way," he said, interrupting my thoughts, "I have another surprise for you. Can you come with me on a brief excursion?"

He wouldn't say where we were going, which made me a bit nervous. But I was beginning to warm to this generous man. His passion for Russian history was insatiable, and as he told me more about his own background, I came to feel certain that I could trust him. After all, we had a strong bond, for he was also the descendant of a Decembrist, Colonal Ivan Pavlo-Shveikovsky. Maybe our ancestors had even met and talked to each another.

We put on our coats, thanked Svetlana Stepunina, and stepped out into the slushy street. The melting snow, mixed with sand and salt, began to ooze into my shoes. We hailed a minibus-taxi, which hauled us and a dozen others to the Belorussian metro station. Dropping our 5-kopeck pieces into the turnstyle, we descended the long but fast wooden escalator into the marble depths. The smell of ozone wafted up to us as the trains rushed by with such a clatter that it was almost impossible to talk. Once on the platform, my companion drew me aside.

"It's not a good idea for me to be seeing you often," he shouted over the roar of the trains. "My work, my son's career, conditions in general . . . you know. If you need to get in touch with me, use this number, and call only from a public phone booth."

We pushed through the doors of a blue subway car. A recorded voice echoed through the carriage: "Caution! The doors are closing. The next stop will be Barrikadnaya."

Svyatoslav Alexandrovich's warning did not surprise me. I

remembered that in the 1960s casual encounters between Soviets and foreigners rarely developed into permanent relationships. Under Stalin, people had been given prison terms for talking to outlanders or accepting presents from them. These days in the Soviet Union, especially in Moscow, the younger generation is oblivious of that bitter legacy; they are less afraid of authority than their elders. But the young are not necessarily more courageous — they are simply naive. The fears of Svyatoslav Alexandrovich's generation are based on firsthand experience. I learned later that his family had suffered horribly in the purges. His mother and father had lived in Paris but returned to Moscow after the Revolution. His father was subsequently arrested and never seen again. For Svyatoslav Alexandrovich, it was a true act of courage to meet me.

After changing from the Ring Line to the Purple, we pulled into 1905 Street, and my guide started pushing his way to the door though the solid wall of bodies. Once outside, we turned left and started walking. I realized we were heading toward Vagankovskoye Cemetery, which I had often visited before. Svyatoslav Alexandrovich, I imagined, planned to show me the grave of his ancestor.

It was a Friday, but there were many people about. Most were elderly, and they were cleaning up the graves for Easter. Several men were carefully painting the wrought iron railings surrounding their plots. The people who visit Soviet cemeteries are not necessarily religious in a traditional sense. They are simply aware of the fragility of life, and few countries are as familiar with death as the Soviet Union. In the Second World War alone, the Russians lost twenty million soldiers and civilians. Not all the deaths were caused by outside aggression, however; an estimated fifteen million people starved to death during Stalin's collectivization of agriculture in the 1930s, and another six million or more disappeared in the purges. The memories of the dead are revered in Russia, and people are surprised that Americans don't visit family graves often, as they themselves do. Furthermore, with such overcrowded living conditions in Russia, the cemetery becomes a private place, a spot where one can ponder the meaning of life. In another two weeks, Moscow's cemeteries would be full of flowers. Relatives would place painted eggs, cakes, oranges, and even bottles of vodka by the grave markers. The offerings — a holdover from pagan rituals — are meant to nourish the dead on their wanderings in the netherworld.

As usual, there was a crowd around the grave of Vladimir Vysotsky, the poet who captured the hearts of all Russia in the 1970s with his stinging verse against arbitrary power and blockhead bureaucrats. He died, at forty-four, from too much vodka during the summer of the Moscow Olympics. I saw a woman emerge from the crowd and arrange a bouquet of red carnations on his grave.

"No country loves poetry as much as the Russians," I commented as we walked down the path lined by oak trees. "But then, Russia always destroys its greatest talents." My friend did not answer.

We walked past the yellow and white orthodox church. Several coffin lids, covered in red, yellow, and blue crepe, were stacked against the wall. In the candlelit interior, the priest would be saying prayers over the open casket. The relatives, women with shawls over their heads and men with hats doffed, would cross themselves silently. At the gravesite, the ancient practice would be repeated: relatives would kiss the forehead of the deceased one last time, and the coffin lid would be hammered down. The box would be lowered, and the closest kin would throw a handful of dirt into the pit. Then the party would probably go home and get drunk, eulogizing the departed far into the night.

We came to an abrupt halt. "*Vot!* There!" Svyatoslav Alexandrovich exclaimed dramatically, pointing to a plot I had walked by absent-mindedly many times before. "Frolov's grave!"

I was stunned. Before me, resting on a stone slab, stood a squat, reddish granite cube, about a yard on each side. A highly polished hemisphere sat atop the cube, cradled by the four raised

corners. At each corner was a sculpted oil lamp; from the lips of
these stone latnerns flowed lines of smoke etched into the hemisphere along with a constellation of stars. A tree and a large bush
filled the rest of the plot, which was enclosed by a black iron
railing. Within that space, beneath that momument, lay the bones
of Alexander Frolov. My flesh and blood! A part of me, a part
of Baboota and of Serge, a part of Caleb and Miranda.

During all the years I had lived and worked in the Soviet Union,
my interest in my family had been intellectual. Baboota's accounts
had been gripping but secondhand. What I had learned in college
came from books. Here, at last, was the emotional confirmation
of my Russian origins. I could be an American and belong to the
United States, as Serge wanted. I could be separated from ordinary
Russians by tongue and passport. But I could not be standing
here if Frolov had not lived. I knew my search would turn into
more — much more — than a remote errand from Baboota.

Svyatoslav Alexandrovich broke the silence by announcing that
he would recite some of his own verse. It was a wonderfully
Russian gesture and sent a tingle up my spine. He stepped away
from the grave, drew himself up, and turned toward me, saying:

Russia is not just birch trees that grow beneath your favorite
window,
Russia is blood and turmoil,
Blood, and sweat, and tears.
Russia lay down to sleep with the sword.
At weddings, Russia rejoiced with the sword.
With sword in hand, her children were born.

I was deeply touched. Clearly, my companion's love of country
was far deeper than the empty slogans shouted in Red Square on
May Day.

I studied the grave closely. A white marlble plaque recorded
that Frolov had died in 1885, at the age of eighty-one. The plot,
it turned out, was also the resting place of another Decembrist,
Bobrishchev-Pushkin, and Frolov's wife. Her name was Yevdo-

kiya Nikolaevna Makarova and she had lived until 1901, the year my own mother was born. I spotted, too, the graves of Baboota's two brothers, whom she had often talked about. Gavriil had died in 1947 and Alexander in 1942, the year of the last letter from Moscow.

The Frolov monument was unusual, I thought. The lanterns and the wisps of smoke probably symbolized the Decembrists' political aspiration of freedom from serfdom and tyranny; the stars meant that their hopes, though unfulfilled, were eternal. Knowing a little about Frolov's life, I wondered why the monument was so elaborate. It raised new questions, beckoning me on. Could it be that Frolov had in fact been an important strategist in the movement? Was that why he got such a harsh sentence? Or did he become famous because he lived so long, a kind of rebel elder statesman? Or maybe his children simply wanted to glorify him beyond measure? I had to find out.

Glancing again at the monument, a patch of red caught my eye. I looked closer and saw three red roses and a sprig of greenery. Someone else had also been visiting the grave. A stranger? A Decembrist enthusiast? My God, I thought, someone else cares as much about Frolov's memory as I do. Could I possibly have living relatives in Moscow?

Six

THERE WAS NO CALL for questioning this Monday morning, September 1. It was a relief, for it gave me a chance to collect myself. Another sleepless night had left me feeling like an old sneaker. Even Stas's solicitousness made me jumpy. He continued to assure me that Lefortovo had good facilities. From the prison store, every month I could order 10 rubles' (about $14) worth of essentials like bread, butter, and tooth powder. The library was the best in the Soviet prison system because, he said, "all the books have been confiscated from intellectuals." It was as if my cellmate was preparing me for an extended stay. "Later," he said, "we'll order up the book catalogue, which comes in a couple of binders, and you can choose a few books for yourself. I get seven books every week and try to read a book a day. In the meantime, feel free to browse through anything I have."

I was quickly losing track of time. Until my watch had been confiscated, I didn't realize how much I depended on it. Now I felt off balance, which was of course the whole idea. Even when I had nothing to do, I still wanted to know how much time there was before the next event, whether it was a meal or an interrogation. Stas boasted that he could guess the correct time to within half an hour. He noted that the prisoner's day is regulated by meals: breakfast at eight o'clock, lunch at one, and dinner at five. "It's also very important to check the clock over the guard's desk when they take you out," he added.

I decided to accept Stas's offer and borrowed a biography of Ivan Michurin, a Russian plant breeder who laid the groundwork for the quack genetic theories of the 1940s and '50s, which asserted that acquired characteristics could be inherited. I sat on my cot, turning the pages mechanically. I found it extremely difficult to read, partly because I didn't have my reading glasses, partly because I couldn't concentrate. Try as I would, I found it impossible to banish anxiety for more than ten or fifteen minutes at a time.

The prospect of more interrogation hung over me like a cloud. I knew that Sergadeyev would use every trick in the KGB handbook to make me look like a spy. Sitting in my cell, I imagined him in a smoke-filled room with his advisers, plotting the next move. The only benefit in my being called to Room 215 was that I could check the time and possibly get a hint about what was going on in the world outside.

Ruth had told me that the American media were outraged at my arrest and were clamoring for my release. That was cheering news, but it was not enough. The big question was: Would Washington be willing to deal? Or would the political hard-liners insist that I be freed unconditionally, leaving Zakharov in jail to stand trial? I knew that I would never walk out of Lefortovo until there was some give in Zakharov's situation. I was arrested, after all, because the KGB takes care of its own. And if Washington did negotiate for Zakharov, would Moscow give on Daniloff?

Gorbachev was a tough player. Under his leadership, the Soviet Union increasinly demanded reciprocity in its relations with the major capitalist countries. On the subject of spy arrests, his policy was tit for tat. In 1985, when Britain expelled twenty-five Soviets from London as spies, Gorbachev ordered twenty-five Britons

out of Moscow. When Prime Minister Margaret Thatcher upped
the ante by sending five more Soviets packing, Gorbachev expelled five more Britons.

In Gorbachev's view, the Soviet Union is a superpower and
should be treated with respect, particularly by the United States.
And in 1986, especially, the Soviet leader was in no mood to
deal charitably with Ronald Reagan. Gorbachev was smarting
from what he considered gratuitous insults following his first
summit with the American president in Geneva. In January, the
White House had brushed aside Gorbachev's comprehensive arms
reduction proposal with an apparent lack of consideration. In
March, unannounced, the Pentagon had ordered warships through
Crimean territorial waters, setting off a Soviet military alert. The
same month, Reagon had ordered a major reduction of Soviet
diplomatic personnel at the United Nations on the grounds that
they were nearly all spies. In April, the United States had bombed
Libya, a Soviet friend, in retaliation for a terrorist attack on a
German nightclub in which American citizens had been killed.
Then, just as preparations were moving ahead for a second summit meeting, the White House sanctioned the arrest of Zakharov.
I could imagine Soviet diplomats asking themselves, If the Americans caught a Soviet spy red-handed, why didn't they inform the
Soviet ambassador and request that the man leave quietly? Why
create a storm now? In Soviet eyes, either Reagan was being
deliberately provocative or someone didn't want a summit.
Whichever, Gorbachev was not going to be pushed around.

As I tried to look at the U.S.-Soviet confrontation over my
arrest from all sides, one thing became increasingly plain. I did
not want to be swapped, one for one, for a Soviet spy. That
outcome would encourage people to think that I really did have
ties to the CIA. Such suspicions could haunt me for the rest of
my life, as they had haunted, and ruined, Sam Jaffe, my colleague
in television.

What I didn't know then, thank God, was that a strong precedent existed for such a swap: in 1972, the U.S. government

agreed to trade a Soviet spy for an American businessman held hostage in retaliation, and that was the approach the Russians were insisting on now. This episode began in February 1972 when the FBI arrested Valery Markelov, a Soviet citizen without diplomatic immunity, for collecting classifed information about the U.S. Navy's F–14A Tomcat fighter. The KGB retaliated, and Paul Sjeklocha of California was the victim. This flamboyant businessman visited Moscow frequently and wanted to organize hunting parties in Siberia. Before, he had passed easily through Soviet customs with expensive presents he allegedly used as bribes. After Markelov's arrest, he received several invitations to come to Moscow to complete his business deal. When he arrived at the airport, he was arrested for importing undeclared firearms and thrown into Lefortovo.

Sjeklocha was held for several weeks while the United States mounted pressure. Finally, a deal was struck, and Sjeklocha was released to the U.S. Embassy. After his KGB investigator read a protocol banning him permanently from the Soviet Union, he was placed on a flight back to the States. Markelov was put on a plane for Moscow just days before President Nixon's first summit with Brezhnev in May 1972. Both superpower leaders were anxious to meet and they managed to hush up the entire affair. The deal would have remained secret to this day if the *New York Times* hadn't reported, months later, that Washington had asked a federal judge to dismiss the charges against Markelov so that $100,000 in bail could be returned to the Russians.

Sitting on my cot, pondering superpower relations and trying to read, I looked up and noticed Stas scribbling his interminable formulas on toilet paper. It reminded me of my old interest in math: as a schoolboy I had been fascinated by plane and spherical trigonometry and by navigation. I continued to study math in college but lost interest after calculus. Thinking it might distract me, I asked Stas to explain differential calculus. Predictably, he was delighted to share his enthusiasm for numbers. He reached for a clean piece of toilet paper, sketched a graph with X and Y axes, and drew a curve in the first quadrant; the object is to determine the area lying beneath the curve. He then proceeded to give me, in Russian, the same explanation of the formula I had heard, in English, thirty-three years earlier at Harvard. When I finally wearied of his lecture, I thanked him and stuffed the scrap of paper into my pocket.

At 1:00 P.M., just as Stas had promised, I heard the lunch trolley coming down the hall. Lunch at Lefortovo is the big meal of the day: soup followed by mashed potatoes and about two ounces of fish or meat, all washed down with tea. We ate slowly, drawing the process out for about fifteen or twenty minutes. Soon after we finished, the *kormushka* banged open.

"Danilov! *Gotovte na vyzov!* Prepare to be summoned!" a guard shouted at me. My heart sank. Now what? Within minutes, I was marching along the balcony with my guard to Room 215.

ဆ ဆ ဆ

The colonel looked up from behind his desk. He signed the usual receipt and handed it to the guard.

I felt at a terrible disadvantage, standing in front of my well-dressed adversary, hands behind my back, trousers falling down, shoes half laced. The stubble on my chin itched, and I reeked of sweat. These indignities made me cringe inside, but I struggled not to let my distress appear on my face.

Sergadeyev let me stand there for a moment while he looked me up and down without saying a word. Then he gestured toward the chair, signaling that the little game between suspect and inquisitor was over.

"And how have you fared, Nikolai Sergeyevich?" he inquired in a friendly tone, as though humiliating me was the last thing on his mind. "Do you have any complaints?"

"None, other than that you are holding me here," I responded. In truth, my hemorrhoid was very painful, particularly when I sat for hours on the hard wooden chairs of Sergadeyev's office. I didn't want to bring it up with him, though, at least not then.

I had exposed enough weakness for one day. Later, I might want to make it a health issue, along with my blood pressure.

"By the way," the colonel said, "did I give you a notebook?"

I shook my head.

Sergadeyev reached across his desk and handed me a notebook with a green cover for my own records. "You know" . . . he seemed to open up . . . 'you are really a very accomplished spy. I can tell. You don't resist arrest. You keep yourself under strict control."

I couldn't win. They could take whatever I did and make me look like a spy. Even my self-control, which I clung to with such determination, worked against me.

"And your wife is also remarkably well trained," he continued. "She is not throwing herself on the floor in hysterics."

"I am not a spy," I insisted. I repeated that phrase ad nauseam throughout my interrogation. "I am not a spy. I am not a spy . . ."

"Not a spy? Well, we shall see," he answered with a smile. I caught a glimpse of his gold fillings. "By the way, you will be having a visit shortly from your son, but I want to go over a few questions from our last chat."

The prospect of a visit with Caleb was wonderful, but I hardly reacted. I held myself still while Sergadeyev flicked a switch near his desk to turn on a red light in the corridor. The interrogation was officially under way.

"Have some tea? Coffee?" he asked. The colonel seemed in no special hurry to get down to business. That, too, was technique. By drawing out the process, the interrogator exhausts and intimidates the prisoner, making him more susceptible to pressure. Being in the presence of Sergadeyev was like being in a dentist's chair without an anesthetic.

He reached over to the white china teapot, filled it slowly with water, and placed an electric filament in it. Then he walked over to the wall and, with infinite care, plugged the device into the socket.

"You don't have to worry that I am going to drug you," he remarked.

"I didn't suppose you were," I said, adding, "If you don't mind, I'd like some tea."

Sergadeyev reached for a glass with a metal holder for my tea and a china cup for his coffee. I noted his preference for coffee; maybe I was right about his Central Asian connections.

While the colonel and measuring the tea leaves, I had a chance to look about the room. The office was rectangular, about fifteen by twenty-five feet. Sergadeyev's desk was on the left. I was seated at a long table, which came off the colonel's desk at a right angle and faced the two windows, which were wide open; I could see the beige bricks on the far wall of the building across the yard. Remembering Stas's advice, I checked the clock between the windows: 3:40 P.M. Over the desk hung the Soviet hammer and sickle, painted gold and covered with dust. On the window side of the desk were two small tables: on one stood a single telephone; on the other, three. A spittoon sat on the floor nearby.

On the right-hand side of the room was a small table, next to the courtyard wall, with a carafe of water and several glasses on a round tray. Next to it stood a large bookcase filled with reference books, including the 1983 *Soviet Military Encyclopedia*, suggesting that Sergadeyev was regularly involved in national security cases. Next to the wall behind me were what appeared to be a child's desk and chair. These diminutive pieces seemed strangely out of place among the heavier furniture. Only later did I discover their purpose.

"I did not call you this morning." Sergadeyev began again as he walked over to a formidable brown metal safe that stood across from his desk by the corridor wall. He fiddled with the combination, pulled the massive door open slowly, and extracted some papers. "I did not call because I went to the Moscow Procuracy to obtain approval for your arrest. Under our law, we may arrest and hold a suspect for seventy-two hours. But then we must have the assent of the procuracy. Here are the formal papers."

He handed me a neatly typed piece of white paper, without any special letterhead, describing my arrest and bearing the circular rubber stamp of the Moscow procurator's office.

"I'm glad you raised that," I told him. "I had been wondering about the legality of your arresting me." But to myself I said: Valery Dimitriyevich, you should have gotten your warrant before you arrested me, not after. In the West, your failure to get a warrant would betray how hastily you threw all this together. And why not the usual simultaneous search of my apartment? Or my car? Why didn't you impound my personal effects?

Sergadeyev handed me the glass of tea and returned to his questioning in a businesslike tone: "You say you met Misha in Frunze. Tell me again the circumstances of your trip."

I repeated the details of my trip to Frunze with Jim Gallagher. The questions and answers continued like a broken record. We met Misha in a restaurant. No, he was not alone. Yes, we met him the next day. A number of the questions seemed totally irrelevant, though I assumed there was some purpose behind them because the colonel wrote down everything on his pad.

"What was Misha's last name?" Sergadeyev asked.

For a moment I couldn't remember . . . we so rarely used family names.

"Come on, come on." Sergadeyev began to push me. "Could it have been Luzin? Wasn't it Mikhail Anatolyevich?"

"It might have been Luzin. I never knew his patronymic." I was still trying to work out in my own mind whether I owed Misha any protection. How long had he been working with the KGB? Was it from the very beginning? Or did the KGB get to him later?

"How then, when Misha called you on Friday, August 29, he said to you — and we know this" — Sergadeyev paused to make sure I got the point that the KGB had recorded the conversation — "he said, 'This is Frunze calling.' Why did you call him Frunze if his name was Luzin? I think you can understand that it looks very suspicious to us. Conspiratorial, I would say."

"My wife and I called him Frunze because we knew a lot of Mishas. We wanted to distinguish him from the others when he called. Also, he was concerned that our relationship might come to the attention of the KGB. He didn't want that."

"And that is why you asked him, from time to time, if the KGB had approached him between your meetings?" The colonel looked at me skeptically. Whatever I did, whatever I said, looked suspicious in their eyes.

Uneasy, I glanced at the clock: it was now nearly 5:00 P.M.

Sergadeyev relented. "All right. We'll continue another time. I did promise you a meeting with your son." Sergadeyev put down his pencil and stood up.

         ဢ ဢ ဢ

We walked out the door, turned right instead of left this time, went by the other offices and around the corner, and walked past the portraits of the outstanding KGB men and into the empty visitors room. Caleb had not yet arrived. The white ruffled curtains that covered the iron bars on the window were drawn. But I soon realized that something was very different. All the furniture had been switched around. The couch, instead of being on the left side of the room, as it had been on Sunday, was now on the right, where the investigator's desk had been; it now occupied the couch's former spot. I guessed that the hidden microphones had had trouble picking up what Ruth and I were whispering to each other.

Waiting for Caleb, I wondered how he would be. Ruth and I had asked a lot of him by bringing him to the Soviet Union, and he had not disappointed us. One of the reasons I had sought a Moscow assignment was to have the oppotunity to pass my Russian heritage on to the children. Mandy had spent a year with us, studying Chekhov and the theater; just this summer she'd come back from London on a Soviet ship and was elected queen of the vessel, Miss Baltika! I'll always be sorry that she wasn't able to spend more time with us in Moscow. Now Caleb was about to suffer with his father in jail. Russia, it seemed, insisted on extracting tolls from our family.

Caleb's adjustment to Moscow had not been easy. Adolescence is a hard enough time without introducing another language in another culture. I recalled that first summer, when we sent him to the Pioneer camp just outside Moscow. We wanted him to gain a better grasp of the language before the school year began in September. Poor Caleb. For an eleven-year-old American to be thrown into a Soviet Pioneer camp was total culture shock. Everything was different — the kids, the food, the language . . . In Washington, Caleb had always swum in beautifully clean, chlorinated pools. At the camp, the pool was dirty, full of weeds and frogs. He complained, too, about the kids; he said they were all gay because they hugged each other constantly. Still, he stuck it out, thanks to a young counselor named Volodya, for whom it was a matter of pride that the American boy should like the Soviet camp. He helped Caleb with his Russian and saw to it that he was part of the group. Before long, he was diving into the slimy green pool with the others. I will always be grateful to Volodya for his kindness. Caleb learned an important lesson that summer: people can enjoy themselves without having a high standard of living.

For the next two and a half years, Caleb was one of thirty-five students in a class in Moscow School No. 80. The Soviet curriculum is standardized, demanding, and largely unimaginative, and although the average Soviet pupil graduates from high school with a better grasp of reading, writing, math, and science than his American peer, he lacks the ability to analyze and think independently.

Besides struggling with the three R's in a foreign language, Caleb also had to distinguish between the classmates who liked him for himself and those who saw him as a source of American chewing gum, stickers, and Beatles tapes. After a time, we felt that Caleb had gotten all he could from the Russian school, so we transferred him to the Anglo-American School, run by the

English-speaking embassies in Moscow. Its classes were much smaller than those in the public schools, and the teaching methods encouraged the children to think creatively.

As it turned out, Caleb made a remarkable passage between his two cultures. In Moscow, he passed for a Soviet teenager, becoming familiar with the adolescent world of secret discos, underground concerts, and *barmatukha* (rot-gut wine). During our last year, he returned to the States to go to boarding school, but he flew back to Moscow for Christmas and Easter vacations.

Now, Caleb was about to leave Moscow for good. In three days, he would have to say good-bye to his Russian friends, whom he was unlikely to see again. For some of them, the war in Afghanistan was about to become a reality when they entered military service. Only a couple of weeks earlier, Caleb had participated in an emotional all-night *provod,* the ritual farewell for a new Soviet recruit. And the afternoon of my arrest, Caleb's friends had been at the apartment playing the guitar. Frightened that the KGB would search our home and find them there, Ruth ordered the boys to leave. They came back a short time later, however, to tell Caleb that they were sure I was not a spy. *"Tvoi otets — matros,"* one of them said, which means in the Moscow vernacular, "Your father is a tough cookie."

◡ ◡ ◡

At last, Ruth and Caleb arrived. Caleb was wearing jeans, a blue T-shirt, and a blue and white school letter jacket. Like his closest Soviet friends, he wore his hair long. The colonel extended his hand to Caleb and, turning to me with a smirk, quipped, "I thought you had a son, not a daughter!" We all snickered at this insensitive joke. Soviet parents regularly chide their long-haired sons for looking like sissies.

Caleb and I sat down together on the couch. Clearly ill at ease, he began to question me. I didn't know it then, but he had prepared for this meeting with a Russian friend who had considerable experience in visiting prisons and labor camps. Standing on our apartment balcony so that the traffic would jam the microphones, they had drawn up key questions for Caleb to ask. They wanted to get as much information as possible, despite the ban on revealing prison conditions.

"How did you feel when you were arrested?" Caleb began.

"At first, shock," I told him. "I couldn't believe it was really happening. Then fear. Once I got here, I wanted to scream and shout and bang my head against the walls so they would let me out. Then I calmed down and realized I had to cope with the situation."

The translator, who was sitting nearby, repeated everything in Russian for Sergadeyev, who conscientiously took notes on his pad.

"What about your meals?"

"They feed me three times a day, and the food is passed through a little window in the door."

"Tell me about the cell," Caleb said.

There Sergadeyev intervened: "We agreed yesterday that you would not discuss our internal conditions."

Ruth broke in: "But I want to know under what conditions my husband is living. It is very important for me to know."

"These are prison rules and we must abide by them," I acknowledged. "So far, with the exception of setting me up, they have been courteous enough." I worried that if Ruth protested too vigorously or was rude to Sergadeyev, our visits and phone calls would be cut off.

Caleb changed the subject to exercise. The question had been carefully chosen to judge how I was accommodating to incarceration without my daily run.

"We exercise for an hour a day on the roof, and we can also pace in the cell," I told him.

"How do you spend your time there?"

I pulled out the piece of toilet paper with Stas's explanation of differential calculus and showed it to Caleb. "My cellmate is a mathematician and has been giving me a refresher course," I explained. "This is written on toilet paper. Look at it, and tell my colleagues about it." I nearly slipped the paper to Caleb, then thought better of it.

"What do you talk about with him?" he asked.

Sergadeyev looked irritated again. Undoubtedly, he guessed that everything I said would be passed on to the press.

"Well, we had a conversation about whether there is extraterrestrial life and whether some birds can fly backward. My cellmate believes that man can fly under his own power, and plans to prove it when he is released."

"Are you getting anything to read?" Caleb pressed on.

"We get *Pravda* every day. They tear it into three sections and pass it to us in the cell. The prison has a library, which I will be allowed to use once I have filled out an application."

Ruth asked if I had received the books on the Decembrists she had brought on Sunday.

"Not yet," Sergadeyev shot back, "but he will be allowed to have them."

Caleb continued: "What sort of thoughts do you have?"

"Well, I have been thinking a lot about Alexander Frolov and how he got through nine months of solitary. I, at least, have a cellmate with whom I can pass the time."

"Be careful of that guy," Caleb said, giving me a knowing look.

I could see that he was fidgeting. I felt sorry for him but was also proud of his self-control. He now confided that he had to go to the bathroom, so I put his request to Sergadeyev. The colonel looked annoyed but summoned a junior officer, wearing civilian clothes and a black vinyl jacket, to take him to the toilet.

Ruth took advantage of the break to request that the food she had brought with her be inspected and passed on to me. The colonel picked up a telephone and dialed a number. A balding man in a white *khalat* coat soon appeared with a plastic basket.

Under Soviet regulations, relatives may bring up to five kilos (eleven pounds) of food for a prisoner once a month. Ruth and

Gretchen Trimble, Jeff's wife, had carefully prepared the parcel with the help of our Soviet friend who had coached Caleb. It included *kolbasa* (hard sausage), smoked ham, cheese, vitamin pills, aspirin, a powdered orange drink, and my blood pressure pills. Ruth had carefully cut the sausage and the cheese into three portions and wrapped each one separately in cellophane. That way, our Soviet friend had explained, if the inspector objected to the quantity, it could easily be reduced on the spot.

Finally the inspection was over. The medicine, vitamins, aspirin, powdered orange drink, toothpaste, and dental floss were rejected. The powdered orange drink might contain dangerous drugs; the toothpaste might carry a message or a razor blade.

Caleb returned from the toilet with a look of disgust. "You know," he whispered as he sat down again, "that man stood right beside me as I took a leak!"

"That's prison life for you," I responded.

I could tell that our meeting was drawing to a close when the colonel started fiddling with his pencil. He rose slowly to his feet and glared at Ruth as he said, "I would like to ask you not to bring the press with you next time you visit your husband." His tone was polite, but there was no mistaking the veiled threat.

The American embassy had also suggested to Ruth that the presence of the media might infuriate the Soviets. But Ruth knew that was our only weapon. Furthermore, the reporters were my colleagues, and she was determined to keep them informed. Secretly, the embassy probably agreed with Ruth, but they wanted to be on record with the KGB as behaving with diplomatic propriety. (They had been careful to advise Ruth over the telephone, which they knew to be tapped.) Naturally, the newsmen had been tenacious. On the first visit, they had pushed into the prison reception area with Ruth. After much telephoning, the nervous KGB guard at the desk finally summoned reinforcements. Half a dozen thugs, their faces contorted with anger, shoved the newspeople out. This time, while Ruth was waiting in a first-floor holding room, she pulled the curtains aside. Before the guard could notice and rush to close them, a television crew placed a stepladder against the prison wall, clambered up, and succeeded in shooting through the window.

"They even put ladders up against the prison wall!" Sergadeyev complained icily. "I strongly advise you to leave them at home next time."

Caleb jumped to Ruth's defense. "She has no control over the press," he said in flawless Russian. "It's their work to follow the story. They are concerned about my father, and no one can stop them from coming."

"What despicable work they do," the colonel retorted.

I couldn't have been prouder of Caleb. Though he was nervous, Sergadeyev had not cowed him. Still, the colonel's words to Ruth were ominous. What did he mean? Did her visits depend on turning off the press?

Both Caleb and I were near tears when the meeting ended. He got up, and I gave him a hug. A few days earlier, Ruth and I had been planning his departure, going over the courses he would be taking at school, lecturing him about working hard. Now I could offer no help at all, and I had no idea when I might see him again.

"Have a good year at school!" I managed to call after him. But he and Ruth were already disappearing through the door; I couldn't tell if he had heard me. Then they were gone.

Sergadeyev, the interpreter, and I sat slumped in our chairs for a few minutes. The room was oddly silent as the tension of the hour dissipated. For a moment, it seemed as if we were just three normal human beings, not individuals torn apart by high politics and criminal charges. The colonel turned to the interpreter and said in an unusually friendly voice, "It's amazing, isn't it? Nikolai Sergeyevich's son has the real *Moskovskii govor*, the real Moscow way of speaking."

◈ Seven

RED ROSES ON A GRAVE, the quick honoring the dead: this was Russia at its very essence.

But I realized that the roses on Frolov's grave did not necessarily mean that I still had relatives in Moscow. Russians habitually place flowers on the tombs of historical figures they admire, and by 1982 a considerable cult had developed around the Decembrists. Russians recall the Decembrists not so much for bungling a revolution as for triumphing over Siberia. Imprisonment and exile feed into the Russian notion of redemption through suffering, which the Orthodox Church has promoted for a thousand years. Just how profoundly the lives of the Decembrists fascinate Russians came home to me when one acquaintance confided, "The Decembrists have become my religion. I read about them to understand how intelligent people survive in a world that is a jungle."

Yet, as I walked away from Frolov's grave that April day, I kept hoping that the roses, like the ring, might lead me closer to my great-great-grandfather and his descendants. As Svyatoslav

Alexandrovich and I passed through the yellow gates and picked our way over the tram tracks, I decided to raise the subject.

"I know the roses don't necessarily mean anything," I said, "but do you think I could have relatives in Moscow?"

He nodded. "It's likely. Give me a little time, and I'll see what I can find out."

We continued walking briskly down Great December Street, past the old crones selling flowers to visitors arriving at the cemetery. We chatted about other matters, but after a while, Svyatoslav Alexandrovich returned to the subject I hoped he had forgotten.

"Have you thought any more about bringing Frolov's ring back?" he asked. I could hear the hope in his voice. "The State Historical Museum is planning an exhibition in the fall about the three stages of the Revolution: the Decembrists, the 1905 Revolution, and, finally, Great October. The Frolov ring would be a wonderful addition."

I did not answer immediately. My companion, sensing my reluctance, persisted. "I know the ring belongs to you," he said. "But, you know, it also belongs to our history. People here would be interested to see it. It's another new find. They would be much more interested than people in America, who probably don't know anything about the Decembrist uprising."

He was right. Frolov's ring was a precious discovery: it had survived more than a century of oblivion. I owed a debt to Russian history as well as to Svyatoslav Alexandrovich, who had been so generous to me. By all rights, Frolov's ring should be available to the Soviet people.

But still I hesitated. I also had an obligation to my role as a correspondent. My chief editor, Marvin Stone, had been explicit when he sent me off to Moscow. I was to be the magazine's representative, nothing more. My job was to report and analyze the news, to solidify the magazine's reputation in the Soviet capital, not to be a cultural emissary or a courier for dissidents. "I expect you to be critical but fair in your reporting," Stone had said to me at our farewell lunch. "Just remember, it's all right with me if you're expelled for something you write. It's not all right if you get expelled for something else." That "something else" was just the kind of thing I was risking with the ring and my personal history.

Stone had an important point: American correspondents in Moscow must be holier than the pope. To change money on the black market, to drink too much or take drugs, to have sex with Soviet citizens, or to become involved in antiquities (such as buying icons from unknown persons) was asking for trouble. Correspondents from Third World countries and nations friendly to the Soviet Union can, and do, violate these unwritten canons, but Americans should not. There was nothing wrong or illegal about bringing the ring back to Moscow, but I knew it could be used against me. My greatest fear was that if I brought it into the country openly, declaring it at customs as a gold and iron ring, the authorities might dispute my ownership and confiscate it as a state treasure.

But these concerns were rapidly losing ground to my desire to help Svyatoslav Alexandrovich. "You'll get it back, all right," he kept assuring me. "A paper will be drawn up. You can trust the museum."

"Okay, okay," I wanted to be persuaded, and I finally relented. "I'll bring it back when I return from vacation this summer." When we said good-bye, I promised Svyatoslav Alexandrovich that I would phone him in the fall. He seemed pleased, and he explained how to contact him without going through the newspaper.

I decided simply to carry the ring into the country without declaring it, since the customs officers in those late Brezhnev years usually took little interest in the personal items a traveler wore or carried in his pockets. I was taking a risk, I knew. I did not discuss the matter with friends or colleagues, and I certainly did not tell my father, who would have considered me a first-class idiot. I did inform the U.S. Embassy, however, in case a dispute should arise. I kept telling myself that in bringing the ring back, I was doing no more than all Russia was doing in 1982: digging up the past.

✎ ✎ ✎

Later that same summer, an unexpected invitation took me a step closer to Frolov. I never ceased to be amazed, throughout my five-year search, how clues seemed to drop into my lap from nowhere. It was uncanny, as though my digging had taken on a life of its own.

Ruth had been working for months on a story about the efforts to restore Russia's churches and icons despite the government's policy of militant atheism. A friend had told us of a group of architects who were restoring the seventeenth-century Krutitsky Monastery in Moscow, located on a bend in the Moskva River. Built by a self-important Russian bishop when he was thrown out of his sumptuous quarters in the Kremlin, it was intended to rival the czar's palace. Catherine the Great, who never lost an opportunity to insult the Church, confiscated the residence a century later and converted it into barracks for her troops. After the Revolution, it fell into increasing disrepair.

Ruth and I first visited the monastery during the summer of 1981. We picked our way over piles of rubble through a court-yard, past one building that is today a military prison, and finally found the restoration office. I pushed open the ramshackle door on the second floor and discovered a small group of people smok-ing and drinking around a small table. Enormous architectural drawings taped to one wall gave a general idea of what the restored structure would look like. On another wall, I recognized a map of Moscow, on which blue dots marked other, similar projects. When I introduced Ruth and myself as American cor-respondents, a look of alarm crossed the face of one of the older men, apparently the chief. But, in the end, the tradition of hos-pitality for the unexpected guest overcame his nervousness, and he rose to offer us chairs and tea. We talked for a while about the plans for the monastery. Then a middle-aged man named Georgii Ivanovich suggested a tour of the site.

We threaded our way through passageways and over bricks and lumber, squeezed through broken arches and scaffolding. It was clear that those dedicated conservationists who want to preserve something of Russia's past face a heroic task. Not only must they preserve what little remains, they must also battle the authorities for permission to rebuild what has been lost. Walking around Moscow today, you can see the results of neglect almost everywhere: fine old churches have been turned into warehouses or abused to the point where trees sprout from their onion domes.

"What happened in the 1930s was cultural suicide." said Georgii Ivanovich, who had prematurely white hair and wore heavy, horn-rimmed glasses. "If I can help restore some of these buildings, I'll consider my life worthwhile." He recalled some of the horrendous destruction that had occurred before and during the Second World War. The official campaign against religion had inspired many Communist fanatics to bulldoze churches and make bonfires of icons. In 1935, Stalin dynamited the Cathedral of Christ the Savior, which had been built by popular subscription to commemorate the victory over Napoleon in 1812. In its place he wanted to build an enormous Hall of Soviets surmounted by a giant statue of Lenin, whose little finger alone was to be ten feet long. The war intervened, and today a swimming pool occupies the site. The Church of St. Basil the Blessed, that fairytale landmark known to all the world, was destined for a similar fate when the Party chief proposed a north-south highway right through Red Square. Stalin eventually backed off when Pyotr Baranovsky, a well-known architect, threatened to chain himself to the cathedral, which had been built by Ivan the Terrible to mark his victory over the Tartars.

"Our past is in somewhat better shape now than during those years of 'proletarian culture,' when some of our finest architecture was wantonly destroyed," Georgii Ivanovich went on. "The turning point probably came after Khrushchev fell in 1964. Conservationists seized the moment and persuaded our new leader, Brezhnev, to create in All-Union Society for the Preservation of Historic Monuments. But some of our more suspicious leaders are uneasy about our society. They think it could spawn dangerous tendencies, like Russian fascism, anti-Semitism, nationalism, or even a political force that might one day rival the Party. On the other hand, the Party has coopted the society's leadership, and, regardless, the Russian Republic Council of Ministers has the power to dissolve it at any time."

Georgii Ivanovich pointed out the section of arches he was working on. Money, he said, was not a limiting factor in restoration: the dues of the eighteen million members of the preservation society and the government itself provided plenty of funds. The real problem was the lack of good building materials and skilled workmen — and of course bureaucratic bottlenecks.

We sat down for a moment on an unfinished stone wall. "By the way," Georgii Ivanovich said, "how did you learn Russian so well?"

I told him about Baboota and our family and soon was recounting what I knew of Frolov's ring.

His eyes lit up. "My wife is a Decembrist descendant, too. I'm sure she would love to meet you."

I wasn't quite sure what he meant and whether it would lead to an invitation. I certainly hoped so. By then, the reticence with which we had been greeted had entirely dissolved, and we parted warmly, exchanging telephone numbers and hopes that we would meet again. Nevertheless, many months passed before I heard anything. Then, sometime after my visit to the cemetery the following summer, Georgii telephoned with an invitation to meet his wife, Natasha, at their apartment.

They lived, by choice, in an old part of Moscow, near Clear Ponds, in a dilapidated building rather than in a new apartment in one of the soulless suburbs. It was the first time that Ruth and I had been in the home of one of the old Moscow intelligentsia. We entered through a door that was elaborately upholstered in leather. Padded doors are a sign of status as well as good protection against winter drafts. We passed through a heavy maroon curtain into a carpeted living room with books stacked to the ceiling. A few of the volumes were elegantly bound in old leather; most had broken spines, testifying to their considerable use. An old-fashioned fringed orange lampshade hung from the ceiling, illuminating the dinner table but leaving the rest of the room in shadows. The antique furniture was threadbare and rickety. A few pieces, Natasha explained, had been in the family for years, the others had been rescued from dumps or donated by friends with more modern tastes.

A handsome woman in her middle forties, Natasha was also an architect and was working on an important restoration project not far from the Kremlin. Her dark auburn hair was arranged in a thick roll around her head, giving her a distinguished nineteenth-century look. We dined on *zakuski* — pickled herring and mushrooms, caviar, slices of tongue, hard sausage, cheese, onions, dark Borodinskii bread, vodka with lemon rinds — to the accompaniment of choral music from the record player.

Soon our conversation took us deep into the Decembrists. Natasha explained that her line came down from a young naval officer, one of the five Bestuzhev brothers who belonged to the Northern Society. "Nikolai Bestuzhev painted watercolors of nearly all the Decembrists against the will of the czar, who ordered that no likenesses of these 'state criminals' should ever be made," Natasha said. "For a long time — a hundred years — his drawings disappeared and were thought to be lost."

I recalled what Svyatoslav Alexandrovich had told me about these drawings earlier in the spring. Natasha explained that Bestuzhev's sister gave the collection to a Moscow art dealer in about 1860 to sell for the benefit of the Decembrists' families. But for reasons that were unclear, he held on to them. Before he died, however, he consigned them to a friend, with instructions to put them up for sale. The friend, too, failed to act and, at the age of eighty-six, was feeling very guilty about never having sold the pictures when Ilya Zilbershtein, an art collector, tracked him down in early 1945.

The story was intriguing. It was almost too much to hope that Nikolai Bestuzhev had painted Frolov and that I might actually see a rendering of my ancestor.

"You should contact Zilbershtein," Natasha advised me. "He lives here in Moscow, not far from the Belorussian railraod station on Forest Street, where Lenin ran an underground press. Who knows, maybe your Frolov will be among them."

We talked far into the night about the Decembrists and the Russian soul. I was taken aback when Georgii totally discounted the avant-garde period at the beginning of the twentieth century, when Russian art was in the forefront of European creativity. He called it "an aberration that went nowhere." Russian culture, he insisted, was rooted in Orthodox Christianity. Ruth and I soon realized that Georgii and Natasha were really Slavophiles, drawn more to the religious mysticism of the past than the rationalism of the present.

Georgii was describing one side of the constant tension of Russian history: whether the country should turn eastward or westward (or inward, toward isolation, which happened in Stalin's last years). Such a conflict is not surprising, considering Russia's geographical location between Asia and Europe. The opposing views are articulated today by the two giants of the dissident movement, Alexander Solzhenitsyn, the modern Slavophile, and Andrei Sakharov, who believes that the destiny of the Soviet Union lies with the West.

If Georgii did not have such fine manners and was not so polite, he would probably have said: "The West has nothing to offer Russia but materialism and decadence. Russia's cultural superiority is tied to its religion, which goes back a millennium. Unlike Roman Catholicism, Eastern Orthodoxy has not been polluted by the Renaissance or the Reformation." Georgii believed that the person to blame for Russia's decline was Peter the Great, who, like Gorbachev today, wanted Russia to tilt westward.

"Are you Orthodox?" Georgii suddenly asked.

"No," I replied. "My father was nominally Orthodox, but my mother was an American Protestant. My grandmother was really areligious, even though she was a great Russian patriot." I knew at once I had disappointed him.

"But you are religious?" he asked in a shocked tone.

"Not in the sense that I believe in a God above or even in a faith," I responded. "But I do have great respect for religion as the conveyor of our heritage and as an ethical system."

I doubt that Georgii and Natasha were satisfied with this answer. But they must have forgiven me eventually because we met from time to time to pursue our common fascination with Russia's past and present. They reminded me of Baboota in their belief that Russia was unique.

Love of country is strong among Russians. They complain endlessly, of course, criticizing the government for everything from the lack of food in the shops to their inability to travel abroad. Yet, given the opportunity, few Russians would choose to live anywhere else. If the Soviet borders were opened, people would flood out to see the world, but I believe that most would return home in time.

ᔓ ᔓ ᔓ

Several weeks after our dinner with Georgii Ivanovich and Natasha, Ruth, Caleb, and I flew to the United States on vacation. Just before returning to Moscow, I collected Frolov's ring from our safe deposit box and put it in my change purse, which I carried in my pocket. It seemed safe enough, but as the British Airways jet descended into Sheremetyevo airport, I began to worry. My concerns mounted when the KGB border guard took an unusually long time to examine my passport, carefully comparing my photograph to my features. He noted my height, eyeballing it several times against the yardstick stenciled in inches and centimeters on the glass front of his booth. He asked my name, address, profession, and current business, carefully entering the information on a computer hidden from view.

I was reminded of the reception that the Marquis de Custine got in St. Petersburg in 1849, during the reign of Nicholas I. This famous French traveler wrote later: "All foreigners are treated like criminals upon arrival in Russia. So many precautions, considered indispensable here but completely disregarded elsewhere, warned me I was on the verge of entering the empire of fear." Not much had changed. The Soviet suspicion of foreingers, the national paranoia about frontiers, are understandable in light of history. With its thirty-five thousand miles of borders, the Kremlin feels vulnerable even today. To the east, Soviet leaders see hordes of hungry Chinese; to the west, aggressive Europeans backed by a technologically superior United States. Looking back over time, the Soviets recall invasions from all quarters: the Tartars, Mongols, and other nomadic tribes; the Swedes, Poles, French, and Germans; even the Americans and their allies, who intervened at Archangelsk and in Siberia in 1918. I recalled one Soviet historian telling me bitterly: "We always acted as a buffer against the barbarians from the East, and during the last two world wars, we siphoned off German aggression from the West. We lost millions of people and got no thanks from the Europeans, who regard us as barely civilized."

Finally, after scrutinizing my passport for a few more minutes, the KGB guard stamped it loudly: *ka-plunk, ka-plunk, ka-plunk.* I passed through the gate into a long line that wended its way toward customs, which I finally reached two hours later.

"Anything to declare?" the female officer asked.

"Just personal things," I said, hoping my face did not reveal my nervousness and trigger a search.

She waved me through with only a cursory examination, and soon I was on my way into the city. I could hardly wait to see Svyatoslav Alexandrovich. We met in an apartment on the western edge of Moscow a few days later. As I took the ring out of a small box and handed it to him, I could sense his excitement.

His hands trembling slightly, he peered at the ring through the jeweler's loupe in his right eye. I waited, nervous that he might pronounce it a fake.

"It looks like the real thing," he finally said.

Excited and relieved, I sat back in an armchair and watched him examine it further. He sat at a card table and placed the ring on a pair of scales, weighing it with great care. Using a pair of calipers, he determined its internal and external diameters. Then he took a minor scrape from the iron to assess its composition. He said he wanted to be sure that it corresponded to the type of iron known to have been used in the chains worn by the Decembrists. Finally, he produced an ancient box camera and took several closeups of the ring.

Next, he turned to the letters cut into the ellipse, the symbols I hoped would lead me to the next clue. To my disappointment, he could offer no explanation for the D and the I. He said he had never seen such markings before on the sixteen rings he had already photographed for his catalogue. But he did note that the letters were not cut in reverse, which meant that Frolov's band was not a signet ring; more likely, it was a symbol of membership in a secret movement.

"I would like to take the ring to the State Historical Museum and have some experts look at it," he concluded.

I wasn't enthusiastic about sharing the ring with unknown museum officials, and I was very reluctant to part with it, even for the exhibition. It was one thing to show it to Svyatoslav Alexandrovich, who gave it back the same day, and quite another to put on display. Still, I had come this far, so I agreed.

In early October, I took the metro from the Lenin Hills to the Lenin Library stop and walked the rest of the way up the cobbled hill to the red brick history museum on the north end of Red Square. This massive building was built in about 1880 by a famous Moscow architect, Vasily Shervud (his Scottish ancestor was called Sherwood, who was himself the grandson of Shervud the Loyal, who betrayed the Decembrists.

I met Svyatoslav Alexandrovich at the entrance of the museum. As we climbed the stairs to the director's office, he drew me aside on a landing. "I have found a cousin of yours," he confided. "Her name is Svetlana Algazina. She is descended from your grandmother's sister Olga."

I was elated. "When can I meet her?"

"Unfortunately, she wants nothing to do with you." Svyatoslav Alexandrovich frowned. He explained that she held an important Party position that included trips abroad. Seeing my disappointment, he added quickly, "You haven't missed much. She is not a particularly attractive person. She is coarse, a heavy smoker, and totally uninterested in Frolov."

I asked Svyatoslav Alexandrovich for her address and telephone number, but he had promised her not to pass it on. Suddenly I resented this woman who refused to meet her American cousin. I decided to dig up her address and telephone number myself. If I was successful, I planned to knock on her door unannounced just before leaving the Soviet Union.

Svyatoslav Alexandrovich and I continued up the stairs until we reached the administrative section of the museum. A secretary ushered us into a paneled conference room, where an officious-looking middle-aged woman with dyed blond hair introduced herself as the chief administrator of collections. I quickly gathered from her remarks about trips of West Germany that she, like my cousin, was a *vyezdnoi chelovek*, a person authorized to travel abroad; in fact, she was a Party official, heavy on loyalty but light on expertise. She invited the director of the forthcoming exhibition, an obviously knowledgeable young man, to join us around a long table.

I described the history of the ring: how it came into our family and made its way to America. When I finished, the administrator reached for the telephone to summon the museum's expert on period jewelry. A few minutes later, an older woman with refined features appeared. Barely raising her eyes, she seemed extremely nervous to be in the presence of a foreign correspondent and the museum management. I guessed she was a highly competent expert who, like many professionals, had been cowed by less knowledgeable but more powerful Party authorities.

Holding out the ring, the administrator asked the specialist in a rather authoritarian tone, "During what period would you say this was made?"

The woman took the ring between her thumb and forefinger and turned it over slowly. Then, without the slightest hesitation, she announced, "Late eighteenth century or early nineteenth."

Confirmation at last! "And the inscription?" I nodded.

She looked at the ring again under the light. "D fourteen . . . Yes, the letters mean D fourteen."

"How do you get that?" I asked, hardly daring to believe I was getting closer to the next clue. "D, after all, is the fifth letter of the Russian alphabet. Shouldn't it be D fifteen, not fourteen?"

"True," she replied. "D is the fifth letter of the Cyrillic alphabet we all use today. But the numbering system on this ring is not based on modern Russian."

I was astonished. How she could tell from only three symbols? "What is it based on, then?"

"This system comes from Church Slavonic, in which D is the fourth letter, not the fifth."

I was ignorant of the various alphabets that preceded modern Russian and knew nothing about Slavonic numbering systems. "Can you explain that?" I asked.

"The squiggle, of course." She smiled confidently. "Look at the squiggle."

"The squiggle!" So there was significance in those letters after all. My heart started to race with excitement.

"The squiggle above the D and the I," she went on, "indicates a contraction. Something — some letter — has been left out. That sort of contraction was common enough in the eighteenth century. When it is used with an I, it means ten. The zero has been left out. When you add the D — that is, the number four — you get fourteen."

"In other words," I said, "this combination of letters could mean December fourteenth?"

"Of course," she said. "The ring could be related to the Decembrist uprising."

"Would you say, then, that this ring might actually symbolize some kind of oath of loyalty to the Decembrist cause? Defiance of the czar?"

"It's possible. Because this ring uses old Slavonic numbering, you could even speculate that it belonged to a member of a radical group that was entranced with its Great Russian origins . . ."

So the pieces were beginning to fall into place. I was exhilarated, like a detective whose instincts and hard work had begun to pay off. I was mulling over this information when the chief administrator spoke.

"You know, this ring really belongs in this country. Would you be willing to put it on display in the Three Stages exhibition?" she asked. "After that, you know, we would probably be willing to buy it from you."

I agreed to lend the ring for a limited period but made it clear that I could not consider selling it without consulting with other members of the family. The museum had already prepared a form, acknowledging the loan of the ring for a year, and now I was asked to sign it.

I hesitated. It wasn't too late. I could tear up the agreement, take the ring, and leave. I glanced over at Svyatoslav Alexandrovich. He had taken many risks for me, and I could not disappoint him now. But, as a precaution, I asked that the loan period be reduced from twelve months to three, with the possibility of an extension. The administrator penned in the correction. And I signed.

As I handed Frolov's ring to people I had known for less than an hour, I wondered if I would ever hold it again. How would I look my children in the eye if I could no longer pass Frolov's ring on to them, as it had been passed on to me? One thought haunted me as I left the director's office: How far could I trust these Russians?

✍ *Eight*

THE KORMUSHKA slammed open. "Out to walk!" the guard shouted. It was time for our daily exercise on this Tuesday morning. September 2. The cell door opened and the guards ushered us out, hands behind our backs. Stas walked ahead of me as we marched toward the midpoint of the prison.

Lefortovo was built as a military prison in the shape of a capital K at the end of the eighteenth century. The architect was an admirer of Catherine the Great, maybe even a lover, for he called her Katya and dreamed up the K configuration from that nickname — at least, that is what Stas told me. The main block of the prison ran southwest to northeast, according to my reckoning, and the two diagonal wings pointed approximately east and south. Our cell was in the east wing, near the midpoint.

Leaving the cell, I had a chance, once again, to look up and down the corridors. The interior cavern of the main block seemed to dwarf us: the sides, with cell doors, catwalks, and wire safety nets, rose five stories. Moving at the very bottom of this space was like walking along a wharf between two immense, black-hulled ocean liners immobilized by wire mesh.

As the "waist" of the K, a guard acting as a traffic cop held up a baton with a red flag about ten inches square. He signaled up and down the four wings to delay any other prisoners while Stas and I were conveyed to the elevator. This practice of prohibiting interaction among the prisoners reflects the general fear of political and social opposition in the Soviet Union as much as concern about prison conspiracies. The authorities react instinctively to any kind of organization they do not control or have not infiltrated. Under *glasnost*, the many unofficial groups that have sprung up have undoubtedly been infiltrated by the KGB. In prison, administrators believe that a furtive glance between inmates is enough to spawn rebellion.

Passing through the intersection, I stole a look at the clock over the guard's desk. It was still early in the morning. We went down the corridor and turned right into a well-lit corridor leading to the elevator.

"It may be chilly on the roof," said Stas, "so grab a *telogreika* from the rack."

About twenty black quilted jackets hung from pegs on the left side of the corridor for prisoners to use in the fall and winter. Most of them were too big for me, but I finally found one that fit well enough. There was something different about this common workman's jacket from the one Caleb had: the prison model had no pockets.

Ahead was the elevator, its doors gaping. Stas and I walked in and stood at the back. The guard operated the cabin from a control panel in the front. Between him and us was a folding steel security door, with windows, which he could bolt when carrying toublesome prisoners. He didn't bother to shut it today. Stas was exceedingly polite, smiling and greeting the guard, who yawned lazily in acknowledgment. Up five flights we rose to enter a dank, uneven corridor dotted with puddles. A series of doors, right and left, led to exercise cages. I called them "bear cages."

"Thirteen!" the guard commanded.

Stas and I obediently entered cage number 13. The door slammed shut and the key rasped in the lock. We were in an enclosure roughly the same size as our cell — about nine by fifteen feet. It was bounded by grimy yellow stucco walls about twelve feet high. Across the top, chain-link fencing foreclosed any escape. At the far end of the cage stood a makeshift shelter, where prisoners could huddle against snow or rain. At the right-hand corner, facing the door, stood a rusty can that served as both spittoon and ashtray.

Running along the top of the door wall was a long, covered gallery. While the prisoners exercised, an armed KGB guard, clad in a *shinyel,* greatcoat, marched up and down. If anyone talked above a whisper or seemed rowdy, he immediately yelled at them to shut up.

"You know why this is the tallest building in Moscow?" Stas asked softly, pausing. He looked as if he was about to spring a joke. "Because, they say, from the roof you can see all the way to Siberia!"

I tried to laugh but had little stomach for it.

Stas continued: "Don't ever look up. On good days you will see blue sky, and it will drive you crazy."

Naturally, I looked up. It was cloudy, but the cottony wisps promised to clear. I understood what Stas meant, and I recalled those lines from Oscar Wilde's "Ballad of Reading Gaol," about "that little tent of blue which prisoners call the sky." I swallowed hard and looked down again.

"How long have you been doing this?" I asked.

"Spring and summer," he replied. "This last summer was really the worst. The sky was so clear, the desire to fly away like a bird was unbearable."

Stas began pacing around the cage as if he knew exactly how much time he had and precisely what he wanted to accomplish. It was while exercising, he told me, that he did his creative thinking, here that he had conceived of a man-powered flying machine. He preferred figure eights, but varied them from time to time with straight shuttling between the walls. Intermittently, he would push against one wall or execute a few pushups and deep knee bends.

I envied Stas. Although I was athletically inclined — I had run marathons, in fact — the shock of my arrest and three sleepless nights had depleted my energy. My body felt hollow, and I sensed a weakness of will. I could not force myself to do even one pushup. I didn't think I was being secretly drugged, but I wondered whether the bland food would turn my body to mush, and how soon. I realized that I had to fight my lethargy and force myself to exercise whenever possible. And the fresh air did invigorate me after the fetid atmosphere of the cell.

As I trudged back and forth, I kept thinking: so the KGB needed a hostage for Zakharov, but why select me? I imagined the lights at KGB headquarters burning late into the night after they learned of Zakharov's arrest. According to former Soviet intelligence officers who defected to the United States, the KGB has material on six Americans ready for use at any given time. Keeping the files up to date with incriminating information is part of their routine. Most of the time the information just sits there and is never used. Out of the six current files, I figured that the KGB's choice probably narrowed down to me and Serge Schmemann of the *New York Times*. Serge and I had similar profiles and were both about to leave. We were both of Russian émigré stock — something the Soviet authorities have mixed feelings about. I used to joke that on Mondays, Wednesdays, and Fridays, I was treated as one of them; the rest of the time I was a White Russian with an ax to grind against the system. Both Serge and I were fluent in the language, so we could become part of Soviet society, develop a wide range of friends and contacts, and thus be difficult for the KGB to track. Correspondents who know little Russian must be accompanied by translators; furthermore, they tend to socialize in the foreign community rather than with Soviets.

However, on August 30, 1986, the KGB had a very good reason not to choose Serge as their target: he was out of the country, looking into what he thought would be his next assignment.

Later, I learned that his Soviet staff had been making inquiries at the time of Zakharov's arrest about when Serge would be back. So I became the perfect choice. I could just imagine my case officer's satisfaction as he pulled the files on me that the KGB had been keeping since 1959, when I first visited the Soviet Union as a student. As I speculated on the many reasons that the KGB might want to get even with me, one incident jumped to mind.

On Monday, April 28, 1986, the Foreign Ministry had held a press conference to tell the world about Oleg Tumanov's redefection to Moscow from Radio Liberty, a U.S.-supported radio station that broadcast to the Soviet Union from West Germany. As I listened to Tumanov's anti-American tirade, I became increasingly angry. Only a few days earlier, *Sovietskaya Rossiya* had printed an ugly attack on Serge Schmemann and Donald Kimelman of the *Philadelphia Inquirer,* accusing them of espionage and drunkenness, including vomiting all over the Transsiberian train. When Tumanov finished, I stood up and asked for the floor. Recalling Forbachev's call for civility between nations, I said that I hoped civility could also be the rule between journalists and the Soviet Government. I then went on to denounce the attack on the two Americans and asked if they would be given the right to reply in the newspaper. I also said that the idea of American correspondents being spies was "laughable."

The conference chairman, Yuri Grimitskikh, tried to cut me off, but I persisted. When I finished, my western colleagues broke into applause. Clearly, my outburst had unleashed a well of pent-up resentment. Several correpondents jumped to their feet and began shouting questions at Grimitskikh, citing examples of unfair newspaper attacks on themselves or colleagues.

Such aggressive behavior at a Soviet press conference was unprecedented, and it clearly upset the press department. A few months later, a Soviet official I met at a party for a departing journalist chided me for humiliating Grimitskikh. Although I had had no intention of embarrassing a press department official and had taken care to be polite, I was pleased that my challenge had caused a stir. It was a step in the right direction. Ideally, Moscow correspondents should form a press association to promote their interests and protest abuses; unfortunately, we are all too busy to organize one.

Pacing back and forth in the bear cage, I recalled a conversation I had had with the deputy director of a Moscow think tank only a few weeks earlier about conditions for foreign correspondents in Moscow. This official was a renowned "agent of influence" — that is, someone who pushes the Soviet line on Western journalists and diplomats while collecting political information from them. His rank in the KGB was reputed to be as high as general. While serving in New Delhi in 1967 — some said as the KGB *rezident* — Svetlana Stalin defected, a scandal that cast a pall over his career for a while. I found him an intelligent unofficial spokesman for the Kremlin and, therefore, a useful contact despite his shady reputation.

Over the last year, he seemed to have toned down his ideological utterances, which I attributed to an awareness of his own mortality. He had already had a heart attack and suffered from kidney problems, and he regularly measured his arterial pressure in his office with an American blood pressure machine. Once, as a favor, I had obtained some Western medicine for him in England, and he tried to press a hundred-dollar bill on me in payment. Not wanting to exchange currency with a Soviet citizen, I refused. The very fact that he carried American dollars in his wallet — a currency violation for ordinary citizens — convinced me of his high status.

"There's a serious question I would like to ask you," he said at the end of a discussion of Soviet-American relations. "How are working conditions for American journalists in Moscow these days?"

"It's really the difference between night and day if you compare it to the 1960s," I replied. "In those days, we had to arrange everything through the press department. They were so inefficient

and uncooperative that we used to refer to them as the anti —
press department."

"Yes, we have been making a great effort to improve conditions," said the deputy, looking pleased. We sat on opposite sides
of his desk, which was littered with papers, clippings, restricted-
circulation TASS news bulletins, and information handouts from
the U.S. Embassy.

"But," I added, "you've got to stop these vicious articles in
the press, calling Western correspondents spies, like the attack
on Don Kimelman and Serge Schmemann." I decided not to mince
words. "Such nasty articles by KGB hack journalists make for
very bad relations. You know as well as I that after the 1977
congressional investigation, the CIA was prohibited from using
journalists."

He noded. "Yes, I know. But you've got to understand that
things change slowly here. Some of the old guard in the KGB still
believe that American journalists are all automatically spies."

I wondered what this man was saying about me now. Was he
remaining silent, staying out of the fuss like some of my official
contacts? Or was he spouting the KGB line? I guessed the latter.
Nevertheless, I believed he was quite sincere when he spoke of
the Foreign Ministry's wanting to help the newsmen. But I couldn't
help wondering: Why arrest a journalist as an instrument to
spring Zakharov? Why not a scholar or a businessman, as in the
past?

I realized that in August 1986 a businessman was out of the
question, since the Soviet government was courting foreign capital. And probably all the visiting American professors had gone
home for the fall term. Arresting a journalist was attractive for
several reasons. It is always easy to make a correspondent look
like a spy. Both journalists and spies gather information, the
difference being that spies file their material to intelligence agencies with intent to harm; journalists file to editorial offices with
intent to enlighten. Interestingly, information sought by Western
journalists is often considered secret in the Soviet Union. Official

secrecy, for example, covers the health of Soviet leaders, certain aspects of nuclear power, and certain statistics relating to both the economy and crime. The weather can be classified, too, as one correspondent discovered when he called the meteorological bureau to find out if he needed to take a coat on a trip to Tashkent. "We aren't authorized to tell you that," he was informed.

The more I thought about it, the more it seemed that there was another reason for choosing a journalist: to intimidate the foreign correspondent corps in general. The authorities have been moving away from the threat of expulsion to the threat of judicial proceedings to force correspondents to toe the line. In 1977, Hal Piper of the *Baltimore Sun* and Craig Whitney of the *New York Times* were actually tried for libel by a Moscow court. During my stay, several colleagues were summoned to the Moscow Prosecutor's Office and questioned, for no very clear reason, about their stories. One of the most outrageous incidents occurred when the Foreign Ministry summoned a *Newsweek* correspondent and accused him of spreading venereal disease among Moscow's prostitutes. The reporter, an aggressive newsman, had reported that General Secretary Yuri Andropov was dying and had only eighteen months to live. A ministry spokesman threatened to file criminal charges against the correspondent if he did not submit to medical treatment as required by Soviet law. He was eventually tested in West Germany and not surprisingly, found to be healthy.

Under Gorbachev's new strategy, which hopes to convince the world it can do business with the Kremlin, a more open press policy had developed. Five years earlier, we journalists had complained that there were not enough press conferences. Now, under *glasnost,* we complained of too many. We spent so much time at official briefings that we didn't have time to develop unofficial or dissident sources who could give us an alternative view. Attacks against correspondents were also designed to limit our access to unofficial informants by frightening ordinary citizens into thinking that all Americans were spies.

To improve the Soviet image at relatively low cost, the authorities have promoted a new breed of spokesmen: the Kremlin "spin doctors" wear well-cut Western suits, speak colloquial English, and avoid Cold War clichés. Not only do they hold press briefings in Moscow, but they also make themselves available on short notice to American news and talk shows. But for all their polish, these propagandists have yet to grasp one vital element: to be credble, you have to establish a track record of telling the truth over a long period of time. Lying on important matters such as the shooting down of the KAL airplane or the Chernobyl nuclear disaster breeds international distrust, complicating possible agreement on arms control and other matters.

Unfortunately, the lie is as natural to many Soviet bureaucrats as breathing. "It's so bad," one friend confided to me, "that we don't even believe them when they are telling the truth." There seems to be a code associated with lying. People make it a point of honor not to lie to family or close friends. Outside that tightly knit circle, however, in society at large, there is little shame associated with deception. In many ways, the Soviet Union is like a tribal society. You do not lie, cheat, or steal from your tribe, but beyond it you do whatever you can get away with. It is a means of survival that begins early in life, as Caleb found out at Moscow School No. 80. This lack of public morality has created a terrible atmosphere of cynicism in Soviet society; it is one of the obstacles Gorbachev must overcome if he is to gain support for his new policies. Without legal or political opposition or an independent press, it may be impossible. Even in the United States, which has a free press and opposition parties, it is difficult to keep public officials honest.

Such thought went round and round in my mind as Stas and I shuttled silently about the cage. I was being enveloped in a shroud of lies with no place for the truth. The accusation that I was an agent of the CIA, gathering information on their instructions, was a lie that needed to be supported with other lies. Sergadeyev was badgering me to make false admissions. And, as I learned from Ruth, the Soviet press was having a field day, spouting every kind of invention. Even official spokesmen were behaving like the archetypal diplomat who lies for his country when abroad. During the purge trials of the 1930s, Soviet prosecutors used to boast: "Give me the man, and I will build you the case." I felt like a rat on a treadmill: watched over every minute, moving in circles, and going nowhere.

The pounding in my temples began again; the palpitations of claustrophobia returned. The yellow walls seemed to be closing in on me, and, as the panic inexplicably rose, I thought I might suddenly collapse.

"I've got to get out of here," I whispered to Stas. "How much longer?"

"About twenty minutes," he replied, breaking his rhythm.

"I've got to get out, I've got to take an urgent leak. I won't last."

"Try to piss in the spittoon when the guard is out of sight," he counseled.

I tried, but it was no go; I was too nervous. "It doesn't work. It's impossible. Get me out of here!"

Stas took pity on me and called the guard, explaining the situation in a few words. The guard looked sullen but relayed an order to unlock the door. Once out of the cage, I felt better. Stas laughed as we descended in the elevator, which helped calm me down a bit.

"Our sudden departure against usual regulations," Stas said, "is what we Russians call a decision at the request of the workers, *po prosbe trudyashchikhsya*. It's a marvelous face-saving device, don't you agree?"

∽ ∽ ∽

No sooner had we returned to the cell than I headed straight for the toilet cone, then flopped, exhausted, on the cot. A few minutes later came the summons: "Danilov! N*avyzov!*"

Again, the forebodings. Again, the march to Room 215. Sergadeyev signed the prisoner receipt, hardly glancing at me. Finally, he picked up his cigarette, inhaled, cleared the phlegm from his throat, and spat ostentatiously into the spittoon beside his desk.

"Nikolai Sergeyevich," he began, "is your wife aggressive?" He looked at me disdainfully and stressed the adjective *agresivna*.

I replied with seeming indifference, "What do you expect? She is defending her husband."

"Well, I must protest to you that the reporters she brought to the prison were very disorderly. One of them even put a ladder against the wall. Against the wall! Against government property! Hooligans!"

He fell silent for a few moments. I feared he was about to embark on another effort to turn the press away, and I braced myself to deflect the attack, but he let me swing in the wind.

Sergadeyev's irritation with Ruth made me realize what an important role she was playing. I was reminded of Nicholas I's annoyance at the wives of the Decembrists when they protested the incarceration of their husbands. Like them, she was a thorn in the side of the authorities, revealing their barbarism to the world.

"Do you smoke?" he asked, breaking the silence and reaching for his cigarettes.

"No," I answered, relieved at his innocuous question. I suppose, instinctively, I wanted to distract him from the business at hand, and I commented, "You shouldn't smoke, either. It's bad for your health. You could develop cancer."

"I'm past that. I'm too old to stop now." Noting that I was more talkative than usual, Sergadeyev seemed to encourage me.

"Perhaps," I went on, recalling my constant struggles with Caleb about smoking. "But think of your family. Are you married?"

"Yes, and I have two daughters," he replied.

"And where do you live?"

"In the Izmailovo section, not far from here. It's a wonderful part of town."

"Do you enjoy Izmailovo Park?" I asked. This former Romanov estate in Northeast Moscow was where Peter the Great first got interested in boats and sailing. The park, with its lake and monastery, provides a large, rustic setting only a short distance from Lefortovo.

"Yes," Sergadeyev said. "Especially in winter. We often go there for cross-country skiing."

It was hard to know whether this turn in the conversation was simply idle chitchat or Sergadeyev's trying to make himself appear more human to me.

"How about a chocolate or a cookie?" The colonel rose from his chair and started boiling water for the tea ritual.

Now, I asked myself, why is he breaking the rules and offering me a stimulant? Did he have an ulterior motive? It was impossible to know. Trying to interpret Sergadeyev's psychological games was exhausting. In the end, I stopped second-guessing and opted for chocolates and tea.

"Now, getting back to Misha," the colonel began.

My stomach tightened.

"You say he did not want to appear in the field of vision of the KGB?" The colonel repeatedly used that term — field of vision — as if it were stadard KGB jargon, meaning under surveillance. Maybe he wanted me to adopt the phrase, thereby making myself seem conversant with Soviet spy lingo.

Again, I said that Misha had warned me against doing anything that might attract KGB attention to him.

Sergadeyev then moved abruptly into an entirely new area. "How does the American community view the KGB?" he asked.

"What do you mean?"

"How does it see the KGB? What do Americans think or say about the KGB?"

It was a strange question. Only later did I realize that Sergadeyev had more than one motive in interrrogating me.

"You must understand," I replied, "that we see you everywhere. We believe our telephones are tapped, our apartments bugged. We believe any Soviet citizen who comes to our apartment is likely to be observed by the KGB. And I think Misha became concerned."

The colonel returned to Misha, asking the same questions over and over again, evidently seeking some small but significant difference in my answers. The great advantage in telling the truth was that I did not confuse myself with my own stories. Stas had warned me to expect that the interrogation would proceed "at a turtle's pace" for a long time. It was another textbook technique, designed to wear down the defendant with repetitious questioning, focusing on the smallest discrepancies until he no longer knew what was true and what wasn't. In this case, Sergadeyev's persistence did turn up a new element, at least for him.

"Describe the photographs that Misha gave you on previous occasions," he ordered.

Again, I described the photographs, adding that they were in black-and-white and therefore not of much use to the magazine.

Sergadeyev stopped me. "What's the matter with that?"

"Our magazine prefers color, so black-and-white pictures are considered second rate, pretty much unusable."

The colonel looked surprised, as if this was an angle KGB counterintelligence had not foreseen when they gave Misha the photographs. He mulled that over for a while. "Any pictures of rockets?" He went fishing again. He kept returning to the subject of rockets as if he knew that missiles were of prime interest to me.

"There were no pictures of rockets," I answered for the umpteenth time.

"No photographs of rockets?"

"No pictures."

Sergadeyev paused. "On whose instructions were you gathering this material?"

"The magazine was always interested in material relating to the conflict in Afghanistan. I gathered it on my own, knowing of this concern."

"No, no," Sergadeyev shot back angrily. "On the instructions of which special services were you gathering this material?"

"Once again, I am not a spy. I tell you again and again that I acted on my own, knowing my magazine would be interested."

Sergadeyev gave me a disbelieving smile. "Do you want to know how I know you are a CIA agent? That article you wrote about the KGB in the March 31, 1985, issue . . ." Sergadeyev seemed to be impressed by the accuracy of the two-page story I wrote when Gorbachev came to power. Called "How the KGB Keeps Its Iron Grip on Soviet Life," it described the KGB's military and financial resources and the inevitable intimidation the police agency created at home. "We all know that the CIA and the KGB are the greatest experts on each other," Sergadeyev said. Then, plunging his dagger home with obvious relish, he declared, "You could not have written that article unless it had been dictated to you by your CIA masters!"

It was ludicrous. Was this explanation the best they could come up with? If so, Sergadeyev was truly reaching. For once, I was cheered by the line of questioning.

"Nonsense! You want to know what I based that article on?" I retorted. "On the work of Western writers, like John Barron of *Reader's Digest,* and on the annual reports of the International Institute for Strategic Studies in London. Also, by interviewing many Soviet citizens who have been questioned by your organization."

The colonel backed off a bit. He flicked an ash from his cigarette and remarked. "When you write your next article about the KGB — that is, if you ever write another article about the KGB — call us up. We'll give you the information you need to know." The KGB's giving a Western correspondent exact details about the KGB? Come on; who was he trying to kid?

Sergadeyev fell silent for some minutes, staring like a sphinx across his desk. These pauses were always uncomfortable. Was he about to spring some horrible new accusation? Either I would not know how to respond or I could fall into a trap.

When he spoke, Sergadeyev again changed the subject and explained that he wanted to draw up a daily record of our conversations. It would work this way: he would formulate a question and I would respond. He would first take notes in longhand. Then he would compose my formal answer and read it back to me. I would comment on his oral rendition and he might adjust it; then he would write it down in longhand again. Overnight, a secretary would type up his record. At the next meeting, we would both review it and sign it if we approved.

"What I am doing," he explained, "is drawing up an objective account of the circumstances. It will be available to the prosecution and the defense at the end of the investigation. You will have a chance to read over the record and correct it. It will be open for amendments until the investigation is finally completed. That could be in six months."

The idea of continuing this exhausting process for six months was horrifying. I knew full well, though, that Sergadeyev was serious, for I had covered the espionage case of Greville Wynne, a British businessman, and Colonel Oleg Penkovsky in 1963. Their investigation went on for more than six months, yet the trial was concluded in a week. Despite his reference to an "objective account," I knew Sergadeyev would use all his skill to incriminate me at every turn. I had no right to legal assistance at this stage. I could have a lawyer — acceptable to the KGB — only after the investigation was complete. I knew from interviews with defense lawyers, long before my arrest, that the investigation was the most dangerous period. Without legal advice, most suspects are trapped into incriminating themselves.

Sergedeyev looked up with a curious expression on his face and said in a less businesslike tone, "Nikolai Sergeyevich, if we were in America, how would we be doing this?"

For a moment, I was bewildered. "In America?"

"Yes, in America. How do they take notes on an investigation in America?"

I shouldn't have been surprised by the question. It was similar to questions I had often been asked by other Soviets. However ambivalent the Soviets may feel about America politically, it is still the superpower standard, the trailblazer, the future that the USSR may one day achieve. Russians constantly measure themselves against Americans, and how things are done in America is endlessly fascinating to them. The Soviet handbook of economic statistics, for example, carries a whole section of U.S. figures for easy comparison. For a playwright or filmmaker to produce his work in America is making it. For a scientist to have research published in the United States means world recognition. European standards are all right, but it is the recognition of the other superpower that really counts. Ever since Peter the Great forced his *boyars* to shave their beards and discard their *kaftans*, Russians have suffered an inferiority complex before the West. The idea of my KGB interrogator's measuring himself, and the KGB, against America by asking his American prisoner struck me as the ultimate irony.

"Valery Dimitriyevich," I replied with all sincerity, "how should I know? I've never been in this situation before. But I would think that if we were in America, drawing up a question-and-answer transcript, the investigator would be using a word processor."

The colonel put down his ball-point pen and sighed. "Yes," he said with a hint of regret in his voice, "we in the Soviet Union are not there yet."

ທ ທ ທ

Back in my cell, I was settling down for an afternoon of reading *The Little Napoleon* and the Michurin biography when the door swung open unexpectedly. A man in a white coat, accompanied by a guard, barged in with a teakettle and two scratched aluminum cups. It was Nikolai Nikolayevich, a prison orderly who dropped by on Sundays and Wednesdays with shaving equipment. Nik-Nik, as we called him, had a rudimentary knowledge of English, which he liked to practice on me.

"Good day!" Nik-Nik pronounced the words with difficulty

and a heavy accent. I found his not too successful efforts to speak my language endearing. "Shave!" He held up a white-handled shaving brush, which looked more like a handful of ragged straws than wolverine bristles, and poured boiling water from the kettle into the two cups. He turned and left the cell while I sat on the edge of my cot and peered into the circular mirror he had left. I was aware that the guards were constantly looking through the peephole to make sure I wasn't cutting my throat.

I lathered my face with the ordinary soap we used for washing and dipped the razor into one of the cups of boiling water. The blade was dull, as if it had already been used by a hundred prisoners. It nicked my skin painfully, barely cutting down the stubble. But I persisted.

"My goodness?" exclaimed Stas. "A shave on Tuesday? Something definitely is up!"

✌ *Nine*

THE LAST MONTHS of 1982 were among the more nerve-racking of my Moscow assignment. After leaving the State Historical Museum on October 10, I tried to put Frolov's ring out of my mind. The exhibition was not opening until the end of the month, and everything seemed to be proceeding as planned. At the request of Yuri Petrov, the dirctor of the exhibition, I had written a short history of the ring. When October 30 came and went with no word from the museum, I decided to call. After dialing the number several times and getting either a busy signal or no answer, I sent Pavel down to ask what had happened. He returned after his usual delay to say that the opening had been postponed "for technical reasons." I started to worry. "Technical reasons" is a Soviet bureaucratic euphemism and usually indicates that something has gone wrong. I conveyed my concern to a Soviet friend, who tried to reassure me: "You foreigners are all paranoid. You see the KGB behind every bush. You can't blame them for normal Soviet inefficiency."

At the beginning of November, I decided to take a break with Caleb and to visit my elderly Russian cousins in France. In one sense, it was a good time to get away: Caleb had a short vacation because of the November 7 Revolution Day holidays, and I badly needed a change. I had already delayed the journey more than once because of Brezhnev's ill health. But I was determined to go this time, for it seemed as though the rumors had been flying around inconclusively for years.

The trip started off badly from the beginning. No sooner had we arrived in Paris than I discovered that my Soviet visa — a separate piece of paper — had disappeared from my passport. Without it, I couldn't return to Moscow. As soon as I reached my father's house, in the suburb of Sceaux, I telexed Ruth to ask the Foreign Ministry to instruct the Soviet embassy in Paris to issue me a new one. Knowing how slowly the bureaucracy moves, I had terrible visions of being stuck in France for weeks with Brezhnev dying in the Soviet Union. My stepmother and I thought it best not to tell Serge about the lost visa. He wasn't well, and I did not want to provoke one of his anti-Soviet tirades.

After Ruth called the next day with good news from the ministry, Caleb and I left on the five-hour train trip to Cognac, where my cousins maintained a vineyard and a modest château. Over a leisurely dinner that evening, Olga and Volodya Matousievitch reminisced about their early years in Tomsk before the Revolution, then described their later efforts to build a successful cognac business in France. They listened with interest to my accounts about life in Moscow and my attempts to trace Frolov. I did not, however, tell them I had taken the ring back to the Soviet Union.

I did not relax for long. The next morning, Armistice Day, I was awakened early by Volodya's frantic pounding on the door. *"Brezhnev est mort!"* he shouted to me. "Brezhnev is dead!"

I leaped out of bed and dressed hurriedly. After eighteen years Brezhnev was gone, and I was far away without a visa. My editors would not be pleased if they found out. Caleb and I boarded the first train for Paris, and early the next morning we rushed to the Soviet consulate. We found the halls draped in black cloth and the staff at a memorial service. Our Air France jet was due to take off in one hour from Charles de Gaulle, so I had no recourse but to create a fuss. Finally, a grumpy official appeared and passed the new document through the visa window. We tore down the autoroute at ninety miles an hour, making the flight with only minutes to spare.

Ruth met us at Sheremetyevo with reams of telex copy, which she had sent on to Washington. She had filed man-on-the-street reactions, for the most part, and details of the funeral preparations. "Now they want analysis," she said. I rushed straight to the telex machine in the office and sent off a long dispatch about the coming succession which managed to reach Washington before the Friday deadline.

It was the end of an era in the Soviet Union. After the Cuban missile crisis and the fall of Khrushchev, Brezhnev had presided over a major military buildup. In his later years, he had allowed the country to stagnate economically. Shortages were widespread, and corruption became a way of life, reaching all the way to the Brezhnev family itself. The world wanted to know what kind of new leadership would now emerge.

I was so busy burying the Brezhnev era and assessing Yuri Andropov, the new leader, that I forgot about Frolov's ring until the beginning of December. A call to the museum established that the exhibition still hadn't opened; the excuse continued to be "technical reasons." Soviet friends told me I was naive to be concerned: nothing ever happened on time in the Soviet Union. I knew they were right, but still I fretted.

Just when I was contemplating whether to confront the museum director, I received some news that took my mind off the ring. Descendants of the Decembrists were planning to commemorate the 157th anniversary of the uprising. The idea of meeting the heirs of the men who had known Frolov intrigued me, and I let all my Soviet acquaintances know how very much I wanted to attend. They were skeptical; Svyatoslav Alexandrovich was noncommittal. I debated about going uninvited, but I didn't want to embarrass anyone. In many instances, of course, going uninvited is the best tactic in Moscow. It is hard for someone to turn you away when you are on the threshold, and if someone in authority notices, your friends can simply blame you: "No, we didn't invite the American. He just came."

Fear of taking responsibility is rampant in the Soviet Union and is largely the result of generations of centralized rule. Without a specific order from the top, no one wants to make a decision. Gorbachev is attempting to eradicate this historical legacy with his policies of *glasnost* and *perestroika,* but people are still afraid, or unaccustomed, to take the initiative. Furthermore, everyone knows that in Russian and Soviet history, interludes of progress and change are usually followed by period of repression. So people are cautious. They remember only too well Brezhnev's regressive policies after Khrushchev's reforms.

I could sympathize, therefore, with the Decembrist heirs' feeling nervous about inviting an American. Yet their attitude annoyed me, too. It was disappointing to discover a lack of courage in the descendants of revolutionaries who had struck for freedom against tyranny. Certainly no one would go to Siberia for inviting me to the gathering. Just when I had decided that the progeny were unworthy of their ancestors, I received not one invitation, but three, over the course of several days. I guessed that Svyatoslav Alexandrovich or Georgii and Natasha had shamed the steering committee into it.

It was cold and snowy on the night of the meeting, December 20, 1982. It took me about fifteen minutes to drive from Leninsky Prospekt to Gogol Boulevard, which forms part of the Inner Ring, a promenade of oaks encircling the old part of Moscow. After parking the car, I navigated the icy sidewalks up to number 10, a handsome yellow and white mansion that once belonged to the Naryshkin family, one of the most famous in Russia. Natalya Naryshkina gave birth to Peter the Great in 1672; a hundred and fifty years later, Mikhail Naryshkin, a Decembrist, met his fellow conspirators and worked out differences between the Northern and Southern societies in this manor house. I wondered how many of the rebels had walked this same path to secret meetings, glancing over their shoulders, as I did; and whether Frolov himself ever passed through the heavy oak doors.

I was apprehensive as I walked through the winter vestibule because I did not want to be recognized as a foreigner. I purposely wore my old glasses, which Caleb claimed made me look like "something out of the fifties." Soviets today are much better dressed than they used to be, but foreign glasses and shoes remain giveaways. As soon as I entered the slightly overheated foyer, I glimpsed Natasha and Georgii. I greeted them warmly, and the three of us lined up with the other guests for the cloakroom. A portly woman in a black smock behind the *garderob* counter gave me a white plastic tag in exchange for my coat.

Walking up to the second floor, I tried to read the faces of the people around me. If they were descended from the rebels of 1825, would noble blood show in their features? I concluded that they looked like almost any crowd at a Moscow literary evening. But the changes in their appearance over twenty years was striking. Faces appeared more refined; people seemed taller and less coarse. It was as though a kind of natural evolution was in process. The Revolution had decimated the Russian intelligentsia; now the old genes were reasserting themselves.

The paneled ballroom where we assembled was already so full that extra chairs had to be brought in. Georgii, Natasha, and I found seats in the front row just before the program began. Natasha leaned over and whispered, "I hope you're not going to be disappointed. These meetings can be very academic and boring." I sensed that both Natasha and her husband had some reservations about the Decembrists. The mutineers, after all, wanted to reject Russian mysticism in favor of Western rationalism.

As fate would have it, the chairman of the meeting turned out to be a Naryshkin himself, a scholar in Moscow whom I had never met before. He might have passed as an Ivy League professor with his tweed jacket, fine features, and pleasing Russian voice. How ironic that he should conduct a meeting in the very house that belonged to his family. To my surprise, he began the evening by acknowledging some of the new faces, including myself. I assumed that Svyatoslav Alexandrovich had told him I would be there. In his introduction, he described me as "a worker, *rabotnik*, for the American magazine U.S. *News and World Report* and gave my name in the Russian style. To the audience, it was not clear from his words whether I was Soviet or American.

Natasha turned out to be right: the first part of the evening consisted of a dry academic paper on a little-known Decembrist, Vladimir Likharev. I had hoped for something more freewheeling, like a discussion of Decembrist ideals, their interest in the American Constitution. Of course, I knew the society's activities had to reflect the Communist interpretation of the uprising as an aborted blow against tyranny rather than a failed attempt to introduce Western democracy to Russia.

At the intermission, Georgii and Natasha decided that they had had enough and got up to leave. Accompanying them to the hall, I bumped into Svetlana Stepunina, who led me across the room to Svyatoslav Alexandrovich.

"There is someone I want you to meet," he said, taking me by the arm and turning toward a frail-looking man with bushy eyebrows and thinning grayish hair, probably in his early seventies. He was dressed like a genteel but shabby English gentleman in a slightly crumpled shirt and a red necktie secured in an outsize four-in-hand knot.

"That," Svyatoslav Alexandrovich whispered to me proudly, "is one of two living grandchildren." He emphasized *grand*. "The other is an old lady of a hundred and one in Leningrad."

I extended my hand, and the elderly gentleman introduced himself as Boris Ivanovich. Looking me straight in the eye, as if assessing my Decembrist association, he said, "Nikolai Sergeyevich, I am pleased to meet you. I have heard about you. It is the justice of history that we meet, because our ancestors got into quite a fight in the 1880s."

I could hardly believe what he was saying. Was it a joke? It was too much of a coincidence to meet a descendant who had something in common with Frolov and me.

"Yes, it is true," Boris Ivanovich repeated, seeing my look of astonishment. "Our ancestors had quite a dispute going."

"Tell me, who was your grandfather?" I asked.

"Dimitri Zavalishin. He wrote an article criticizing the way the Decembrists conducted themselves in prison, and your ancestor defended them. It was published in the Moscow journal *Russkaya Starina.*"

I had heard the name Zavalishin before but knew nothing about him. I asked his grandson to tell me more.

"Well, briefly," Boris Ivanovich continued, "he was a young naval officer from Astrakhan who sailed with Admiral Lazarev on his voyage around the world in the early part of the last century. He wanted to promote Russian-American trade and visited California in the 1820s. His first wife died in Siberia, and he married again late in life, living until 1892. Your ancestor was from the Crimea, if I am not mistaken, and served as a lieutenant with the regiment quartered in the Ukraine." Our conversation had to stop, for it was time to return to our places. Before we parted, Boris Ivanovich added that he was a widower and lived with his daughter in Leningrad. From time to time, his health permitting, he would come to Moscow to work in the archives.

"Maybe we shall see each other again one of these days," he said.

The second half of the meeting consisted of a slide show presented by a female enthusiast who had traveled throughout the Soviet Union, photographing the graves of the Decembrists. Frolov's grave was the most impressive monument of them all, I thought, and in excellent condition. Many of the others had been neglected in the course of time; others had disappeared entirely.

I was ecstatic after the meeting. I was discovering more about Frolov's life and finding new clues to follow.

ᨦ ᨦ ᨦ

Toward the end of December, I received more good news. The "technical reasons" had been overcome and the Russian Liberation Movement exhibition had finally opened, more than six weeks late. I rushed down to Red Square to see if the ring was included. There it was, in a glass case, along with other Decembrist relics. Frolov's band carried a brief identification: "Ring of Decembrist Frolov, A. F.; Property of Danilov. N. S., U.S.A." Maybe some relative would pass by the case and wonder about N. S. Danilov.

There was one slight hitch. According to my contract, the ring was to be returned to me on December 31, 1982, three or four days hence. It seemed churlish to ask for it now, so I called the museum to suggest that it remain on view until June 30, 1983; they agreed and, in early January, sent me an amendment to the contract.

The new year started off well enough. I finally managed to hire a secretary, Zina. A cultivated woman in her early fifties, she was a secretary and translator of the old school. Her English was excellent, and she wasn't afraid of hard work And work was something we had a lot of that spring.

Politically, Brezhnev's twilight years had been unexciting. Now that a new man was in control, my editors kept me on the run with story requests. Andropov, a former KGB chief, was determined to eradicate the Soviet Union's three major evils; drunkenness, absenteeism, and corruption. Long before Gorbachev, he saw that unless a stop was put to the economic stagnation, the Soviet Union would fall further and further behind the rest of the industrial world. No one wanted to buy Soviet goods, not even the Soviet people themselves. Shoddy workmanship and erratic service were reflected in continual complaints. Soviet living conditions had gradually improved, but nowhere near enough, and people had a thirst for more. With increasing numbers of foreign tourists coming to Moscow and more imports available, the Russians had greater expectations and increased their demand for quality. It was sad to see many of the Soviets heap scorn on everything made in their own country.

That summer, before going on vacation, I went down to the State Historical Museum to collect Frolov's ring. As I drove to Red Square, I realized I was about to get an answer to my question about trust and the Russians. Several disturbing thoughts passed through my mind: the ring would still be in the display case and could not be removed — "technical reasons," of course. No: it had been removed, but the staff could not discover where it had been stored. No, neither of those. My grandparents had left Russia illegally and, therefore, so had the ring. By special decision of the Supreme Soviet, the ring was being repossessed without compensation.

I was very nervous as I made my way to the administrative section of the museum. This time, I was ushered in to see the dirctor himself — not a promising omen, I thought. A graying man in a gray suit, he spoke a rather coarse Russian in the authoritarian tone of a Party official used to getting his way. He seemed impatient and had little time for small talk.

"We would like to purchase this ring from you," he announced, "and we are prepared to offer you two thousand rubles."

I pretended to consider the offer — some $2,800 — then shook my head. "My family will not agree. I understand you would like it, but really, it is a family heirloom and is precious to us."

The director looked disappointed, but he picked up the telephone and ordered the person at the other end to bring him the ring. He handed it to me, thanked me for the loan, and showed me briskly out of the office. Clearly, he was annoyed. The museum had wanted the ring; nonetheless, they had returned it.

Driving home, I felt somewhat ashamed of all my suspicions. Perhaps there was a lesson in this experience for Soviet-American relations as well as for me, personally. Where there is mutual interest and a clear contract, it is possible to do business with the Russians. If we are to avoid nuclear war, the two superpowers must take a step to break down the corrosive distrust between them. And that will involve, on occasion, taking a risk, because there is no absolute guarantee.

           ✍ ✍ ✍

When I returned from vacation in August, Moscow was rife with rumors that Andropov had become seriously ill. He had disappeared from view after receiving a U.S. congressional delegation in his Kremlin office in mid-August. On the diplomatic side, however, there were small signs that relations between Moscow and Washington might be improving. A U.S. team had completed a new grain agreement with the Soviet Union and, in late August, American journalists were invited to witness the signing at the Foreign Ministry. As we gathered in its wedding cake skyscraper that afternoon, none of us dreamed that a few hours later Soviet air defense forces would shoot down a South Korean airliner over Sakhalin, plunging Soviet-American relations into a tailspin.

The ordinary Soviet citizen was indignant that the world condemned Moscow for shooting down what the government insisted was a spy plane. This attitude was understandable, for Russians can read almost daily stories in the press about the Machiavellian schemes of the CIA.

"I don't understand it," a taxi driver told me as we drove to a press conference at the Foreign Ministry. "A spy plane deliberately violates our territory; we shoot it down. Then we get blamed and everyone hates us. Why?"

Late one evening, as I was upstairs sending a long report on the KAL catastrophe to Washington, there was a timid — and unexpected — knock on our apartment door. Through the peephole, Ruth saw a slight figure in an old brown raincoat standing near the elevator. It was Boris Ivanovich. Ruth called me down from the office and we invited him in. He was very courtly and kissed Ruth's hand. This time he insisted on speaking a correct, if somewhat halting, English. "I had an English nanny," he explained when Ruth complimented him on his rich vocabulary.

Over tea, Boris Ivanovich explained that he had been doing research in the manuscript department of the Lenin Library when he came across some references to Frolov. "I wanted you to know about them," he said, opening his battered briefcase with shaking hands and taking out half a dozen pages. "These references concern the police records that were kept after Frolov returned to the Crimea, following the amnesty of 1856. You should get access to them if you can."

I was extremely touched by the old gentleman's visit. I admired his courage, too, in coming to a foreigner's apartment. Later, when I learned more about his life, I understood courage was not something he lacked. During the terrible three-year blockade of Leningrad in World War II, he had helped organize the lifeline across Lake Ladoga which provided the city with supplies during the winter.

ᔑ ᔑ ᔑ

Until Boris Ivanovich's visit, I hadn't thought much about seeking access to the Moscow archives. From talking with American scholars, I knew how difficult it was to extract any information from Soviet sources. Part of the problem was that the Soviets often had no idea of what was in each file, and they did not want foreigners uncovering material that could prove embarrassing. Nevertheless, I asked Zina to start tracking down any material on Frolov. It had turned out that she shared my enthusiasm for the Decembrists, and she was already trying to contact Ilya Zilbershtein to find out if Nikolai Bestuzhev had painted Frolov.

Now she contacted the Central State Archives administration to learn where the Frolov papers might be. After much telephoning, we eventually received a reply: to give me access, the archives needed a letter of recommendation from the Foreign Ministry. We wrote to the ministry's press department, which agreed at once to send a letter. I had made no secret of my research and always discussed it openly with Soviet press officials, who generally responded with interest.

The central archives then presented me with a Catch-22 situation. They could not find documents related to Frolov unless I could give them the catalogue numbers. Since foreigners aren't allowed inside the archives, however, I couldn't use their catalogues. I wasn't sure whether there were any reference guides in the Lenin Library and suspected I might have to go to all the way to Helsinki to consult its Slavic Library, which was one of the leading repositories of imperial Russia before Finnish independence in 1918.

As I struggled to find a way around this latest roadblock, Zina presented me with a wonderful piece of news: Zilbershtein had given all of the Bestuzhev watercolors to the Pushkin Museum. And, yes, there was a portrait of Frolov. She called the management of the Pushkin, which confirmed her information. If I was interested in seeing the sketch, I would be welcome. Interested? I was on my way to meet my ancestor!

Knowing that it might be my only opportunity to see a likeness of Frolov, I asked my friend Sergei Petrov to come along and bring his special lenses for photographing art objects. At the museum, we were met by two female curators in brown smocks who led us to a second-floor room, where the watercolors were being examined and prepared for storage. The curators listened, fascinated, as I told them the family history and the high points of my search. We moved to a trestle table, and one of the women lifted up a thin package and unfolded its brown covering. She handed me the original watercolor of Frolov, painted in about 1832, when he was performing hard labor in Siberia. I can hardly describe my feelings as I held this portrait. The paper was in superb condition. The picture had lain, well wrapped, for over a century, so it retained all its initial brightness.

The portrait showed Frolov seated on a chair and turned three quarters toward the viewer, his left hand over the back, wearing a full-sleeved white shirt under a dark gray vest. He had a fresh, clean face, pork chop sideburns, and a slightly drooping ginger mustache. His brown eyes were clear and penetrating, the hump of his Greek nose obvious. He looked more like a poet than a convict.

I moved toward the open window to examine the picture more closely in daylight. At that moment, Frolov ceased being some ancient relative remembered by Baboota on a rock in New Hampshire and commemorated in Moscow by a cube of red granite. He was a real human being, a man who had lived and struggled and survived. I was speechless, but I knew one thing: I would go still deeper. I was going to dig up Frolov's traces: the objects he must have made, the letters he must have written. I was going to uncover what he had passed on to his children, and his children's children.

✑ *Ten*

I **WAS CURIOUS** about the unexpected shave and what it might mean. Imminent release? That was too much to hope for. A visit from an American embassy official? My guess was that it would be a meeting with Mort Zuckerman, my editor in chief. Ruth had told me that he was trying to get a visa to come to Moscow. I had worried how the magazine would react to my arrest. Zuckerman was a Boston real estate tycoon with relatively little experience in the news business or in dealing with Soviet bureaucracy. When he acquired *U.S. News and World Report* in 1984, there were many changes, including the inevitable hirings and firings, which resulted in predictably ill feelings between the old-timers and the new command. I considered myself lucky to be abroad through that period, and was generally the last to hear the office gossip.

Now I wondered how strongly the magazine would support me. After all, I was one of the old-timers. I barely knew Zuckerman, and I had had little contact with the new editor, David Gergen, who once served as chief of communications for President Reagan. Would they understand that a tough initial response was vital? I recalled Robin Knight's bitterness when he told me the magazine's former management had reacted to his drugging episode: "Instead of protesting immediately, the editors started making inquiries about whether I had a drinking problem. It completely undermined my position and gave the Soviets the idea they could act with impunity."

I pulled the blade one last time over my sore chin; then the KGB guard and I climbed the iron staircase to the second-floor balcony and marched to Room 215. My *konvoyir* opened the door. Inside, Sergadeyev was talking to another official. The clock between the windows read 4:45 P.M.

"Well, Nikolai Sergeyevich, what do you make of this Tuesday shave?" asked the colonel, looking pleased with himself. He took a black comb from his pocket and stroked it straight back over his head several times.

"I'm going to have a visit with my top editor, Mr. Zuckerman," I replied.

"Right!" exclaimed the colonel sarcastically. "You really orient yourself very well."

So — there was no interrogation for the moment, thank God, and I was going to see Zuckerman. More than anything else, I needed the reassurance that the magazine was behind me.

Sergadeyev indicated that it was time for us to leave, and we made our way to the visitors room. It was empty when we entered, and I immediately cast my eye over the furniture. The reproduction antiques had not budged an inch since Monday, which meant that the hidden microphones were probably now working. Sergadeyev walked over to the desk, pulled out his notepad, and sat down.

Within minutes, Zuckerman entered the room with Roger Daley. Zuckerman wore a beautifully tailored glen plaid suit, a blue shirt with a white collar, and a paisley tie. He exuded cool self-confidence, as if it were the most natural thing in the world for him to be visiting Lefortovo prison. He extended his hand. I took it and turned it quickly into a bear hug, whispering in his ear, "You sure did the right thing by coming. Thanks!" I was anxious to show Sergadeyev that there was no rift between us. Zuckerman understood instinctively and reciprocated; I need not have worried about his response. Daley sat on the chair nearest the colonel. Zuckerman and I sat down on the couch with the interpreter.

Then Zuckerman began talking. It was hard to know if he was talking more to me or Sergadeyev — probably to both of us. "It would make your ears turn red to know what your colleagues are saying about you in Washington," he began. "Meg Greenfield wrote a wonderful editorial in the *Washington Post*. Marvin Kalb talked about you on NBC."

Sergadeyev listened to the interpreter and took notes at the bowlegged desk.

"This is really the number one story of the day. It leads the news every night," Zuckerman continued. I hoped that the point about American television would not be lost on Sergadeyev, but it was impossible to gauge his reaction. His face remained expressionless.

When Zuckerman completed his summary of the reaction in the United States, I gave him a detailed account of my arrest and incarceration. I repeated that I was innocent of the spy charges and had formally denied them. I went on to describe my cell, the open toilet, the prison routines. At any moment, I expected Sergadeyev to stop my narrative, given his earlier prohibition.

"It would never do to put me in prison," Zuckerman said in jest. "I'd be overcome by claustrophobia."

I then outlined my relationship with Misha, his unexpected telephone call after Zakharov's arrest, and the photographs from Afghanistan.

Zuckerman turned to Sergadeyev: "We are very interested in the situation in Afghanistan." He was trying to make it abundantly clear that I had been under orders to come up with material on the war. "We send correspondents there from time to time to get a firsthand look. It is important for Mr. Daniloff to write stories about the war for us."

At this point, Daley broke in with a question for Sergadeyev: "What has happened to Misha?"

For some reason, I replied before the colonel could say a word: "I have been told he was arrested under Article 64, for treason." I gave Daley a quizzical glance. He looked as if he did not believe this official explanation any more than I did.

"Have you actually seen him in prison?" Daley asked me.

"No," I said.

Daley then pressed Sergadeyev about their failure to have me meet with Misha. "Will they be brought together?"

Sergadeyev remained silent and impassive, as if he had not heard the question.

After nearly an hour of conversation, Zuckerman moved to the area that interested me the most: how to resolve the whole affair. He explained that, despite enormous outpourings of support, there was a growing sentiment in the United States that there should be no direct swapping of Daniloff for Zakharov. It was hard for me to weigh Zuckerman's words. Was he trying to pass a message to Sergadeyev about the American stand, or was he trying to prepare me for the long haul — or both?

"President Reagan," Zuckerman continued, "has said there can be no exchanging an innocent journalist for a Soviet spy."

Sergadeyev listened, poker-faced, while making notes.

News of the Reagan administration's no-bargaining policy made me very apprehensive; I felt like the captain going down with the ship. Intellectually, I agreed with it. When the Soviet Union engages in international brigandage, the United States should come back hard. Moreover, the idea of my being equated with a Soviet spy was extremely offensive. But Emotionally, of course, I wanted out of Lefortovo in the worst way. I was stuck there, however, with the prospect of a long prison term hanging over my head. Nevertheless, I managed a few words of support for the policy.

"I understand the president's position and I support it. I certainly do not want to be equated with a spy," I told Zuckerman. Then I added, knowing full well that unless the administration agreed to negotiate with the Soviets, I could remain in custody indefinitely, "Obviously, the two legal systems have to work themselves out for a bit."

Zuckerman's visit dissipated my worries about any lack of support from the magazine. It was coming out with all guns firing, including constant press interviews and FREE NICK DANILOFF T-shirts. Former Secretary of State Cyrus Vance had been hired to give legal advice, and a round-the-clock crisis center had been created to give Ruth and Jeff constant support.

We had talked for nearly an hour and a half when Sergadeyev sat back in his chair, signaling that he wanted to end the meeting.

"Have you any messages for your family or anyone else?" Zuckerman asked as he stood up to leave.

For the past four days I had been on an emotional roller-coaster. All my feelings — anger, helplessness, fear, despair — were close to the surface. Once again, I thought of Caleb — his courage, his sadness at leaving his friends, all the things I wished I could have said to him and had not. I struggled to control myself. Feigning indifference and calm had become extraordinarily important, even if Sergadeyev tried to turn it against me.

"Please tell Caleb — I hope he has a good year at school, and I love him." Suddenly I thought, To hell with Sergadeyev. Let him think twice about my being the cold-blooded CIA professional. I coughed and sobbed noticeably for a couple of seconds.

Turning away with some embarrassment, Zuckerman addressed Sergadeyev: "I am leaving for the United States tomorrow and I would like to take Mr. Daniloff with me."

The colonel rose to his feet with a self-satisfied smirk and responded, "I think Mr. Daniloff will be taking another flight."

What did he mean? That the authorities were thinking about releasing me, or that it would be ten years or more down the road before "another flight"?

As Zuckerman and Daley prepared to leave, I caught the consul's eye and said, "I really hope you folks are doing something to get me out. I hear what you're saying, but I can't feel anything in here."

Daley did his best to reassure me: "Just hang on. We're pursuing all sorts of avenues. It'll work out in the end."

After they left, I felt very depressed as I returned to my cell. From everything I had learned, the superpowers had come to a standoff. The United States was refusing to talk directly to the Soviet Union, insisting that all charges be dropped and I be released. Now what? My arrest had taken on a momentum of its own. What it boiled down to was that I was a pawn with no control over my fate. That Tuesday night I slept badly.

๛ ๛ ๛

Soon after breakfast the next day, September 3, it was back to interrogation. As I entered Room 215, Sergadeyev was waiting behind his desk. Any fantasies I had had of sudden release evaporated when I saw the unpleasant look on his face.

"So, Nikolai Sergeyevich," he began nastily, "we've had nice visits from family and friends, haven't we?"

I braced myself, seeing that he had shifted into his bully mode.

"The editor is full of sweetness and light, full of praise for his brave correspondent. The American consul has good words, too. 'Just hang in there, and we will get you out.' It all shows what a valuable spy you are!"

I sat there silently, telling myself that the investigation was a smokescreen to camouflage the political nature of the case. Sergadeyev had the upper hand for now; I was simply a dog who could be kicked about mercilessly. I tried to convince myself not to take the bullying, the accusations, the lies, too much to heart. But one of the problems of answering questions at all is that inevitably you do take the process seriously. Although I knew the investigation was rigged against me, I still tried to defend myself. I still put energy into formulating my denials. Defending against a lie, I discovered, is as instinctive as raising a hand to fend off a blow. Stas had warned me once about the difficulties of rebutting an accusation: "It's hard to disprove a negative. It's like trying to prove you're not a camel."

Sergadeyev continued, "I want you to explain something to me. You tell me your magazine has no correspondent in Afghanistan, yet your editor claims that he sends reporters there all the time."

Zuckerman had obviously meant to explain why the magazine pressed its Moscow correspondent for material on the Afghan war, and Sergadeyev was turning the remark against me. I groped for the right words, saying, "We don't have someone there permanently. The magazine asked me to go, and I applied for a visa from the Afghan embassy here, but I couldn't even get an answer from them."

The colonel snapped back, "Even so, you go around asking men of military age for photographs."

"The magazine constantly needs photographs from Afghanistan. I tried to get them in Moscow. I approached a military photographer, Yakutin, at the magazine *Sovietskii Voin [Soviet Soldier]*. He said he would sell me some photographs through the copyright agency VAAP, but it's such a long bureaucratic process that I never followed through on it. I asked Soviet television for photographs by Mikhail Leshchinsky, their correspondent in Kabul. But they had only videotape, not film. The magazine was interested in pictures of the everyday lives of soldiers in Afghanistan, not pictures of secret maps that wouldn't mean anything to our readers."

Sergadeyev stared at me as if he considered me the world's worst liar. Then, without a word, he rose from his desk and turned his attention to making the tea while I sat uncomfortably, wondering which strategy he would use next.

"Tell me something," he said as he handed me the glass of tea. The nasty edges had disappeared from his voice; he was switching back to Mr. Nice Guy. "Tell me . . . They say you have a free and independent press in America. How does it actually work?

Does the government tell the *Washington Post* or the *New York Times* what do print or send out instructions on what to cover?

The question confused me momentarily. His sudden switches took me off guard. But I thought I perceived the direction he was taking. Since the Central Committee briefs Soviet editors regularly in order to promote the Party's views, many functionaries in Moscow imagine that the White House does the same with the American press. They are only too eager to believe that a White House press conference in Washington or the American ambassador's briefing in Moscow conveys mandatory guidelines. Furthermore, Soviet diplomats return to Moscow from Washington and report that frequent press briefings are held in Washington to give U.S. editors their "instructions." So Sergadeyev probably believed that any requests I received from the magazine were actually orders from the CIA via Zuckerman.

For the next half hour, I tried to explain the essentials of newspaper publishing in America. I steered away from words like "free press" and stressed "independent from the state," trying to distinguish between persuasion and compulsion by the government. Once our tea was finished, I steeled myself for Sergadeyev's next move. He sensed my discomfort.

"Nikolai Sergeyevich," he chided, "why is it you always look at me as if I was pointing a pistol at you? Why don't you ever smile or crack a joke.?"

"Because you are pointing a pistol at me, Valery Dmitriyevich! Another time and another place, I'll joke with you."

The colonel shuffled the documents in the brown paper file on his desk, carefully putting one on top of the pile and smoothing it with his hand.

"Tell me again what you talked about with Misha."

It was exhausting. Over and over, he was asking the same old questions. Again, I regurgitated the same old details, trying not to omit any point that he could later say I had been trying to hide.

Sergadeyev frowned. He glanced at the page on top of the pile and banged it with his hand. "That," he said with finality, "is not what Misha says. Misha is being interrogated here, and he has fully reported his suspicions about you. He says you gave him the following assignments:

"One: try to get descriptions of secret factories in Frunze. Two: get pictures of military equipment being used in Afghanistan. Three: obtain the home addresses and the places of work of demobilized soldiers who served in Afghanistan. Four: gather details of deployments and numbers of military subunits getting ready to be sent to Afghanistan . . ."

My mouth seemed to fill with cotton, and I found it hard to breathe. For a moment I felt as though I would pass out. None of it was true, yet a conviction based on these accusations could put me behind bars for years. I came back at Sergadeyev in the same vein. "Not true," I said hoarsely. "I've told you everything Misha and I talked about."

Misha could not have said those things if he had been honest. If he really was saying that now, it was on the KGB's command. And on the KGB's command he would stand up at my trial and bear false witness against me. I realized then that even if I had not accepted Misha's package or had refused to meet Misha, I would still have been arrested. The KGB would have manufactured whatever evidence it needed for a public trial in order to put pressure on the United States to return Zakharov.

Sergadeyev got up angrily and moved closer to me. For a moment I thought he was going to hit me. But he only twisted his oral knife. "You may not be associated with the CIA, but you are certainly an agent of RUMO!"

"RUMO?" I said incredulously. "What is that?" My surprise annoyed my inquisitor, who seemed certain that I was being disingenuous.

"RUMO! RUMO! That is . . . that is . . ." Sergadeyev stumbled, as if he had momentarily forgotten what RUMO was. I had never heard the term before or seen it in the Soviet press; I had no idea what he was talking about.

"RUMO — Razvedovatelnoye Upravlenie Ministerstva Oboroni — the Intellgence Administration of the Ministry of Defense." The colonel finally got the words out.

"Oh, you must mean the Defense Intelligence Agency. It's not true. I have never had anything to do with them," I retorted.

"We know that you are a military expert, Nikolai Sergeyevich. You are very good on military equipment and rockets. Especially rockets. We know about all your activities in Washington."

"It's perfectly true that I covered the hearings of the Strategic Arms Limitation Treaty in the summer of 1979 before the Senate Foreign Relations Committee," I said. "It's also true that in Washington I had briefings with American generals and admirals. But the same thing goes on in Moscow, I'm sure you know. Your top journalists meet with members of the General Staff, but that doesn't make them agents of the General Staff. Nor am I a spy because I talked to a general in the Pentagon."

Sergadeyev was silent for a moment, almost as if he were conceding the point. Once again we returned to Misha. This time the colonel chose to pursue the official protocol of questions and answers. It was a laborious process: Sergadeyev asked me to approve his formulation of every one of my answers.

At one point, he stopped and asked with seeming sincerity, "Should it be: 'I consider Misha to be my friend' or 'I considered Misha was my friend'?" The difference in the verb carried a very significant meaning — at least I thought so. If I allowed Sergadeyev to write that Misha was still my friend, I would be giving credence to Misha's allegations. If I insisted on the past tense, I emphasized my split with Misha. I pondered the choice for a minute, then said, "Everything in your formulation is in the past tense, so keep it in the past."

ᗌ ᗌ ᗌ

When I returned to the cell, Stas was all smiles. "How did it go?" he asked.

I shrugged. I was exhausted from the questioning and in no mood to talk. I also didn't want to discuss it with him.

"It's important, Nick," he added as if he was trying to guide me, "to keep on the good side of your investigator. He controls everything about your life." Stas always urged cooperation; he never once suggested how I could fend off the colonel's blows.

My cellmate was sitting on his bed. Next to him, spread out on the little blue table, were several sheets of toilet paper covered with his interminable mathematical scribblings. Hoping to change the subject, I pointed to his notes and asked, "What on the earth are you figuring?"

"It's a three-hundred-year-old mathematical riddle — Fermat's last theorem," he replied. "So far, no one has been able to solve it."

To keep him talking, I nodded with feigned interest.

"Pierre de Fermat," Stas went on with relish, "was a seventeenth-century French mathematician and a friend of the philosopher Blaise Pascal. Fermat was fascinated by the Pythagorean theorem and its implications for number series. He conjectured that when the Pythagorean theorem is written in its general form — $a^n + b^n = c^n$ — the equation will not hold true if n is a whole number greater than two. Apparently Fermat developed an elegant proof to which he alluded in a handwritten note in the margin of a book he was reading. But he never wrote it down, or if he did it has been lost. Ever since, mathematicians all over the world have tried to reconstruct Fermat's proof without success." Stas paused for a moment, then added somewhat theatrically, "But I think I've found the answer. I've worked through it several times now, and I really think I've got it!"

"Good for you!" I told him. "That's really clever."

Then, to my utter amazement, Stas turned to me and said earnestly, "Nick, when you are released, would you take my solution out with you and take it to the West? In the nineteenth century, the Royal Academy of Sciences of Göttingen established a prize for anyone who solved the problem. You could claim it for me."

I could hardly believe my ears. Here I was, an American suspected of espionage, sitting in a cell with a secret scientist who was asking me to smuggle out some mathematical formula. How was I to know that the endless figures on Stas's toilet paper weren't some code that would be produced at my trial as evidence of guilt? Then I thought Stas must be joking, but he looked quite serious and quite innocent at the same time.

I stalled. "Let's get me released first, then I'll think about it."

I was just beginning to unwind when the *kormushka* opened with a bang. A guard pointed his finger at me: "Danilov? Out!"

Hands behind my back, I stumbled out of the cell and followed him, dreading what might happen next. We turned left and climbed up the iron staircase to the second floor. I glanced at the clock over the guard's desk at the prison's midpoint: 7:35 P.M. It felt as if it were the middle of the afternoon, and I concluded that the clock was broken. Or was it? Maybe the guards had reset the clock in order to disorient me. Impossible; that would be going too far. Maybe the clock was just broken. Still, after Stas's request, anything was possible. In prison, it was sometimes hard to keep a grip on reality.

I was headed, it turned out, for mug shots and fingerprinting; it seemed strange that this standard procedure had not been done earlier. Two guards ushered me into a small studio with old photographic equipment — no quick color shots here. The studio was about ten feet square and had seen better days. The walls were dirty; the lighting, primitive. At one end, by the far wall, was a swivel chair; near the door was an ancient view camera with bellows on a tripod.

The guards sat me down on the chair and adjusted the height. One of them wrestled with the photographic plates, then disappeared under the black hood at the back of the camera and focused. I once again extended the middle finger of my right hand — probably a useless gesture, since my hands would almost certainly fall outside the picture.

The fingerprinting was done in the same room, at a narrow shelf attached to the west wall. One of the guards pressed and rolled each of my fingers in the sticky black ink and pressed them on a white form. He took prints of the individual fingers, then four together. When it was over, the guard motioned for me to wash up under a cold water faucet with coarse soap and a worn-out brush.

We left the studio and walked directly across the hall to a second small office to record my biographical data and physical description. Would these particulars be preserved for eternity in the archives, I wondered, to be discovered in a future century by some investigator? (One of the advantages for a historian in a police state is that the bureaucracy churns out endless details about millions of individuals.) The guards weighed and measured me. One of them sang out: "Weight, sixty-eight kilos; height, one meter, fifty-three centimeters. Hair, brown. Eyes, brown . . ."

The words echoed strangely in my head, as if they were coming to me from the distant past. They were very familiar, but how could that be? All at once, it came to me. I took off my glasses, turned my face so that the guard could glimpse my profile, and said deliberately, "And how would you describe my nose?"

He looked up, studied it for a few seconds, and replied matter-of-factly, "Large nose with a hump."

It was uncanny. Only six months earlier I had read those very same words — "large nose with a hump" — in a nineteenth-century document I had unearthed after the evening cup of tea with Boris Ivanovich. The words had been written in 1827 by the guards who took down Frolov's particulars at the Siberian penal colony of Chita. The concurrence of my description and Frolov's thoroughly unnerved me. As the guards marched me back to my cell, I remembered that I had extended my Moscow tour twice, once two years earlier and a second time the previous fall. I had become so caught up in my search for Frolov that I wanted more time to pursue the many leads. If I had not been so currious, I would have been back in Washington now, out of the reach of the KGB. A thought flashed through my head. It was not the FBI's arrest of Gennadi Zakharov in August 1986 on a New York subway platform which precipitated my arrest. It was Nicholas I's couriers seizing Alexander Frolov in February 1826 in the Ukrainian town of Zhitomir.

ᵓ *Eleven*

IN THE WINTER OF 1984, I began to make some progress in cracking the archives, thanks largely to the efforts of my Soviet friends. Once they learned I was looking for a Decembrist ancestor, they threw themselves into the hunt with typical Russian generosity. Not only did they visit libraries for me, they lent me precious books, introduced me to historians, and offered good advice. Frolov would have been amazed at how many doors, usually closed to foreigners, were gradually opened to his American descendant. "Moscow," my colleague Jim Gallagher once told me, "is a real dump, but in every dump there are treasures." The trouble is, most foreign correspondents are too busy covering the daily routine to search out those treasures.

One evening, we had a visit from a good friend who had lost his job as a mathematician when he applied to emigrate. He seemed very excited and, pulling a sheaf of papers from his briefcase, announced that he had found the call numbers of documents relating to Frolov's arrest in 1826. Covering several pages, the figures looked like some secret cypher: "Fond I, Opis I, Delo: 6285, 6287, 9708, 9769, 10347 . . ." They seemed to go on forever. The following day, with great anticipation, I submitted them to the historical archives; within a few days, I received word that they did not exist. Disappointed, I concluded that the archives had simply resolved to deny me access.

The matter might have died there had not another acquaintance invited me to visit his mother-in-law, who had one of the best Decembrist collections in Moscow. One snowy afternoon in January 1984, I took the metro to the Novokuznetsk stop to meet Ilya, an intellectual who had spent four years in prison and exile for allegedly possessing stolen icons. We trudged along Klimentov Lane, past the Church of Consolation of All Who Sorrow. Stumbling over rusting pipes discarded from the summer heating overhauls, we finally turned right into a side street that led to an apartment building with a dark gray concave façade. The elevator lurched haltingly to the fourth floor.

Ilya opened the apartment door, introduced me to his wife, then ushered me into the library. This relatively large room with a parquet floor, dark paneling, and indirect lighting was definitely one of Gallagher's treasures. Floor-to-ceiling bookcases contained such rareties as Burkgauz and Efron's eighty-six-volume, leatherbound *Encyclopedic Dictionary,* which was published at the end of the last century, and the *Great Soviet Encyclopedia* — both its original sixty-four volumes, edited by Nikolai Bukharin and others in the 1920s and '30s, and the most recent edition of the 1970s. There were also countless memoirs written by Decembrists after the amnesty of 1856 and monographs by leading scholars, like the historian Militsa Nechkina. Ilya told me to make myself at home (his mother-in-law was out) and to browse as long as I liked.

What caught my attention almost immediately were three green volumes, published in 1975, which I had never seen: they contained the call numbers of the individual reports on the more than one thousand Decembrists originally arrested. I flipped open the last volume to the F's — F comes at the end of the Russian alphabet — to find six Frolovs listed, including Alexander Filippovich. Opposite his name were about seventy-five numbers that looked familiar. As I checked the title page of the catalogue, I realized why the archives hadn't been able to find the numbers. I had simply submitted them to the wrong place. The Frolov documents were in the military-historical archives, in the Lefortovo district, a stone's throw from the KGB prison. This was both good and bad: good, because the documents were really there; bad, because it was unlikely that I would be allowed to see them.

Over the next few days, I tried to figure out how to approach the military archives. Finally, I had an idea: along with a formal request, I would offer to donate a copy of General Yuri Danilov's unpublished papers concerning World War I. Some of my Russian friends tried to dissuade me from this tactic, arguing that Le Général's manuscripts would be consigned to a closed collection because he had been a White officer. But I felt strongly that the Danilov papers should have a home on Russian soil. They might not be made available immediately, but in a hundred years . . . ? It was a roundabout way of repaying friends who had helped me.

ఌ ఌ ఌ

On April 12, a telephone call from an unknown woman brought my search to a temporary halt and threw me into my first real confrontation with the KGB. Ruth picked up the receiver to hear the female voice, which refused to identify itself, say in English: "Your friend David Moiseyevich has suffered a heart attack. He is in serious condition, but under no circumstances should you visit him." The woman hung up without further explanation.

My relationship with Dr. David Moiseyevich Goldfarb, an eminent scientist, began shortly after I arrived in Moscow in 1981. I had been given his telephone number on the front porch of our house in Washington minutes before leaving by his son, Alec. The younger Goldfarb had emigrated to Israel in 1974, then moved to New York City as a professor at Columbia University.

David Moiseyevich, I quickly discovered, is a remarkable man. Had he not been Jewish, he would probably have won a Lenin Prize for his pioneer work in genetics, which included an inexpensive screening test for ten childhood diseases, called the Goldfarb Method. An astute political observer, he is also honest and, above all, courageous. We met regularly to discuss current events, and the more we talked, the more I valued his insights into a system he had known for sixty years. Ruth called him "my wise old man."

David Moiseyevich was born in 1921 into an intellectual family living in a Jewish pale at Zhitomir, the same Ukrainian town near which Frolov had been arrested so many years earlier. The family managed to survive the pogroms after the Revolution and escaped the famine of 1921–1922 by fleeing to Moscow. The only boarding school the elder Goldfarb could find for his son in those days was the ballet school run by Isadora Duncan, the American dancer whose marriage to Sergei Yesenin ended with the young poet's suicide in 1925. Eventually, David Moiseyevich transferred to the state system and graduated with outstanding honors in 1936, heading for higher education.

His first year at Moscow University coincided with the Great Terror and its devastating onslaught on academic freedom. He had wanted to study history, but, on the advice of one professor, he transfered to medicine, a discipline far less subject to political pressure. David Moiseyevich recalled the professor's words for me: "You, who were children only yesterday, have chosen a very thorny path. You must always remember what can and what cannot be said. You must understand that whatever your interpretation is today, it may have to be the opposite tomorrow." This duality — what can be said truthfully and what cannot — remains an agonizing problem in Soviet life today.

David Moiseyevich had not completed the five-year medical course when the Nazis launched their surprise attack on the Soviet Union in June 1941. He was mobilized that summer and sent to the Stalingrad front as a medical corpsman. Before the year was out, he had been wounded and lost his left leg. Back he went to Moscow to finish his studies.

By the time we met, David Moiseyevich was already a burr in the side of the authorities. For seven years he had been trying to emigrate and join his son in Israel. His departure was denied on the grounds that he had access to state secrets, something he categorically denied. Actually, a tug-of-war was going on behind the scenes between the KGB and the Academy of Sciences. The KGB wanted to keep genetic research secret because of its military implications; the academy, knowing how far Soviet genetics had fallen behind Western studies, favored a more open policy and cooperation with European scientists. Against that background, the younger Goldfarb, a man of unusual political imagination, precipitated a letter-writing campaign among Western scientists, including thirteen Nobel Prize winners, in support of his father. In June 1984, the issue came to a head because the Academy of Sciences was due to host the annual meeting of the Federation of European Biological Societies, and the organizers wanted to avoid a Western boycott over the Goldfarb case. Finally, the president of the academy intervened at a very high level; the KGB was overruled, and the Goldfarbs were given permission to leave.

They immediately began winding up their affairs and selling their possessions, including David Moiseyevich's invalid car. On April 8, I went to see him for what I thought was the last time. I was happy he was going to join his son, but I knew I would miss my mentor. Saying good-bye was hard; I had no idea when I would see him again. He gave me a rare book about the Russian civil war and lent me a briefcase so that I could carry it home — in the Soviet Union, one never carries unwrapped objects in public.

Then came the strange phone call of April 12. On April 14, after forty-eight hours of anxious waiting, the old man's son-in-law contacted me with hair-raising news. The KGB was accusing David Moiseyevich of smuggling secret biological strains out of the Soviet Union with my help, and he had asked a female colleague to warn me to stay away. I was horrified. I barely knew what a biological strain was and had certainly never discussed these organisms with David Moiseyevich. What I did know, however, was that smuggling strategic materials out of the country was a serious crime that could put both of us behind bars. Apparently, two days after our farewell, David Moiseyevich had been summoned to the blue and white mansion on Dzherzhinsky Street which houses the KGB's Moscow field office. Colonel Viktor Gusev confronted him with photographs, taken surrepti-. tiously, showing me arriving at his apartment empty-handed, then leaving with the briefcase. Gusev told him of the charges and said his exit visa had been revoked.

By launching a case against Goldfarb, the KGB hoped to solve two problems at once. If there was a trial, the KGB would prove to everyone, including the Academy of Sciences, what a treacherous person the Jewish scientist really was. It would also incriminate a Western correspondent and yet again warn the Soviet people to stay away from foreign journalists. If the case did not come to trial, the information against the journalist could be held for some future purpose.

"I am an old, one-legged Jew," David Moiseyevich had said to Colonel Gusev, "and it's no use threatening me. Whether I go to Israel doesn't make that much difference. I haven't got long to live, anyway."

At first, Gusev tried hard to be polite. After all, Goldfarb was an internationally known geneticist as well as a war veteran who had lost a leg in "the Great Patriotic," as the Soviets call World War II.

"David Moiseyevich, don't underestimate our organization," Gusev said. "We have always respected you for your contributions to the nation, and we have allowed you considerable latitude. But I must tell you now, it is a shame you have been selling your possessions. You will be leaving Moscow soon, all right, but you'll be going east, not west."

Months later, David Moiseyevich told me, "I could see that

Gusev was very annoyed. We left with a posse of ten men in three cars, gray, black, and white, to search my apartment. From early evening until two in the morning they turned the place inside out." In time, they found the strains — all dead — in test tubes on top of the bookshelf. Goldfarb tried to explain that these autotrophic mutants of *Escherichia coli* K–12 had nothing to do with national security. He had received the originals from Western scientists in the first place, and he wanted to take some of the strains to Israel, where he would be working at the Weizmann Institute. Throughout the search, Gusev tried to learn about his American friends and asked him to summon me to the apartment with the briefcase while the search was in progress. David Moiseyevich refused, suspecting that if I did show up, one of the KGB officers would plant incriminating evidence in the briefcase.

"If you thought Daniloff was smuggling biological strains for me, you should have arrested him at that time. Then there would be no argument," David Moiseyevich told Gusev.

On April 11, Gusev's assistant returned to the apartment to bargain for Goldfarb's cooperation in implicating me. The KGB officer insinuated that all suspicions against Goldfarb could be dropped if he would be "helpful." Recognizing his stubbornness, the KGB officer took Mrs. Goldfarb aside in the kitchen and asked her to exert pressure on her husband. David Moiseyevich temporized: "I'll think about it." When Gusev phoned, a few days later, the old man said, "I've decided, and the answer is no."

Articles soon began appearing in the West, criticizing the Soviet government for harassing a prominent scientist. Such a groundswell of indignation cheered me: one of the few checks on the abuse of power in the soviet Union is strong condemnation from the West, and Soviet moderates understand the ability of the United States to act as a restraint on the Kremlin. "What those naive American liberals don't comprehend," a Moscow writer once told me, "is that we look to you to rein in our government.

We have no institutional brakes of our own. America is the only force that can save us from ourselves."

With no exit visa, David Moiseyevich was left in a terrible situation. Furthermore, the KGB's harassment had undermined his health. The longer he waited for the treatment his son had now organized for him in New York, the more his health deteriorated. In addition to his diabetes and cardiac problems, he was developing lung cancer and his eyesight was failing. Sensing that his scientific career was receding, he turned increasingly toward his granddaughters and began to rebuild his library in the hope of leaving them something that would stimulate their curiosity about Russian culture and the world as they grow up.

Over the next year, as I watched David Moiseyevich struggle with uncertainty, I concluded that the Soviet system brings out the very best and the very worst in human character. Soviet citizens are tested in ways that we in the United States rarely experience: our political system does not force us into situations where we must choose between betraying a friend and losing a job. Most people lack the moral courage to withstand such pressure. Those who do, like David Moiseyevich, set an example for us all; they confirm that human decency can survive the meanest test.

For months, David Moiseyevich and I lived with the threat of a KGB case. He had survived far more dangerous times, under Stalin, and he tried to reassure me. Since the mutant strains had originated in the West and were already dead, he believed the KGB would not risk the international outcry that a trial would create. In the end, David Moiseyevich was proved right: the KGB dropped the investigation in April 1985.

Fortunately, there was plenty of political news to keep me busy during this period. In February 1984, after only fourteen months as the Soviet leader, Yuri Andropov died, and again I was covering a succession. Konstantin Chernenko, once Brezhnev's right-hand man and a representative of the Old Guard, became the general secretary over the opposition of the Young Guard, headed by Mikhail Gorbachev. Then in May, prodded by Andrei Gromyko in the Politburo, the Soviet Union announced it would boycott the Olympic Games in Los Angeles. Any chance for a new attitude in the Kremlin would have to wait.

ᖫᖫᖫ

Since I doubted that the military archives would grant my request, I continued to cast my net for the Frolov material through the rest of 1984. That summer, a friend put me in touch with Sergei, a researcher in Moscow who had a passion for the nineteenth century and occasionally undertook projects for scholars who worked for the state. His real mission, however, was to rescue and preserve prerevolutionary materials at all costs. At first, Sergei hesitated to receive me, but our mutual friend, a strong-willed woman, shamed him into it, arguing that it was a great opportunity for us both: I needed his help in tracing Frolov's descendants; he needed my help in obtaining bibliographies of Russian collections in the United States.

I drove to his apartment, on the edge of town, and parked the Volvo with its distinctive license plates a respectable distance away. I found his building on a semicircular street and climbed the broken cement steps to the front door. The elevator seemed so rickety, I decided to walk up the six flights to his apartment. I gave the doorbell three short bursts, the usual Russian signal when a friend is calling. Sergei, a small leprechaun of a man, ushered me into the kitchen and put the kettle on the stove. While we waited for the pot to boil, he gave me a tour of the two-room apartment. The living room, which served as his study, was crammed to the ceiling with yellowing newspapers, priceless bibliographies, rare photographs, and posters and pamphlets from the turn of the century. He had amassed so much material, he was forced to store some of it in boxes under the beds. The whole apartment smelled of crumbling, acid-laden paper, and he sternly forbade smoking.

Sergei had catalogued all his treasures and now had a card file, written in a meticulous Russian hand. "I have no idea what I will do with all of this, but someone has to preserve it," he confided. "There are so many individuals in this country who try to preserve things in private collections, but their apartments are so small." The issue of how to handle these materials is a growing problem in Soviet cultural life. People are reluctant to will cherished artifacts to museums, for there is little space and the objects will disappear into basements; children aren't interested in their parents' collections because they take up precious room. The Ministry of Culture promises to do something about the problem, but, like everything else in the Soviet Union, it takes a long time for good intentions to become reality.

On this first visit, I showed Sergei the family tree I had put together since my first visit with Svyatoslav Alexandrovich two years earlier. I explained that Frolov had had three children and showed him how the line came down to me through Frolov's elder son, Nicholas, his daughter Anna Nikolaevna (Baboota), and my own father. He was immediately taken by this road map and quickly started referring to the principal figures as *nashi geroii*, our heroes. He assured me he would find traces of the family, since Frolov's descendants were sufficiently prominent.

On my second visit, I could tell immediately by the grin on his face that Sergei had discovered something. Since there was barely room to stand in his study, let alone its, we moved to the kitchen table again. Setting the kettle to boil, he left the room without a word, undoubtedly to build up my suspense. He returned with an ancient volume, several inches thick, whose pages were falling out of the binding. The title page read: *Vsya Moskva (All Moscow)*.

"It's the Moscow phone book for 1898," he announced proudly, "and look here." With a flourish, he opened it to a leather marker at page 268 and read out the entry: " 'Frolov, Nik. Aldr. Col. Kremlin. Arsenal Bldg. 450.' That's the telephone number of your Decembrist's older son, your grandmother's father. Turns out, he became the commanding officer of the Kremlin artillery arsenal and lived in apartments overlooking the Alexander Gardens."

He closed the book with a thump. For me, it was as though I had been shot back into the previous century by a time machine. Surrounded by those musty books, those posters of czarist generals with their fulsome beards and mustaches, I felt I was drifting into another world. Baboota was alive again, living in Paris, and I could sense her urging me on. She was being vindicated, too; those New England matrons who used to snicker at her exaggerations were wrong. She really had lived in the Kremlin with her brothers and sisters. It felt strange to wake from this reverie and look out Sergei's window onto a stretch of green and realize that this was Moscow in 1984, not Moscow in 1898. Sergei smiled with satisfacton and promised to find still more.

က ကာ ကာ

The death of Chernenko in March 1985 — the third general secretary to die on my watch — threw me back to work with full force. Once again, the lying-in-state ceremonies at the House of Trade Unions, the solemn march to Red Square with the body on a caisson, the meeting of the Central Committee to elect a new leader. We had reached a historic moment: the older political generation, nurtured under Stalin, was at last surrendering power to the younger and elected Gorbachev as their leader. At that time, none of us imagined the extent of the shakeup ahead. Unlike Nikita Khrushchev a quarter of a century earlier, Gorbachev moved cautiously at first, consolidating power. He seemed to be more of a disciplinarian in those early days than the reformer we have come to know.

Throughout this busy period, I asked Zina to keep after the central archives about my request for the Frolov papers. The answer was always the same: the question was under active review. Then, in early June, more than a year after my original request, the military archives came through. They were sending some Frolov microfilms to the central reading room in downtown Moscow, where I could see them.

Once again, I had overreacted to the Soviet bureaucracy. We foreigners tend to assume that when a Soviet organization stalls, doesn't answer letters, or says *nyet,* there is a sinister motive behind it. Of course, it is sometimes true that they are hiding something, but often the delay is simply due to the dynamics of a large organization being governed from the center.

In mid-June, Zina and I drove to Bolshaya Pirogovskaya Street on a sunny morning. We obtained the required passes at a side window, then walked around the corner to the main entrance. We paused in the vestibule, where a militiaman examined my credentials and checked my name on his list. I had time to notice the faded beauty around me — a large wall mirror in an elaborate gold frame and blue vaulting trimmed with white.

When the policeman waved us through, we walked slowly up the grand staircase to the second-floor reading room. Inside, in a chamber about twenty-five feet square, were long tables at which various scholars, all foreigners, were sipping tea and turning their pages. The attendant, a slim young woman named Yevegniya, greeted us with a cheery smile and unlocked the shelves where our material was being held.

Zina and I took the dozens of cassettes over to one of the projection machines. The machine had been abused by previous users, and I had trouble threading the celluloid through the spindle and moving it forward, since the handle was partly broken. At last the writing came into focus on the screen. There, in report after report, were references to Frolov in a precise, flowing Russian cursive. As the frames progressed, I could follow Frolov's journey through his prison life in one secret document after another: his arrest near Zhitomir on February 8, 1826; his arrival at the Winter Palace in St. Petersburg on February 17, 1826; his sentencing five months later; his dispatch to Siberia on the night of January 21, 1827; his arrival at Chita, in eastern Siberia, in March of the same year.

One document threw new light on the length of his sentence: a handwritten *ukaz* to the Senate in Petersburg, signed by Nicholas on the occasion of his coronation in Moscow, on August 22, 1826. In it, the new emperor announced that he was reducing the sentences of all the Decembrists for "reasons of compassion."

Another document, sent by General A. Ya. Sukin, commandant of the Peter and Paul Fortress, to Nicholas on January 21, 1827, reported that Frolov and three other "state criminals" had been shackled in iron and dispatched to Siberia. Then came the monthly dispatches from the penal colony at Chita on the prisoners' status. One listing, signed by Major General S. R. Leparsky, the Siberian commandant, described my ancestor thus: "Frolov, A. F., 23 years of age, height 2 *arshin*, 5⅞ *vershki*. Face somewhat dark, round, clean; eyes dark brown; large nose with a hump, and twisted slightly to the right; hair and eyebrows, dark reddish brown."

As the documents flashed before my eyes, I seemed to be looking at Frolov through a telescope. The more I magnified the image, the more the details came into view. I was now seeing the real man, the prisoner caught in the net; I could almost reach out and touch him. Yet I sensed a barrier, as if the telescope refused to enlarge the image beyond a certain point. These were dry police reports, recording Frolov's passage through various way stations. They told me nothing of what was going on inside his mind, his struggle to stay alive in hopeless circumstances. I could study these pages forever, come to know his jailors superficially, feel the urgency of the reports to the czar, and still fail to find the Frolov I wanted to know. Nevertheless, I was thrilled by this view, and I made arrangements to hand over copies of Le Général's papers later that summer in return for copies of these microfilms.

In July, another call came to the office, this time from the archives of literature and art. At the request of the central archives, this depository had searched its stacks and come across several folders relating to Frolov — further proof that once archivists and other professionals receive word from the top, they approach their tasks with intelligence and enthusiasm.

Zina and I drove to this archive off the Leningrad Highway, not far from the Moscow's northern river port. We parked beside several smelly garbage bins and made our way to the beige brick building hidden behind trees and puddles on a quiet side street. This time, we were allowed inside the reading room used by the Russian scholars; we chose a table near an open window.

A female clerk in a brown smock brought in the faded gray folders. Inside were hundreds of sheets of paper that had languished on the shelves for sixty years. The main document was a nearly illegible manuscript of one hundred and fourteen pages. It had been prepared in 1925 for the hundredth anniversary of the Decembrist uprising for a magazine called *Land and Factory* (*Zemlya i Fabrika*). Zina whispered the notation that ran across the bottom of the first page: "Recollections of the grandson of Decembrist Alexander Frolov, professor of art and engraving A. V. Manganari."

When I heard the last name, I was electrified. Manganari?"

"Yes," said Zina matter-of-factly, "Manganari. Take a look for yourself." The name meant nothing to her.

I looked closely at the page — sure enough, Manganari. I had not heard or thought of that name in thirty years, yet the Greek syllables resonated in my brain. A few more seconds and I had it: Baboota's cousin Sasha Manganari, the boy who jumped off the bookcase with homemade wings. The A obviously stood for Alexander, for which Sasha, of course, is a common nickname.

I skimmed the pages swiftly. The text was difficult to follow; still, the places jumped out at me: the Peter and Paul Fortress, Chita, Nerchinsk, Zhitomir, Kerch. And the people: Nicholas I, Countess Volkonskaya, Count Trubetskoi, the Muravyov-Apostol brothers. Here, at last, was what I had hoped for. Manganari had written it all down, not wanting Frolov's story to be lost and forgotten. Even so, his account had almost disappeared, undetected by Soviet historians, unknown to the general public.

I realized then that we are all links in a chain, each one inter-secting and determining the next. Unless we understand these links, we can hardly know ourselves. I now felt sure I was going to find the real Frolov: who he was, how he reacted, what he experienced during his eighty-four years. I was going to learn why he was forced to spend decades in Siberia and, perhaps most important, how his link joined mine.

↶ Twelve

"BANYA TODAY!" Stas announced cheerfully when we woke up on Saturday morning, September 6.

A *banya* is a public bath, and going to the bathhouse is an ancient ritual in Russia. Not only is the steam room a place to get clean, it is also somewhere to relax with friends. Serious *banya*-goers alternate steaming with rolling in the snow or jumping in icy water; the real enthusiasts beat each other with *veniki*, birch twigs.

"*Da, da,*" Stas went on. "We get a shower today. That's why prisoners call Saturdays *banya* day." Joking, obviously, helps inmates overcome the darker moments of prison life, but Stas's quips were getting on my nerves. A real *banya* at Lefortovo? Ridiculous!

This Saturday marked my first full week in prison, and there was no break in sight. In this time, I had overcome the initial shock of the arrest and was beginning to adjust, as Stas had predicted. My anxiety level had subsided, and my mind seemed to be functioning with more clarity.

I knew from my meetings with Ruth and Mort Zuckerman

that the United States was in an uproar over my arrest. When would that pressure become apparent in the interrogation sessions? So far, Sergadeyev had given no hint of it, which made me apprehensive. Still, I kept reassuring myself that at least I had not been indicted. The decision to charge or release me did not need to be made until the tenth day after my arrest, three days away. I knew an indictment would create complications for a rapid diplomatic solution, and, with any luck, the Soviets would stop short of that step. I counted the days: I could be out by next Tuesday, September 9. In the meantime, I would take a shower and at least find temporary relief in being clean for the first time in a week.

ᗯᖇᖇ ᗯᖇᖇ ᗯᖇᖇ

Half a world away, the political wheels of the U.S. government were beginning to churn. My arrest had caught the Reagan administration at an awkward moment; in late August, key officials were on vacation: Reagan himself was in Santa Barbara; Secretary of State Shultz was at the Bohemian Grove in northern California; and even Mark Parris, the chief of the Soviet desk at the State Department, was away. Larry Speakes, the White House spokesman, announced that preparations for a summit would continue despite my arrest, giving the Soviets the impression they could act with impunity. In Moscow, the political configuration was significantly different. Gorbachev had left for his summer holiday, but top aides remained in town, including Anatoly Dobrynin, for more than twenty years the Soviet ambassador to the United States and now Gorbachev's leading foreign affairs adviser.

The first weekend of my arrest, the National Security Council in Washington created a subcommittee to monitor developments and prepare options for the president to consider on his return. This group, under Deputy National Security Adviseres Alton Keel, now pulled the files on the three cases similar to mine from the previous twenty-five years. Each case began with the arrest of a

Soviet spy in the United States and was followed by the KGB's taking an American hostage in the Soviet Union as a bargaining chip.

The most recent incident had occurred in May 1978, when the FBI detained two Soviets without diplomatic immunity in New Jersey, Vladik Enger, an assistant to the undersecretary general of the United Nations, and Rudolph Chernyayev, a personnel officer in the U.N. Secretariat. They were charged with attempting to buy classified information on antisubmarine warfare from a U.S. Navy officer. Moscow retaliated two weeks later by arresting F. Jay Crawford, a Moscow representative of International Harvester, and charging him with currency violations. After intense negotiations, the Russians were released to the custody of Ambassador Dobrynin, and Crawford was turned over to Malcolm Toon, the U.S. ambassador. Armand Hammer visited Brezhnev in the Crimea to urge a speedy resolution of the case for the good of Soviet-American relations.

Brezhnev blustered, but in September Crawford was put on trial and found guilty; he received a five-year suspended sentence and was expelled from Moscow. The Soviets claimed they had a "gentleman's agreement" with the Americans for a speedy resolution of the Russians' case; U.S. officials denied it. The two Soviets were tried later in September by a federal court and sentenced to fifty years in prison for espionage. Moscow denounced this outcome as "monstrous," and negotiations continued over the next eighteen months. First, Dobrynin suggested trading two U.S. citizens held in Moscow on drug charges for the two spies, but Washington rejected that idea. After more diplomatic haggling, Moscow finally agreed to release five important dissidents for the return of the spies.

The other two cases, of course, were those of Professor Barghoorn in 1963 and Paul Sjeklocha, the California businessman, in 1972. In the first case, President Kennedy obtained the Yale scholar's freedom by personally assuring Nikita Khrushchev that Barghoorn was not a spy. Khrushchev, who had a sneaking respect for Kennedy, accepted his word and authorized Barghoorn's release "for humanitarian reasons." According to Yuri Nosenko, a KGB defector familiar with the case, Khrushchev also castigated KGB officials for framing "a friend of Kennedy's."

The NSC advisers hoped that a presidential assurance would similarly spring me. After making sure that I had no connection with any intelligence agency, they drew up a letter for Reagan to sign; it was dispatched on Thursday, September 4. In it, the president urged Gorbachev to dispose of the mushrooming problem for the good of Soviet-American relations. He stated: "I can give you my personal assurance that Mr. Daniloff has no connection whatsoever with the U.S. Government."

This first U.S. initiative fell flat. The Soviets were determined to get their man back. And, unlike Khrushchev, Gorbachev did not have a soft spot for the U.S. president. Furthermore, Soviet aides with long memories were still smarting from what they considered the unequal deal in the Barghoorn case: the professor went free, but Igor Ivanov served ten years. Nor did Gorbachev care for the outcome of the Enger-Chernyayev-Crawford case. Under Hammer's influence, Brezhnev had undermined his own bargaining power by not sending Crawford to a labor camp. An American citizen rotting in Siberia would have given the Kremlin leverage over the White House. The Kremlin clearly preferred the one-on-one swap of the Markelov-Sjeklocha case; it corresponded to Gorbachev's views about reciprocity in Soviet-American relations. The 1972 case had also occurred on the eve of a summit. Then, both sides managed to handle the case quietly and prevent a showdown, so why not follow the same tactic now?

As Stas and I were preparing for the Lefortovo *banya*, a storm between the two nations was gathering momentum. Gorbachev's response of September 6 to Reagan's letter angered the president. Not only did the Soviet leader deny the request that I be released unilaterally, but he also brushed aside the assurance of my innocence. Gorbachev claimed that I had abused my foreign correspondent's status, adding, "Now an investigation is being conducted, and we are going to make a conclusive judgment." At the same time, he urged that the Zakharov-Daniloff incident not be allowed to disrupt the projected summit.

The same day, President Reagan fired off a response that brought the superpowers even closer to a head-on collision: "I have given my assurances that he [Daniloff] was not conducting any activity on behalf of the U.S. government. If he continues to be held, we can only consider this an attempt by the Soviet authorities to create a hostage, and we will have to act accordingly."

In accordance with diplomatic practice, the White House remained silent about these exchanges. However, at the celebration of Harvard's 350th anniversary on September 5, Secretary of State Shultz spoke out angrily, letting the world know of the administration's increasingly tough stand. "Let there be no talk of a trade for Daniloff," he said. "We and Nick have ruled that out. The Soviet leadership must find the wisdom to settle this case quickly and in accordance with the dictates of simple human decency and of civilized behavior."

During this first week, unofficial initiatives were also developing behind the scenes. As in 1978, Armand Hammer once again became a player, despite his advanced age. Furthermore, the eighty-eight-year-old industrialist was probably the only American who knew the private telephone numbers of many Soviet officials. At the time of my arrest, he was touring the Soviet Union with his art collection, discussing with top officials the new Soviet rules governing joint ventures with foreign investors, which had been adopted in mid-August. On September 2, my third day at Lefortovo, Hammer met with Premier Nikolai Ryzhkov. No reference was made to my situation, suggesting that Moscow was not particularly concerned about the American reaction at this stage. It was only when Hammer returned to New York on September 4 that he understood the mounting outrage could be disastrous for diplomatic relations. After a sleepless night in his Greenwich Village apartment, he decided to call Dobrynin in Moscow and warn him.

Hammer reached his old friend at his spacious *dacha* outside Moscow which had once been assigned to Marshal Georgii Zhukov, a great Soviet military hero. Hammer cautioned Dobrynin that the Reagan administration and the American media were taking a very hard line. Unless the crisis was defused, Hammer argued, the projected summit might be canceled. He offered to write directly to Gorbachev, urging a solution. Dobrynin encouraged him, but added ominously that he could not discuss the Daniloff affair further and suggested that Hammer call again on Monday, when the situation would be clearer. The Soviets were planning a preemptive move, but Dobrynin had no intention of revealing it to Hammer.

ఎ ఎ ఎ

Not a ripple of these events penetrated the walls of Lefortovo. Inside our basement cell, I was still fending off Stas's jokes. My cellmate had been under investigation for more than five months (so he said), and he acted as though it were perfectly normal. Like many Russians, he seemed to take the prison experience for granted. I imagined his thinking: Nick has only been in prison a week and he is already complaining. I could also hear some of my Soviet friends telling one another: "Wait until he has been there for seven years, then he will know what so many of us have experienced." To that I could only reply: "Sorry, I'm an American. Training for prison is not part of our culture. It is part of yours because of your long tradition of imprisoning people for political beliefs. Frankly, I think living in a cell on soup and kasha is nothing to boast about. You launched a revolution in 1917 and struck a blow for the rights of man. You redistributed wealth, expropriating it from the rich and giving housing and land to the poor. But your idea of human rights is having a roof over your head, a job, free medicine and education. You have not secured the civil liberties we take for granted in the West: the right to free speech, travel, worship; the right to assemble, to vote, to have a fair trial . . . In fact, I have fewer legal rights today under the Soviet criminal code than I would have had in Russia a hundred years ago, when juries existed and defense lawyers could influence the outcome of a trial."

For now, all I wanted was a break from interrogation and Stas's company, a chance to wash the prison stench out of my skin and to read the Decembrists' memoirs. The books had finally been delivered to me after the prison authorities checked them for secret messages, razor blades, and drugs. No doubt they remembered how one Soviet citizen, caught working for the CIA, committed suicide during an interrogation session by swallowing a lethal poison hidden in the eraser of his pencil.

I thought there was a fair chance I would get a respite from interrogation. It was, after all, the weekend, and since the Kremlin abolished the six-day work week some twenty years earlier, weekends were about as sacred in Russia as in America. Kremlin leaders and high Party officials habitually retire to well-appointed government mansions northeast of the capital, at Barvikha and Zhukovka; cosmonauts disappear to their retreats on the Moskva-Volga Canal; and literary folk seek seclusion at writers' colonies — Kotebel in the Crimea or Tarusa or Peredelkino outside Moscow. Ordinary people without special privileges rent *dachas* or rooms wherever they can find them.

Sometime after breakfast, the guards arrived to march Stas and me down the corridors to the large hall where I had been taken on the day of my arrest. Numerous doors led off this holding room. Opening one, they locked us in a small cubicle about five feet square, with walls paneled waist high in unexpectedly clean green and white tiles. We undressed and sat silently on a rough wooden bench. After a while, the guards reappeared and marched us to the shower, a short distance away. We entered a room with a sloping cement floor and opened the hot spray from two overhead showers. I found the coarse laundry soap and with great difficulty tried to make it lather. The guards allowed us ample time, maybe twenty minutes or more, before they began shouting for us to wind it up.

Standing under the water, I couldn't help compare this shower with the real *banya*, which had been a regular feature of my Moscow weekends, mostly on Saturday nights. I used to go with friends to the Voikovskie Baths, in a northeast working district of the city. We were a mixed bunch — all Soviets except me. Among us were upstanding members of the Communist Party, several computer programmers, an environmentalist, and a man connected with the Academy of Sciences. The group, which we called the *obshestvo;* or society, also included a number of men who wanted to emigrate but who had been denied exit visas. Among them were the talented pianist Vladimir Feltsman, who has since settled in New York, Sergei Petrov, the meticulous fine arts photographer who was married to an American woman, and Sasha Kalugin, an artist who had been thrown into psychiatric hospitals several times on false charges.

Sitting naked in the sauna broke down all barriers; we shed our inhibitions as well as our clothes. Some of the participants I never knew by name. Some I never saw more than once. Some, I suspect, never realized I was an American. In the steam room, no subject was taboo — from the existence of God to the machinations of the KGB.

In time, I came to know the organizer of these sessions well. We jokingly called him our *starosta,* the prerevolutionary term for village elder. Yuri had grown up totally within the system, advancing through the hierarchy of the Communist Party to responsible positions in the Moscow trade and building professions until he became disillusioned. When I first met him, he had lost his job and was driving a gypsy cab; his wife, a trained engineer, was selling ice cream from a sidewalk kiosk. Now in his early forties, he was an energetic bear of a man, with one blue eye and one brown eye and a bulging belly half covered by an immense red birthmark. An eternal optimist, Yuri never descended to self-pity over his loss of status.

In his heyday, he had enjoyed the privileges the system bestows on its faithful: a Soviet-made Fiat and a three-bedroom apartment with high ceilings, a well-appointed bathroom, and a kitchen with modern conveniences and gadgets. He had a network of well-placed friends in the bureaucracy who could obtain almost anything for the asking. In the mid-1970s, Yuri won the crowning perk: the position of Soviet trade representative in New Zealand. In Wellington, he had the opportunity to compare the success of free enterprise with the sluggish economy of his own country. Swilling beer and eating salty *vopla* fish in the private lounge next to the sauna, Yuri would regale us with stories of life in the Soviet compound in Wellington. "Like all Soviet embassies, it was a rat's nest of fear, stupidity, and corruption," he said. He recalled how KGB officers at the embassy would tail him and his wife and listen in on their telephone conversations. Everyone was constantly reporting on everyone else. Within weeks of his arrival, Yuri came into conflict with the ambassador. Unlike most of his countrymen, Yuri thrived on hard work. The New Zealand businessmen immediately took to his gregarious nature, and he was able to arrange some excellent lamb and mutton deals. But his popularity with the capitalists quickly made him suspect. "Here I was, making a profit for my country and waving the Soviet flag in the community, and all those idiot security people started suspecting I was a spy."

If he had not had aging parents in Moscow, Yuri would have defected then and there. Instead, he returned home, resigned from the Party, and applied to emigrate legally. For this disloyalty he lost his job, and his exit visa was repeatedly denied. The refusal was not surprising. For a man to want to give up the best the Soviet system could offer was incomprehensible, if not unforgivable, to the authorities. Yuri was not a disaffected intellectual or a Jewish refusenik. He was an ordinary Soviet citizen.

He understood the system: he knew how to avoid regulations, how to keep the state security people off his back, what to give the manager of the grocery store to get fast service. For years he had played by the rules and been handsomely rewarded, but in the end it had not been enough. Why did he give it all up? As

he said, he had a lot of energy. He liked to work, but he never
felt that he accomplished anything. Soviet inefficiency was ultimately demoralizing. Sitting in the *banya,* he once told me, "I
used to suffer from ulcers — probably from all the deceit and
games I had to play. As soon as I handed in my Party card, I felt
liberated and my ulcers went away."

For me, the *banya* was a place to gain a sense of how ordinary
people viewed the latest political events in Moscow and abroad.

ও ও ও

On leaving the shower, Stas and I were handed clean underwear
and bedding by an orderly in a white coat. This time, I donned
the dark blue cotton shorts and light blue tank top. For a week,
I had been living in my own underclothes day and night; they
were uncomfortable and smelled foul, and I was happy to relinquish them. But I continued to wear my own street clothes, since
prison uniforms were not required.

The Lefortovo underwear was pleasantly soft from many wash-
ings. The top was marked "SN30 — year 84." Getting dressed,
I noticed that my trousers were hanging farther and farther down
my hips. In one week, I had lost about five pounds. I didn't know
it then, but I had been subsisting on a near-starvation diet. Although the prison rules called for an average diet, it was also
standard procedure to weaken newcomers with a diet low in
calories and protein. I kept track of what I was given to eat that
first week, and it amounted to between 1,250 and 1,500 calories
a day instead of the 2,200 I needed. I had never been one to carry
excess weight — how much more could I afford to lose?

No sooner did we return to the cell than the *kormushka* flopped
open: "Danilov! *Na vyzov!*" Impossible! It was Saturday. My
heart started to thud; my mouth went dry. In the Soviet Union,
when someone works on a day off, it's serious business. I picked
myself up, and within a few minutes I was marching along the
catwalk to Room 215.

"I know today is Saturday," Sergadeyev greeted me as I walked into the room, "but business is business. *Dela yest dela.*" He sighed. "We have to go through the protocol and sign it," he announced, opening the file on his desk. "Read these pages and make sure they reflect what you said."

Working on a Saturday seemed to please Sergadeyev no more than it did me. Was he under pressure to produce "evidence" for either a trial or diplomatic haggling with the Americans? I could imagine the scenario: Zakharov would be tried and convicted in New York. I would be put on trial in Moscow. Whatever sentence Zakharov got, I would get one year more. If I was lucky, lengthy negotiations would then begin, and eventually there would be some sort of exchange. In the meantime, I would rot in some godforsaken prison camp.

My mind started to race. Should I sign these documents? Had I been arrested in America, the *Miranda* ruling would have guaranteed me the assistance of a lawyer. I would have been informed that I did not have to answer any questions if I chose not to do so. Here in Lefortovo I was isolated and at the mercy of a highly skilled KGB officer who was pressuring me to incriminate myself at every step. It was impossible to think clearly. Should I refuse to sign? If I didn't, I would probably be subjected to pressure. What kind of pressure?

I toyed with idea of using a phony signature. I have two styles of handwriting: one slanting to the right, which is my usual style, and one straight up and down, which I call my scientific style because I always used it when doing mathematics. I thought about using the scientific style. Then, if the protocols were published, Ruth would spot the difference and understand that I had signed them under duress. But I argued myself out of that idea: to sign is to sign.

"You will write at the bottom of each page the following words," Sergadeyev intoned. " 'The protocol has been read by me. The answers are correctly recorded. I have no amendments.' " Sergadeyev repeated the phrases slowly, articulating the syllables distinctly, emphasizing the grammatical inflections as though he were talking to a simple-minded child. " 'The protocol has been read by me. The answers are recorded correctly. I have no amendments.' "

I knew that other Western journalists who had been interrogated by the KGB had signed the protocols of their sessions. Bob Toth did. Allison Smale did. Jacques Abouchar, arrested in Afghanistan and interrogated by both the Soviet and Afghan secret police, did. I felt there was no way to refuse without courting major trouble. Because of Sergadeyev's deliberate omission on the first day of my arrest, I was unaware that Article 142 of the procedural code states that a defendant may write a statement explaining why he refuses to sign. In the end, I decided that my only recourse was to read each page three times to make sure I had no major objection to its contents.

"Under our law, you can make amendments later if you need to, before the investigation is completed," Sergadeyev told me. He was prodding me.

Was he telling the truth? I had no idea, but I decided to take him at his word, and later I did request some amendments. So I began to sign. I was moderately satisfied with the protocols. Still, I knew that even total accuracy was no protection. Soviet officials have a way of omitting the context, twisting the words, adding public commentary to the stated facts — all to their ultimate advantage.

After signing my name in Russian to each page, a terrible sense of gloom came over me. Sergadeyev, however, looked satisfied. He had won another victory for his side. He leaned back in his chair and, as if reflecting out loud, said, "Yes, you really are a very polished spy." Then he turned to me and asked casually, "Tell me, which intelligence school did you finish?"

"I am not a spy, and I have never been to a spy school," I retorted. "After finishing college, I applied to join the diplomatic service but was rejected because of high blood pressure. How about you?"

"I did graduate from an intelligence school," Sergadeyev conceded. Then, to my utter surprise, he volunteered: "And also of a counterintelligence school." I had the impression that he would have liked nothing more than for me to confess to being a CIA agent so that we could drink tea and swap spy stories together.

Then I had a sudden glimpse behind his façade of objectivity. Of course! As a counterintelligence officer, Sergadeyev had a hidden agenda. His main goal was to incriminate me, but he was also wanted to know how Americans respond to KGB surveillance — how alert American residents of Moscow, not diplomats, are to wiretapping, apartment bugging, routine monitoring — and any other incidental intelligence he could glean.

Assembling the signed protocols in a neat pile, Sergadeyev pushed back his chair once again. "Nikolai Sergeyevich," he said melodramatically, "you will return to the United States one day and you will write a book. And you will give me hell. You will be a national hero and make a lot of money." He paused for several seconds, waiting for my reaction. Then he added, "But when you will return, nobody knows!" As an afterthought, he said finally, "I'm getting on in years, and frankly, I don't think I'll live to read your memoirs!"

I said nothing. His chilling message was not lost on me. The colonel was a master at manipulating emotions.

"Now let's return to those photographs Misha gave you." Sergadeyev resumed the interrogation. "Where did you send them?" I was surprised that he hadn't pursued this subject earlier. I was ready. He needed to demonstrate that I was guilty of what the criminal code describes as *peredacha,* transmission of materials constituting a state or military secret. It was exactly the same question Misha had asked me during our walk. My erstwhile friend had received excellent coaching.

"I kept them in my office for a long time," I replied.

"Where did you send them?" Sergadeyev was getting increasingly insistent, hardly able to restrain his irritation. He leaned forward over his desk and, with a piercing look, shouted, "You took those photographs to the *rezidentura,* the CIA station, didn't you? Go on. Admit it!"

"I did not!"

"What did you do with them, then?" He was not going to give up.

I didn't want to tell Sergadeyev that I had given them to a traveler to take out of the country. He would twist that to mean that I had given them to a CIA officer. "I told you the photographs were not very good and would probably not have been used by my magazine. I was in no particular hurry to send them to our Washington office, and I took them out when I went on vacation in August. I had them with me when I went through customs."

Sergadeyev looked skeptical but dropped the subject. He had failed to get the answer he needed, and he never raised the subject again. Then he embarked on an entirely new tack. "Nikolai Sergeyevich, you wanted to know if your son reached home safely. Would you like to call your wife?"

I was taken aback. What was behind his offer? He had already told me that Caleb had returned home safely. I had asked him to find out from Ruth when she called about another meeting. Did he want me to tell her about the unusual Saturday interrogation, thereby signaling that the Soviet side was proceeding at full speed toward a trial? I had no idea.

I stood up. "May I?"

The colonel nodded and summoned the interpreter from another room. It was nearly noon. I got up from the long table and walked around to the small table with the three telephones at Sergadeyev's desk. I dialed the office number; Ruth picked up the phone.

I greeted her, then heard her sing out, "It's Nick." She conveyed to me obliquely that Gary Lee of the *Washington Post* was there, interviewing her. She wanted him to listen in so that he could record accurately what was said and have something exclusive for his report.

I began by explaining that Sergadeyev was allowing me to inquire about the children. Ruth seemed puzzled, too, at first. "But I told him everything when I talked to him yesterday," she said. She then launched into a description of the mounting outcry in the United States. I responded cryptically, hoping that Sergadeyev and the interpreter would not catch the drift of the conversation. Journalists and friends from around the world had been calling, she said, expressing both sympathy and outrage.

"So far the Soviets have not cut off the telephone completely, although the line is usually so bad, it is impossible to hear," she said.

I told her that the Soviet side was moving quickly. "They seem intent on bringing the matter to trial, although there have been some fuzzy hints about a swap." I asked her to obtain my medical records from Washington, outlining my history of hypertension. I also asked her to dig up the file containing accounts of the various KGB provocations against me.

She immediately understood that I was planning for a trial. "I'll do it," she said, "but never forget that this is a political case, not a legal case. A defense is irrelevant."

At this point, Ruth changed the subject to the packing we had been doing when I was arrested. Our major shipment had left the Soviet border the day before I was seized, with the exception of a few items that customs refused to authorize. "Can you believe it? They are trying to accuse us of smuggling our own jewelry out of the country.

"Customs called up and wanted me to drive out to Butovo. They plan to start a legal case against us," she said. "I told them I'm too busy and have passed everything over to the British embassy. I can't deal with this on top of everything else." Ruth, who retains her British citizenship, then added for the benefit of the telephone monitors, "They should know that they will have to deal not only with President Reagan but also with Her Majesty's Government." The threat would not deter the KGB, but it would let them know that she would not be intimidated. They were clearly trying to harass her in order to frustrate her efforts to create publicity about my case.

Ruth next told me that she had arranged to visit David Goldfarb, who was hospitalized in the Vishnevsky Institute. I had planned to visit him the afternoon I was arrested. His health had become critical, and still the Soviet authorities were refusing to allow him to travel to New York for treatment. Twenty percent of his remaining foot had been amputated because of the onset of gangrene. Now there was talk of amputating his other leg, and no one believed he would survive such an operation. On that unhappy note, we ended our conversation.

ᴖᴖ ᴖᴖ ᴖᴖ

I returned to my cell in a black mood. Goldfarb's situation was grim. As I descended the iron staircase at the cellblock intersection, I steeled myself for more of Stas's humor. But this time he seemed sensitive to my mood. After the door slammed shut, we chatted casually for a while. I told him about my search for Frolov's cell in Leningrad and the time I spent with the door closed.

He picked up on that. He told me a story about a Soviet journalist who asked to be imprisoned. "He also wanted to get the feel of what it was like. He asked a judge to lock him up. After a few days, he read in a newspaper that his judge had suddenly died. The journalist went into a panic. When he finally managed to persuade the authorities to let him out, he learned that the judge was really still alive and had planted the article on purpose.

" 'Why the hell did you do that to me?' the journalist castigated the judge.

" 'You wanted to know what it means to be buried alive,' the judge replied."

Stas's story did nothing to improve my morale. On the contrary; I wondered if he had recounted it deliberately. In any event, I no longer wanted to talk. As always when I was upset, I reached for one of my Decembrist books. This time I took down from my shelf the memoirs of Nikolai Basargin, a young captain who had passed up a chance to flee to France after the uprising because he wanted to share the punishment of the other Decembrists. As it happened, Basargin had served time in the Peter and Paul Fortress and was shipped to Siberia in the same convoy as Frolov.

❧ Thirteen

"HE WHO HAS NOT EXPERIENCED fortress detention in Russia cannot imagine the gloomy, helpless feeling that seizes a man when he steps over the threshold and into his cell." Basargin was writing in 1856, having served thirty years in Siberia. I knew just how he felt. Reading about the Decembrists and thinking about Frolov always helped to put my own situation in perspective. Basargin continued: "The prisoner stands alone against that unlimited autocratic power that can make of him anything it wants; at first subjecting him to every conceivable privation, and later even forgetting about him."

I closed the book and pushed it aside. How little had changed in Russia. Finding parallels between czarist and Soviet rule became one of my few mental distractions — that is, as long as I did not allow the similarities to unnerve me. Frolov's misfortune invariably made me wonder if Siberia would be part of my destiny, too.

I reached over to the shelf for a piece of toilet paper from the shelf and wrote down the Basargin reference, tucking it between the pages of the book. In the week I had been in prison, I had tried to map out the book I intended to write about Frolov and even made a sketchy outline in the back of my green interrogation notebook. But mostly I organized my thoughts in my head; my notes might be confiscated later.

Fortunately, by the time of my arrest I had collected almost all of the important facts about Frolov's life, but it wasn't until I was in prison that I began to digest them, to put the pieces together. After "lights out," gazing at the naked bulb in the ceiling through my handkerchief, I thought again of the questions that had prompted my search in the first place: Why was Frolov sentenced to twenty years of hard labor and eternal exile? How did he survive that terrible punishment?

ᵍᵒ ᵍᵒ ᵍᵒ

Alexander Frolov's association with the Decembrists began during the summer of 1825, only a few months before the uprising, in the Ukrainian town of Old Konstantinov. At the time, he was a twenty-one-year-old lieutenant with the Penzensky Regiment of the Second Army. He came from a military family in the Crimea: his father, Filip Frolov, was the commander of the small fortress at Kerch, which guards the strait that connects the Sea of Azov with the Black Sea. The family was not wealthy, so Alexander was educated at home with his brothers, Nicholas and Peter, and his sisters, Elizabeth, Claudia, and Pelageya. At fourteen, he entered a military school at Sevastopol, intending to emulate his father.

That summer, like most summers on the flat steppes west of Kiev, was hot and uneventful. Frolov passed the time with other young officers, drinking and smoking in the taverns and discussing the ideas stirred up by the French Revolution. Although Frolov was too young to have marched on Paris in 1813 with Czar Alexander, he loved to listen to the others reminisce about their encounters with Napoleon's Grande Armée. Coming from some of the best families in Russia, the young men exuded the bravado and self-confidence that Frolov himself lacked. But the more he listened, the more he agreed with his comrades: Russia needed reform. Serfdom should be abolished and a constitutional government, based partly on the U.S. Constitution, should be instituted.

One evening in May after a boisterous gathering, Frolov's tentmate, Pavel Mazgan, accosted him drunkenly in a courtyard. Would he join a secret society, the Union of the United Slavs, and contributed fifty rubles to the restructuring of Russia? Mazgan showed him the eight-cornered star — the society's symbol — and suggested he take the secret oath, the Slavonic Catechism. Frolov could not afford the sum, so he tried to stall. "I did not read the oath, nor do I know its contents, nor did I ever hold it in my hands," he said many years later. As it happened, however, this encounter with Mazgan turned out to be one of the main pieces of evidence used against him.

Several weeks later, Frolov's commanding officer, Captain Aleksei Tyutchev, invited him to a meeting with Nikolai Bestuzhev-Ryumin, a charismatic, nineteen-year-old lieutenant who acted as the liaison between the Southern Society and the United Slavs. The Southern Society, led by Colonel Pavel Pestel, hoped to form an assassination squad from the ranks of the Slav radicals. The conversation of the men assembled in the ground-floor apartments of a fellow officer soon turned to the idea of overthrowing Alexander.

"The time has come," Bestuzhev-Ryumin declared, arousing his listeners' patriotism, "for the liberation of the people from their exploitation and enslavement. It is unthinkable that the Russians, who have made such a name for themselves by their brilliant accomplishments in war, liberating Europe from Napoleon, would not throw off their own yoke." The young officer was prepared to do anything to depose czarism, even killing the whole Romanov family.

The idea of assassination made Frolov uncomfortable. Like most Russians, he believed that the czar, however despotic, had a god-given right to rule. "And why should we kill the empress?" Frolov protested. "After all, she does so much good for the poor."

"It's for the good of the nation," one of the officers responded. "We must sacrifice father, mother, children!"

Bestuzhev-Ryumin scowled. Such objections threatened to undermine his mission. Major Ivan Spiridov, one of Frolov's superior officers, drew the young firebrand aside and whispered, "Don't worry about Frolov. He's young, and we can turn him any way we like."

Frolov overheard the remark and flashed with anger. He was about to respond when there was a sudden commotion in the yard and a face appeared at the window. A government spy? No one was sure, but Frolov took advantage of the distraction, grabbed his cap, and broke through the circle of officers.

"I won't agree to this crime, and I ask you not to consider me a member of your society!" he shouted over his shoulder as he hurried from the room.

The meetings continued throughout that summer, though Frolov did not attend them. When he was told that most officers in the South were members of the southern Society and that they had collected more than a million rubles toward the uprising, Frolov contemplated writing to his father for permission to leave the army. Instead, he consulted his commander, Major Fyodorovich, who arranged for him to be reassigned to a training battalion near Zhitomir, an important grain center in the Ukraine.

It was there that Frolov got word of Alexander I's sudden death at Taganorg in November 1825, an event that threw Russia and the conspirators into turmoil. Konstantine, the emperor's younger brother, was expected to become the new czar. But, in a secret letter, he had abdicated his right to the throne. As the Russian viceroy in Poland, he preferred living with his Polish mistress to taking on the burdens of his country. Nevertheless, the throne was offered to him twice. He refused, causing one observer to remark that the Russian crown was being passed around like a cup of tea nobody wanted. Finally, in early December, Alexander's second brother, twenty-eight-year-old Nicholas, agreed to become the next Romanov czar.

The Decembrists had originally planned the assassination for the following summer, when Alexander would have reviewed troops in the South. Now they had to develop a new strategy. Although they were not prepared, the societies decided to use the confusion following the czar's death to kill Nicholas before he could consolidate his power. The coup was set for December 14, when the military and civilian institutions in St. Petersburg would swear allegiance to their new ruler. Prince Sergei Trubetskoi, a hero of 1812, was elected to lead the rebels in Senate Square; Colonel Pestel would head the revolt in the South.

Thanks to the traditional network of informers in Russia, Nicholas learned of the uprising several days in advance, and Pestel was arrested on December 13. Even though the Northern Society suspected leaks in its organization, the members voted to go ahead. "Better to be arrested on the square than to be taken in bed," the naval officer Nikolai Bestuzhev, who was also a painter, told Kondratii Ryleyev, the fiery Petersburg poet was was one of the Northern leaders. "Let the people know what we will die for rather than allow them to be surprised when we mysteriously disappear from society and nobody knows where we are."

The rebels planned to assemble eight thousand troops in Senate Square. They would demand the creation of a provisional government and a constitution abolishing serfdom forever. But they were doomed from the start. Nicholas seized the initiative, holding the first allegiance ceremony in the Senate at 7:00 A.M. The mutineers were slow to leave their barracks, and Prince Trubetskoi, who considered the attempt a lost cause, failed to show up at all; the so-called dictator of the uprising took refuge in the house of his father-in-law, the Austrian ambassador. In the end, only three thousand troops took up their positions outside the Senate. Even the weather worked against them. The day was dark and cold, with the mercury hovering at ten degrees below zero.

A bitter wind was whipping off the Neva River, and by afternoon a light snow began to fall.

Nicholas viewed the uprising as a serious challenge to his power as he began his reign. He contemplated fleeing but instead retired to pray for the strength to do his duty to God and Russia, even if it meant firing on his own men. Then he left the Winter Palace for the square, passing his six-year-old son, the future czar Alexander II, to loyal soldiers in the street in a dramatic demonstration of trust. Making a final effort to persuade the troops to disband peacefully, Nicholas ordered the governor-general of St. Petersburg, General Mikhail Miloradovich, to address them. Sitting on a white charger, the former commander in the war against Napoleon harangued the soldiers, declaring them a disgrace to their uniform, to the czar, to Mother Russia.

Suddenly a shot rang out; the white horse reared, and Miloradovich tumbled to the ground. Instead of assassinating the czar, Lieutenant Peter Kakhovsky had mortally wounded one of Russia's military heroes. As the afternoon light faded, Nicholas gave orders to fire. The shooting lasted little more than an hour; by five o'clock the mutiny was over and a thousand victims lay dead or dying, their blood draining into the snow. Watery holes dotted the ice on the Neva where many had tried to escape.

As soon as quiet descended, Nicholas ordered the arrest of the ringleaders. Three days later, he established a special commission of inquiry and stacked it with friends and allies, including his brother Michael. Its primary goal was to excise the cancer that could undermine the czar's power, not to uncover the truth or to see that justice was done. Nicholas himself was not inherently evil — he was not a Hitler or Stalin or even a Peter the Great. He was a hard-working disciplinarian who wanted the best for Russia, so he did what any strong leader does when his power is threatened: he moved to protect it.

The conspiracy was also a personal humiliation for Nicholas. Many of the rebels were his friends, not peasant riffraff with the usual grievances. He had ridden into battle at their side; he had

danced at court balls with their sisters and wives. But their political ideas were beyond his comprehension. How could Prince
Trubetskoi, one of the wealthiest men in the empire, be such a
fool as to betray the crown? Or Prince Volkonsky, who had
fought with his brother Alexander against Napoleon? They were
the cream of the Russian nobility. Princes, generals, outstanding
army officers, had turned traitor. It enraged Nicholas that they
had drawn up various constitutions for Russia in which the Romanov czar would play little or no role and that they had plotted
to kill his entire family.

If the czar's anger with the leaders was understandable, his
obsession with tracking down everyone associated with the revolt
was maniacal. His couriers traveled far from the capital, to Moscow, Kiev, and Warsaw, in search of suspects. Even those with
only a passing involvement in the rebel societies were subject to
arrest, including such officers as Alexander Frolov — who had
been four hundred miles from Senate Square and played no role
in the uprising.

From the moment Frolov learned of the disastrous revolt, he
knew he was in danger. In late December, he shared his concern
with Ivan Ivanov, the secretary of the United Slavs, who tried to
calm him. "You have nothing to fear," he said. "You refused to
join the society, and your name is not on its rolls. Anyway, the
courts of Britain, France, and Austria will intervene to defend
us." Frolov was not convinced. His own major and several other
officers from his regiment were arrested in January, and he worried that they would betray him — which is precisely what happened. On February 8, 1826, the czar's *feldjaegers* arrived with
a warrant for his arrest. He did not resist.

Nicholas insisted on a personal interview with most of the
suspects, and on February 17, Frolov was delivered to the Winter
Palace. His hands manacled behind his back, he was led by guards
through the imperial palace, chamber after chamber, until they
entered a magnificent gold-and-white-embossed salon overlooking the Neva. Through the frosted windows, Frolov could make

out the silhouette of the Peter and Paul Fortress, which Peter the Great had built a century earlier to defend his "Window on the West" from Swedish attack. Shimmering in the distance was the gilded spire of Trinity Cathedral.

At the far end of the room stood the imposing figure of Czar Nicholas. His waist tightly drawn in, his chest thrust forward aggressively to display his military honors, he wore the uniform of brigade commander with the light blue sash of the Order of St. Andrew. Nicholas scowled contemptuously when the guards pushed forward the disheveled young lieutenant. Then he exploded in rage.

"You!" he barked. "How old are you?" He used the second-person singular to underscore his disdain.

"Twenty-two years from birth, your majesty," Frolov stuttered.

"Miserable urchin! Treading the same path, eh? Cur! I'll teach you."

The sight of the junior officer in his tattered uniform infuriated Nicholas, who had inherited an obsession with the military from his father. Paul and Nicholas seemed to think that well-drilled troops in beautiful uniforms would save Russia from any unrest smoldering beneath the surface. The czar approached the prisoner and kicked his shins so hard that Frolov almost fell to the ground. Nicholas then turned to General Vasily Levashov, his chief investigator, snatched a pen, and scribbled on a piece of paper: "Imprison and hold under harsh conditions." He would show Russia what happened to disloyal officers.

Frolov was carted off to the Peter and Paul Fortress and the following day thrown into Cell 15, where he spent the next eleven months in solitary confinement. He fell into deep despair: he was penniless, his military career ruined. Worse still, he had brought disgrace and tragedy to his family. Upon hearing of his son's fate, Filip Frolov suffered a stroke from which he never recovered.

The cells in Peter and Paul were damp and small, about four paces by four, with no plumbing or running water and little light.

Cell 15 had a barred window looking north, but the panes were smeared with whitewash, blocking any view. Frolov's diet consisted of buckwheat groats, stale buns, a few bits of rotten meat, and tea. Some of the other prisoners fared better: Basargin, for example, received beer; Ryleyev was offered wine.

In accordance with the czar's instructions, Frolov was not permitted writing materials or books, not even a Bible, which prisoners commonly received. He had no idea why he was being treated so harshly, but he realized that to keep his sanity, he had to occupy his mind. One Decembrist, Colonel Aleksei Bulatov, became so disoriented by his incarceration that he cracked his skull against the wall and died a few days later, his brain oozing through the fracture. The only occupation Frolov could think of was to remove the whalebone stays that puffed out his uniform jacket and to fashion them into crude knitting needles. Then he unraveled his woolen socks, winding the yarn into balls. His fingers were so stiff from the cold that it was an act of will to twist the wool over the makeshift needles. "Now I had yarn and needles," he reminisced decades later with his grandson Sasha Manganari, "so I could continually be knitting my socks. I would knit, undo, knit and undo, and so my thoughts gradually became happier."

Clearly, Nicholas wanted to make a example of Frolov and the other members of the United Slavs who had plotted an assassination. Harsh prison conditions, out of public view, were not enough. Severe sentences trumpeted throughout the land were necessary to assert the crown's authority. It was easy to arrange. Although Nicholas pretended he had nothing to do with the commission of inquiry, he was active behind the scenes, reading its secret reports, dictating prison diets and treatment.

The trial of the Decembrists in July 1826 was a charade carried out in the middle of the night. Nicholas named seventy-two government, military, and religious leaders to a special criminal court that never even cross-examined the hundred and twenty-one defendants, never allowed them any kind of defense. Rather, the court accepted the findings of the commission and immediately ranked the prisoners according to levels of guilt. Then it imposed punishment in the tradition of eighteenth-century Russian justice. The five ringleaders, who were judged so heinous as to belong to no category, were to be drawn and quartered. The "first category" prisoners were to be beheaded, and the "second category," which included Frolov, received hard labor in perpetuity. Nicholas, not wanting to appear a barbarian before Europe, altered the sentences by decree. Disemboweling gave way to hanging, beheading turned into perpetual hard labor, and perpetual labor became twenty years of bondage.

Frolov's case was serious from the start because Lieutenant Mazgan, Captain Tyutchev, and Major Spiridov had all implicated him before the commission. They stated that he had attended at least one meeting, possibly three, of the United Slavs. Any association with this extreme group was damning. When Frolov was questioned before the trial, he tried to answer honestly and simply.

> QUESTION: Did you swear allegiance to the emperor?
> FROLOV: I did swear loyal subordination to the present emperor.
> QUESTION: How did you become involved in free thinking and liberal ideas: from others or from reading books, and how did these opinions take root in your mind?
> FROLOV: I was introduced to free thinking by Lieutenant Mazgan, Lieutenant Gromnitsky, and Captain Tyutchev, who invited me to their society; but why I became involved I can attribute only to my inexperience and my desire to please my unit commander Tyutchev.

When his questioning was over, Frolov tried to lighten his fate with an appeal to his interrogator, General Levashov: "I am placing my hope on you, your excellency. I did betray the emperor, I did break my oath, and for that I shall be severely punished, but believe me, your excellencey, I did this without ulterior motive and only out of a desire to please."

After May 1826, Frolov was called no more. Then, on the

night of July 12, well after midnight, the defendants were called by categories to the commandant's house, where the court was sitting. Frolov and the others had no idea they had already been condemned and assumed they were to be questioned further. When they assembled, they were surprised to hear the clear call out their names. A wave of bravado swept over the men when twenty years of labor was announced. This was the first time they had been brought together in a group, and they began talking eagerly to each other. Someone shouted, "Remember, the sun also shines in Siberia!"

Immediately after the sentencing, Frolov and the others were ordered out of the fortress to the northern embankment. The night sky glowed with the light from bonfires, the flames illuminating the loyal troops who had come to witness their comrades' humiliation. To the roll of drums, the Decembrists were ordered to their knees. The loyal troops broke the mutineers' swords over their heads, ripped off their epaulets, and commanded them to throw their tunics into the flames. In a defiant gesture, Mikhail Lunin, a prominent southern Decembrist, started to urinate. *"La belle sentence doit être arrosée,"* he shouted. "The glorious sentence must be celebrated!"

Trooping back to their cells, the men spotted the five gallows on which the ringleaders were to be put to death. Later that morning, at five o'clock, after the others had returned to their cells, the five doomed men were led out in white sheets bearing the word CZAR-MURDERER. They had killed no czar, but the nooses were drawn tightly around their necks. A shot resounded, the traps fell away, and two lifeless bodies swung in the air. The witnesses gasped when they saw that three of the ropes had broken and three badly injured men, covered with blood, picked themselves up from among the broken planks. One of the victims found the strength to shout out to the new goverenor-general of the city, "General, you came no doubt to watch us die. You can gladden your sovereign's heart with the news that his wish is being fulfilled. We are dying in agony!"

Colonel Sergei Muravyo-Apostol then struggled to his feet and spoke his last words, which have reverberated through history ever since: "Poor Russia! We cannot even hang properly!"

✍ ✍ ✍

As I contemplated Frolov's fate from my own cell, I thought about political power and the struggle of the American founding fathers in 1787 to limit abuse by dividing the power among equal branches of government. In Frolov's time, as in the Soviet Union today, no system of checks and balances limits political power. It was in the czar's interest to make an example of Frolov and the others. Similarly, if the Politburo judged it to be in the Soviet interest to send me to Siberia, no courtroom defense, no appeal machinery, no "independent judiciary," was going to oppose it. "The new regime is hardly better than the old," I remembered my father telling Baboota whenever she criticized the Romanovs. With these depressing thoughts, I turned over and tried to sleep. But it was no good. I kept imagining a slight, emaciated figure with a drooping ginger mustache, sitting in his cell, knitting and unraveling his socks.

I pictured the cold night of January 20, 1827, when the gurads burst into Frolov's cell, handed him a tattered sheepskin coat, and ordered him out. With no explanation, he was again led to the commandant's house, across the inner courtyard of the fortress. Inside, Frolov met three other prisoners for the first time: Lieutenant Basargin, Major General Mikhail Vonvizin, and Dr. Christian Volf. Soon, the prison commandant, General A. Ya. Sukin, hobbled into the room and announced, "By order of the czar, I am dispatching you this night to Siberia." He wheeled on his wooden leg and departed.

The guards hauled in an anvil mounted on a wooden block, and a blacksmith began fitting the men with leg irons. "I remember only too well with what emotions I put my foot on the anvil," Frolov recalled. "The smithy was not just beating out the irons, he was riveting my soul."

Nicholas had authorized that the prisoners travel by sledge rather than on foot, a decision motivated less by compassion than by a desire to avoid further political embarrassment. He was determined that the sons of Russia's noblest families not be turned into martyrs. He laid down stringent rules for the journey, however; there was to be no misunderstanding about the perfidy of the crime. The prisoners were to move at full speed, day and night — no rest stops, no halts at taverns or inns, no exchanging of gifts or messages. Identities were to be kept secret at all times. But, then as now, the rules were largely ignored. Fortunately, the convoy commander, Vorobyov, had a kind heart, and the farther the sledges traveled from St. Petersburg, the more he bent the rules to accommodate his "gentlemen prisoners."

The chimes of Trinity Cathedral struck two and sounded out the hymn "God Save the Czar." The gates of the Peter and Paul Fortress swung open, and the five sledges, each drawn by a troika of horses, headed down onto the frozen Neva. Once on the ice, the convoy picked up the track, heading northeast toward Lake Ladoga and the Shlisselburg prison fortress. Four of the sledges carried a single prisoner accompanied by an armed guard; in the fifth, Vorobyov shouted commands and brought up the rear. Their destination: Siberia.

෴ ෴ ෴

Frolov tried to bring the blood back to his frozen limbs by stamping his feet, but the leg irons were too heavy. Solitary confinement had sapped his energy and left him depressed and lethargic. He wondered if he would live to see Siberia, for he knew that many convicts died before reaching that distant wasteland, particularly on winter convoys. The dreaded *myatel* — the white-out blizzards — disoriented the most experienced drivers, sending the sledges careening off into mountainous drifts. If the bodies were not devoured by wolves, they would be found in the spring when the snow melted.

At the first post stop, some twenty miles north of St. Petersburg,

Vorobyov halted the convoy. While the horses were changed, he allowed the prisoners to warm up inside. This was Frolov's first chance to talk with his fellow prisoners. Basargin, who was a few years older than Frolov, seemed distraught. Shortly before the uprising, his wife had died in childbirth. Now he feared he would never see his son again. Vonvizin, a retired general, was also depressed. His young wife had rushed to meet him at the post stop with the news that the convoy was headed for Irkutsk, the capital of East Siberia. Dr. Christian Volf was the son of a Lutheran pharmacist and had studied medicine in Moscow. As a nineteen-year-old medical student in 1812, he had cared for the wounded during Napoleon's siege of the capital. Later, when he became surgeon-general of the Second Army, he had helped Colonel Pestel draw up the sections of his constitution dealing with medical treatment for the poor. After half an hour, Vorobyov ordered the prisoners back into the sledges, and the convoy moved on.

The drivers were using the northern track, which passed well beyond Moscow, through Tikhvin, Cherepovet, Nikitino, and Kotelnich. As they rushed on, Frolov's spirits improved: the cold air was invigorating after the dank atmosphere of the Peter and Paul dungeons. He was pleased to discover that, instead of being seen as traitors, he and his fellows were often hailed as heroes along the way. The townspeople were curious to see the hotheaded aristocrats and pressed food and money into their hands, sending them off to Siberia with God's blessing.

After several weeks of relentless driving, the sledges arrived at the low-lying Ural Mountains, the divide between Russia and the great landmass of Siberia. In the summer months, convicts walking into exile would scoop up a handful of Russian earth, to be placed in their coffins when they died. They were going to an inhospitable country peopled by pagan tribes; in Siberia, said Basargin, "you are no longer an inhabitant of this world."

After passing through Kostroma, Vyatka, Perm, and Yekaterinburg, the sledges reached Tobolsk, the halfway mark on the four-thousand-mile journey. The governor of the town, who happened to be a relative of Vonvizin's, welcomed the prisoners into his custody and allowed them to rest for three days under the roof of the police chief. One of the czar's numerous spies along the way sent a report from Tobolsk on the mental state of each prisoner. He stated that Frolov and Basargin were depressed and Vonvizin was tearful and full of remorse; only Volf seemed inexplicably cheerful.

On March 27, a bit more than two months since leaving St. Petersburg, the convoy approached what was called sarcastically "the Paris of the East." Across the plain, Frolov saw the reassuring sight of Irkutsk, a multitude of golden cupolas glittering in the sun. Originally a customs post for collecting fur taxes from Buryat tribesmen, Irkutsk had grown prosperous in recent years from its gold, silver, and furs. By the middle of the seventeenth century, Russian hunters had spread across the whole of the northeast territory. On their heels came government officials, who claimed the lands for the crown. With the conquering of Siberia, the czars ruled over the largest state in the world — a land the size of Europe, the United States, and Alaska combined — stretching from the Baltic to China and the shores of the Pacific.

Soon the sledges passed under the arch of the city gates and proceeded along the wide streets lined with small wooden houses. They came to a stop in Irkutsk's palisade fortress, where, under police supervision, they were allowed to rest for a full week. There Frolov learned that their final destination was Chita, a penal colony beyond Lake Baikal. He and his fellow Decembrists were about to encounter the reality of *katorga* — hard labor.

As their journey continued, Cossacks replaced the Russian gendarmes. These mounted warriors, used to defend frontiers, possessed none of Vorobyov's decency; they had lived too long on the edge of civilization. To save time, the convoy crossed Lake Baikal, perhaps the most spectacular inland body of water in the world. The icy track was especially treacherous in winter, and Frolov feared that the Cossacks, who drank vodka constantly, would send them all to the bottom of the mile-deep lake. Concentration was required to guide the sledges. In some places, the surface was black glass; in others, it heaved up into icy crags, exposing the inky water below. The sledges traveled so fast, they were in constant danger of running down the horses.

Frolov's first sight of Chita was a shock. As the sledges approached, he saw a miserable frontier settlement of tumbledown cabins, a rickety church, and prison buildings surrounded by a wooden stockade made from hefty poles, fifteen feet high and sharpened at the ends. The penal colony contained several thousand common criminals; the commandant, Burnashev, was a sadist and was nicknamed the Executioner.

Frolov's first years in Chita were backbreaking, even though Nicholas soon replaced Burnashev with a more civilized commandant, Major General Stanislav Leparsky. In the beginning, the new warden was determined to establish his authority. He was so unsympathetic to the prisoners' petition that they called him Kommandant Ne-Mogu, Commandant No-Can-Do. His brutal suppression of a prison revolt in 1828 at one of the outlying mines horrified Frolov. The executions that followed were marked by the same ineptitude as those in St. Petersburg; rifles malfunctioned, and several of the prisoners had to be finished off with bayonets.

Frolov was assigned to a road gang, moving sand in a gully that the Decembrists called "The devil's grave." As the prisoners dug, sand cascaded down, penetrating their clothes and hair and working its way under their fingernails. Frolov was constantly dirty and itching.

"We labored in chains, tied to our wheelbarrows," he said. "Sometimes we would get orders to move faster, and the guards would make us shovel ten hours a day. We were punished for any unguarded grimace or a rude remark."

Frolov's group was quartered in a small house inside the stockade. "At first, in the Chita prison our conditions were truly terrible. Sixteen men lived in a small room with plank beds. When we lay down to sleep, we had less than an *arshin* [twenty-eight inches] for each. You couldn't turn over at night without waking up your neighbor." The food was nearly inedible — the usual bland fare of groats, tea, bread, scraps of meat, and little fat. In good weather, the prisoners ate in the courtyard, but in bad weather they squeezed inside like sardines.

In time, Leparsky began to improve conditions. An educated man, he was well aware of the caliber of his charges. By appointing a respected figure like the former commander of the Northern Cavalry Regiment to oversee the Decembrists, Nicholas hoped to dampen the protests from the families of the more influential prisoners. Eventually, Leparsky reduced hard labor from ten hours a day to only two or three. In the remaining time, the men were free to do as they liked. Without the commandant's lenience, the Decembrists would not have left such a large imprint in Siberia or on Russian history.

The nineteen women — wives, fiancées, and sisters — who insisted on following the Decembrists to Siberia despite the czar's opposition also played a role in their legacy. "Our guardian angels," Frolov called Princess Volkonskaya and Countess Trubetskaya. Normally, the government encouraged the families of convicts to accompany them, hoping they would stay and colonize the area. Nicholas, however, did not want St. Petersburg society stirred up on behalf of the state criminals by the constant agitation of highly placed women. Frolov held these women in awe: they had given up everything to come to Siberia. He made wooden toys for the children and jewelry boxes for their mothers. He also cobbled boots with special hiding places in the soles for the secret postal service the women organized.

"Usually there were three servants on the go such that when one arrived in St. Petersburg, another was en route, and a third was just leaving Siberia," Frolov noted. "In this way, Petersburg and Siberia were always fully informed about what was happening in either place."

Having failed to establish a new order in Russia, the Decembrists turned their energy to creating an ideal society behind bars. They formed two cooperatives: the Greater Artel, through which they pooled their financial resources, and the Lesser Artel, to help departing prisoners settle in exile.

Rarely had so much intellectual and scientific talent been concentrated in one spot. This extraordinary group of men held workshops, planted vegetable gardens, and set up an open university that they called the Academy of Chita. Dr. Volf lectured on anatomy and chemistry; Bestuzhev painted portraits and produced a dictionary of the local Buryat language. Muravyo spoke on military strategy; Lunin, on political philosophy. Zavalishin offered instruction in eight European languages as well as ancient Greek and Latin. Before long, people from the surrounding area were attending the academy. Frolov felt honored to be a member of such an illustrious society.

He himself, however, was not cut out for the academic life. Thanks to the encouragement of Dr. Volf, who had become his mentor, Frolov gravitated to practical subjects such as agriculture, medicine, metalwork, and handicrafts.

"Volf instantly understood that my restless, volatile nature was no good for the high sciences," Frolov recalled. "For that reason, I did not try to learn languages, philosophy, or gracious speech — something my more talented comrades did. Instead, I studied the natural sciences." When asked, Frolov would attribute his survival at Chita to the good doctor. "It seems as though one of the great purposes in his life was to make something worthwhile out of me. It's not for me to judge whether I justified the time he spent," he said with humility, "but I am in his debt in that he gave me a chance to live life to the full and not fear any kind of work."

In 1829, word came from St. Petersburg that Nicholas had approved Leparsky's proposal to remove the leg irons from all the prisoners. The Decembrists had lived so long with the chains that their clanking had come to symbolize their solidarity in a common fate. Someone suggested hiding a set of shackles to turn into jewelry in memory of the uprising. As one of the better metalworkers, Frolov agreed to help pound out some of the bracelets, crosses, and rings. On the surface of the ring he wore for the rest of his life he cut the cryptogram D14.

In the fall of 1830, a permanent prison for the Decembrists was completed at Petrovsky Zavod, four hundred miles west of Chita. This ironworks had been supplying East Siberia with tools since the end of the eighteenth century. Leparsky ordered his prisoners to pack their belongings and begin the long trek on foot; only the most feeble were allowed to make the six-week passage in carts.

Resettling brought many new problems. The area was swampy and not so suitable for agriculture as Chita. The prison, which had been built with Nicholas's approval, had no windows. Construction was poor, and there were chinks in the walls. Windows were cut and the holes filled only after the women complained to the authorities in St. Petersburg.

When Frolov was not helping Dr. Volf in his medical practice, he busied himself in the workshop that Leparsky allowed him to build outside the prison walls. "I always had a guard with me," Frolov noted, "but most of the time he slept. Once, when Leparsky was coming, I tried to wake him up. Leparsky immediately understood what was going on. 'Leave him alone,' he said, 'I know it is you, not he, who is on guard.' "

Frolov did not serve out the full fifteen years of hard labor because in 1832 Nicholas reduced the sentences yet again. Frolov's servitude came to an end on the tenth anniversary of the mutiny, December 14, 1835.

The first Decembrists to leave were those in the lesser categories, who had completed six years or less. They were sent in groups of four, six, or eight to isolated villages across Siberia. For those assigned to desolated areas, the real hardships were about to begin. "The self-discipline we learned at Petrovsky helped us bear that burden, but there were cases — rare, it is true — when some went out of their minds," Frolov recalled.

In June 1836, Frolov's group was called to say good-bye to Leparsky. It was an emotional farewell. The prisoners' resentment of the commandant during the initial period of incarceration had dissolved, and after a decade of coexistence, they felt great respect for him. According to Basargin, the old general was so moved by their thanks that he brushed away a tear or two and replied, "Your words are the best award I could ever receive and I must give you all your due. You have all behaved, gentlemen, like [George] Washingtons."

Frolov described his existence at Chita and Petrovsky Zavod as "life in a golden cage," but he was quick to add that "a cage is still a cage." Though his original participation in the conspiracy had been negligible, he seemed to become more of a Decembrist as he grew older, and he wore his ring with pride. I often wondered what he would have thought of the ring's going to America. Would he have preferred it to stay in a Russian museum as a reminder of the Decembrists' ideals of freedom? Considering that unanswerable question, I finally fell into a fitful sleep.

✐ Fourteen

SUNDAY, SEPTEMBER 7, turned out to be even more strenuous than the day before. Shortly before 2:00 P.M., I was again summoned for interrogation. Collecting my notebook, I marched to Room 215. As soon as the guard opened the door, I sensed the ominous atmosphere. Sergadeyev was not alone. Beside him stood a portly man in a white turtleneck sweater and a well-cut reddish-brown jacket. Another stranger, a youngish man in civilian clothes, was also present.

"Gospodin Danilov." Sergadeyev began with the more formal style of address. "Please sit down." The colonel pointed to the child's desk in the right-hand corner of the room. My mouth went dry as I walked over and squeezed behind the table. This was no ordinary interrogation. My temples began to throb as I braced myself for the next round.

Sergadeyev paused, as if savoring my discomfort. "I want to introduce you to General — — — from the military prosecutor's office." I did not catch his name.

The general merely glowered at me with contempt. I found it hard to believe that this ill-tempered person in civilian clothes was really a general. He looked more like a prosperous, self-satisfied peasant. I assumed the young man at his side was either an aide or an translator.

"As you know, Gospodin Danilov," Sergadeyev continued, "under our law you may be held for ten days on suspicion of criminal activity. Then we must either indict you or release you." My heart sank. I knew what was coming. Sergadeyev paused for a few seconds, glaring at me over his glasses. "Today," he announced, "we are here to indict you." I struggled to maintain my composure. Why were they rushing through the indictment? Was it related to Zakharov in New York? The general picked up a document and started reading from it in a monotone. The Soviet Union was formally accusing me of being a spy. Specifically, I was being charged with:

1. Collecting, on the instructions of the CIA, and transmitting to the CIA information of an economic, political, and military character detrimental to the Soviet Union.

2. Assisting the CIA to make a conspiratorial contact with a Soviet citizen.

3. Other unspecified espionage activities.

When the general finished reading, he looked up and addressed me: "Espionage is a very serious crime against the state, Gospodin Danilov. Our law provides penalties from seven to fifteen years, including the highest measure of punishment — death."

The word "death" winded me for a moment — it was a blow to the solar plexus. Like my kidnap/arrest, I couldn't believe this was happening to me. I thought I might pass out. A nauseating heaviness seized my head; my forearms, knees, and calves seemed to float in the air; my heart pounded against my ribcage; my fingers trembled.

"I would advise you to cooperate with our authorities. In the end, you will find it to your advantage." The general's voice brought me back to reality. Suddenly, my mind cleared. Samuel Johnson was right when he said there is nothing like the prospect of hanging to concentrate the mind.

The whole affair was becoming increasingly serious. My initial reaction, once I recovered, was to be businesslike: to take notes on exactly what was happening, anything to focus the mind. I opened my notebook, took out my ball-point pen, and started writing. I made no comment on the indictment and displayed no reaction. Neither did I acknowledge the general or Sergadeyev. My only defense against them was self-control and seeming indifference. They probably wanted me to grovel or at least offer to cooperate in exchange for leniency.

My passivity clearly irritated the general. "Aren't you troubled by the gravity of the charges against you?" he demanded.

"Of course I am troubled," I answered hoarsely. It was an effort to speak. I barely looked up from my notebook and kept on writing.

"So why did you go around asking this Misha for photographs?" the general insisted. "If you wanted photographs, you should have gone to *Red Star* [the newspaper of the Defense Ministry] and requested them. They would have supplied what you needed. You should not be going around talking to unauthorized individuals."

I continued writing. The idea of requesting photographs from the Defense Ministry was as laughable as calling the KGB to ask for information about the secret police.

"And how do you intend to plead, Gospodin Danilov?" Sergadeyev finally asked.

I looked up from the page. "I deny all charges," I answered, looking him straight in the eye.

The two men seemed disappointed. Sergadeyev picked up the telephone and dialed. A few minutes later, a secretary entered the room. Sergadeyev handed her the indictment and his notes to be typed. While we waited for her to return, the general sat at the end of the long table, strumming his fingers impatiently. I guessed he had been called from his *dacha* and was itching to return before his Sunday was completely wasted. Finally, the secretary returned with a piece of white paper about eight by ten inches. The terms of the indictment were typed at the top of the page. A middle section contained my denial. A final section, divided from the rest by a line, stated that I had been given an opportunity to acquaint myself with the charges, that I had read them and understood them.

I read this document very carefully. If I was to sign, I wanted to make sure that my signature did not indicate agreement with any of the charges. The only section I would sign would be the final section, confirming that I had read the document. I read the papers one last time, then signed my name. Suddenly, I noticed the date: September 7, 1986. My God! My father's birthday! He would have been eighty-seven. Again, his words about the salt mines came back to me. He was right: I was one step closer to Siberia.

The general stood up, said good-bye to Sergadeyev, and left with his interpreter. I rose from the little desk, hoping the session was over. All I wanted to do ws return to my cell and collect my thoughts. But Sergadeyev was not ready to quit. He returned to his desk and motioned me to sit down closer to him. "Now, Nikolai Sergeyevich," he said, "we have something more to discuss. Father Roman. Tell me about Father Roman."

I sat down, but my whole body tensed. First, the indictment; now, Roman. The noose was tightening. All week I had prayed that Sergadeyev would not raise the subject of Father Roman.

"We know you received a letter from Roman," he continued. "What did you do with it?"

If there was one subject guaranteed to raise my blood pressure, it was the letter that the man who called himself Father Roman Potemkin put in my mailbox. Of all the suspicious characters who approached me in Moscow, he was the KGB masterpiece. Even his last name was ingenious: Potemkin was the eighteenth-century prince who built fake villages to deceive Catherine the Great about the population of his dominion.

❧ ❧ ❧

The Roman incident began on Monday, December 10, 1984. I was working in the office when I received a telephone call from a stranger who described himself as a Russian Orthodox priest. It is not unusual for correspondents in Moscow to receive such unexpected calls. When the man said he would like to meet me, I told him that I was too busy and to call back the next week. Over the years I had built up a network of trustworthy sources on most subjects, and I did not like to meet unknown people off the street who could possibly be linked to the KGB.

Usually, when told to call back, the strangers disappeared. But exactly a week later Father Roman called again. I suggested that he come to the office, hoping that the inevitable KGB microphones would discourage him. He was not deterred and, in the end, I agreed to see him. When I heard the office doorbell ring at about eleven o'clock that Tuesday morning, December 18, I was irritated. I was in the middle of a story that I had to telex to Washington that evening. Before opening the door, I had decided to get rid of my visitor as soon as possible. However, I was pleasantly surprised by the young man standing before me. Father Roman, I judged, was in his late twenties and wore blue jeans and a ski jacket. A priest so dressed did not surprise me, since the Soviet authorities forbade clerics to wear their religious vestments in public.

I invited Roman in, then suggested we take a walk so we could converse more freely. I could also end the interview more easily by pleading urgent business in the office. Roman readily agreed; I got my jacket and we left. Going down in the elevator, Roman apologized profusely for bothering me. That made a good impression. Many Soviets who approach foreign correspondents act as though you have nothing else to do but listen to them.

Once out of the apartment complex, we walked across to the central, tree-lined promenade that runs down the middle of Kosygin Street. A light snow was falling as we began walking. In the course of the next hour — the one and only time I ever met him — Father Roman explained that he was involved in promoting religion among Russian youth. He spoke intelligently and I was interested in what he had to say, since an increasing number of young people were attending services. He explained that he was a member of a quasi-dissident organization called the Association of Russian Orthodox Youth, founded in the early 1970s. I had never heard of it, and now I doubt it ever really existed. Its purpose, he said, was to spread information about church functions, times, and places among young people. He said he wanted foreign correspondents to know about this association and asked if I could put him in touch with other reporters. In return, he would keep me abreast of the religious movement among the young.

As we walked along the boulevard, he began telling me about the campaign against religion that the Soviet government was mounting before the one thousandth anniversry of Christianity in Russia, in 1988. He spoke about other, more sinister subjects, too, like the experiments the KGB was conducting on mental patients at an infamous psychiatric hospital on the outskirts of Moscow called Beliye Stolby. "It is done without the patients' knowledge," Roman said. "I know of a case in which a nurse was supposed to give an injection, but asked the guard to do it for her. The guard was drunk, naturally. Instead of injecting a milligram, he injected the whole syringe. As a result, this patient went mad for two months and doctors doubted he could be saved."

The reporter in me recognized Roman as an interesting source, and I later wrote an account of our talk in my journal. But I was also cautious. Father Roman did not appear to be an obvious KGB plant, but one could never be sure. After he finished telling me that the Patriarch Pimen was seriously ill and not expected to live, I decided to throw him a few questions to test his credibility.

"Tell me something about your own work in the Church," I said.

"I serve as a deacon quite often, filling in for other priests in some of the outlying churches." As if to explain his low status, he went on to reveal that he had been falsely accused of harboring stolen icons and sent to a labor camp in the Komi Autonomous Republic. When I asked how long, he replied that he had been there two years. "At first I did hard labor, chopping down lumber. Later, when the camp authorities realized I had a good head, they let me work in the office."

Two years struck me as a short sentence for such a crime. It was surprising, too, that he had been allowed to work in the office. Had he made a deal with the devil? I then moved on to some of the well-known religious dissidents who were in trouble. Did he have any new information on Yuli Edelshtein, a Hebrew teacher whom the police had set up by planting a pistol in his apartment. When Roman said he didn't know anything about Edelshtein, a warning flag went up. Then I asked about Alexander Riga, the Catholic priest who had been sent to Siberia for preaching ecumenism. Again, Roman had never heard of him. Another flag arose. Finally, I asked how he had found my telephone number.

Roman said he had wanted to contact a correspondent who spoke Russian and had asked a friend who knew a secretary in the press department of the Foreign Ministry if she could suggest someone. "She looked over the list of correspondents and said, 'Here is Nick Daniloff. They say he is an extremely interesting correspondent, the sort you can talk with. And he speaks Russian.' She gave me your telephone number."

His calling me "extremely interesting" seemed suspicious. Was Roman making a play for my ego in order to hook me into a relationship. Toward the end of our walk, Roman returned to his desire to contact other Western correspondents. I suggested he return to the office with me. There I managed to find an old copy of *Information Moscow,* a privately printed guide that lists foreign news bureaus and other useful numbers. Before leaving, Roman gave me his telephone number, saying, "Give me a call when you have time and we'll get together."

Thanks," I replied, making no commitment. I had already decided that I would seek no further contact with him. I analyzed our conversation with Ruth, sentence by sentence, when we took Zeus for a walk the next morning. In the end I concluded that this interesting young priest had useful information, but certain things about him did not jibe. If I needed information about religious matters, I could turn to more reliable sources.

I had forgotten about Roman when, on January 22, 1985, he called the office and told my secretary he was going to drop off some information for me on the Russian Orthodox Church. Two days later, I arrived for work as usual at about 9:30 A.M. and opened the large yellow mailbox on the office door. Among the newspapers and other letters was an unstamped envelope addressed to me in a Russian hand. I assumed this was Roman's material on the Church. Opening the envelope, I was very surprised to find another envelope, this one addressed to Ambassador Hartman. Suddenly, my suspicions about Roman returned, sensing a trap. Planting incriminating documents is a classic KGB trick — witness the cases of Robert Toth and Professor Barghoorn. My first reaction was to get rid of the letter as soon as possible.

I rushed downstairs to the apartment to warn Ruth, signaling, without speaking, that I needed to talk to her urgently. She threw on a jacket and we went into the courtyard. "Burn it, rip it up — anything — but get it out of here," Ruth said, just as upset as I. "The KGB could come by at any time and find it here and accuse us of God knows what."

I decided that burning the letter was succumbing to paranoia. After all, it was addressed to the ambassador, not me. If it was a provocation, I wanted the embassy to know about it. The press office kept a list of incidents involving journalists which they would periodically protest with the Foreign Ministry. Knowing what I know today, however, I would not hesitate to destroy the letter, no matter to whom it was addressed.

We decided to deliver the letter immediately, and I asked Ruth to accompany me. If the secret police waylaid me, I wanted a witness. As I drove along the Ring Road to the embassy, I kept glancing in the mirror to see if we were being followed; I expected to be pulled over and searched at any moment. We drove along Zubovsky Boulevard and through Smolensk Square, past the Foreign Ministry. Ruth insisted on removing the envelope from my briefcase and placing it in her purse, thinking that the KGB would be less likely to stop her. We finally reached the embassy, made a U-turn, parked the car, and almost ran to the entrance of the building. I remember thinking that if we made it past the two Soviet militiamen at the gate, we were home free. The guards smiled and waved us through.

With an enormous sense of relief, we entered the compound. Ruth handed me the envelope, and I took the elevator up to the office of Ray Benson, the senior press and cultural affairs officer. I told him that I suspected the letter was a KGB provocation and explained everything I remembered about Father Roman. We opened the envelope to find a third envelope, which contained a handwritten letter, covering six or seven pages of very thin paper. We tried to read it, but neither of us could decipher the writing. On one page, I did make out *raketa,* rocket.

Benson did not look any too happy at having been handed this problem. But he was calm as he said, "I'll take care of it." He did not explain further, but I was relieved to have disposed of the letter. Nevertheless, I continued to feel uneasy. The incident was puzzling, and I had no idea what was behind it.

Two more months went by. I was desperately busy covering the death of Chernenko and the rise of Gorbachev in early March 1985. My concerns about Roman had dissipated under the pressure of work until one day when I received a telephone call from Curt Kamman, the number two man at the embassy, asking me to drop by his office. When I arrived, Kamman said he had a confidential matter to discuss and led me to "the bubble," the embassy's safe room. Security was tight; I wasn't even allowed to take my briefcase with me for fear that the KGB had planted a bug in it before I came to the embassy. Kamman switched on the air conditioning and invited me to sit down at the oblong table that takes up most of this Plexiglas room-within-a-room. It was like being in an incubator. Kamman explained that he wanted me to repeat the facts about Roman which I had relayed to Benson. I had just started to recall them when the door of "the bubble" suddenly opened, admitting a middle-aged man with a swarthy complexion and a deeply lined face whom I had never seen before. Kamman introduced him as Murat Natirboff. In time I learned that his family came from Circassia and had fought as Whites in the Revolution before emigrating: Murat Natirboff himself was raised on the Upper West Side of New York City in an émigré Russian community. I remembered seeing his name in the embassy directory as counselor for regional affairs, indicating that he belonged to the political section dealing with Afghanistan.

In an obvious appeal to patriotism, Natirboff explained his interest in having me relate everything I knew about Roman. He said the letter was of interest to the United States; it appeared to be from a dissident Soviet scientist trying to contact the CIA didn't make sense to me. In my judgment, Roman was KGB, and I emphasized my suspicions about him. But apparently Natirboff knew something I didn't. Driving home later, I became increasingly distressed by the encounter with Natirboff; I had been given no warning that he would walk into "the bubble." CIA, KGB — whatever was going on, I wanted no part of it. In Moscow, I had deliberately avoided military attachés or anyone I suspected of being involved in intelligence work. An American journalist who is seen frequently with CIA officers is an easy target for the KGB, and I didn't want to make my job any harder than it was already. Should I have stood up and stomped out of "the bubble"? Perhaps, but it was too late now. I also wondered if the safe room was really KGB-proof. Was there any way they could find out about my conversation with Natirboff — whom I later discovered was the CIA station chief? I prayed that that talk marked the end of the Roman episode. But two weeks later it took one more nasty turn.

∾ ∾ ∾

I was working in my office on the afternoon of Good Friday, April 5, 1985, when the telephone rang. Zina had already left for the day, so I answered. It was Father Roman, speaking in an agitated voice: "I'm calling from a telephone booth and I'm in a great hurry." Before I could speak, he added, "The meeting on March 26 did not work out because your guys did not choose a good place. A militiaman was standing nearby. My friend is still willing to talk to your guys, but please be more careful."

For a moment I was disoriented. His words came as a shock. What meeting on March 26? What the hell did he mean, "your guys"? What was he talking about? Before I could protest, Roman hung up. Then I was angry. As I thought about it, I realized that Roman was trying to implicate me in something over a monitored telephone line. I cursed myself for not being quick enough. I should have slammed down the receiver before he could finish.

When Ruth arrived in the office a few minutes later, I exploded. I hoped at least the bugs in the wall would pick up my indignation and relay it to the KGB. In the next few days, when I talked to other correspondents on the phone, I told them I was being harassed by the secret police. I sensed that my indirect protests to the wall and over the telephone were probably useless, however. I felt I was being sucked into something but had no idea how to protect myself. When Zina came on Monday, I told her that if a Father Roman called again to tell him I was out.

After the encounter with Natirboff, I was of two minds whether to inform the embassy about Roman's latest call. On the one hand, if the KGB was dragging me into something, the embassy should be informed for my own protection. On the other, I wanted to distance myself from the embassy, particularly the CIA, who made me almost as nervous as the KGB. For the moment, I decided to say nothing.

On April 11, I went to the ambassador's nineteenth-century mansion to cover a press conference being given by Speaker of the House Thomas P. O'Neill, Jr., the first high-ranking American to meet with Gorbachev. At the entrance I ran into Curt Kamman, and since we were early, we decided to take a short walk. Toward the end of our conversation, Roman's name came up, and I decided to tell Kamman about the strange call. He listened without commenting. I reiterated my belief that Roman was a trap and asked him to keep me out of it. That evening Ruth and Mandy left on a two-week trip to China, and I drove them to the airport. They were very nervous about my being alone in Moscow and wanted to cancel the trip, but I insisted they go ahead. On principle, I did not want to appear to succumb to KGB intimidation.

A few weeks later, Kamman again invited me to the embassy. He didn't say what he wanted to talk about, but I had a premonition it was Roman. With some reluctance, I went to his office and we retired to "the bubble." Kamman began by perusing a folder he had brought along. Then he said, "We have carefully analyzed the situation and we believe the KGB is indeed setting a trap. Our advice to you is to avoid any further contact with this Father Roman. Try to be squeaky clean."

I was relieved that the embassy had come to the same conclusion as I had. Nonetheless, there was something odd about Kamman's warning. I myself had warned him about Roman. Why was he now reading back my own message? What did he know that he wasn't telling me? Many months later, I learned he had been acting on instructions from Washington. I found Kamman's warning extremely unsettling. Yet he hadn't suggested I wind up my assignment and go back to the States. Throughout the whole unnerving affair, leaving the country never occurred to either Ruth or me. The last thing correspondents should do is to allow the KGB to frighten them into leaving the country or altering their copy. Either action would play straight into the hands of the secret police, setting a very bad precedent. I considered writing a report to my editors, but rejected the idea. First, the office was preoccupied with management upheavals resulting from Mort Zuckerman's new proprietorship, and second, I wasn't sure just what to report. Instead, I kept detailed notes in my journal.

On the morning after Kamman's warning and on many subsequent mornings, Ruth and I tried to make sense out of Roman. As we walked with Zeus along the river near our apartment, we played out enough scenarios for several third-rate spy thrillers.

"Let's suppose for a moment that Roman is for real," Ruth would speculate. "Suppose he is a courier for some dissident scientist who wants to pass information to the CIA . . . Suppose Natirboff and his boys really believe Roman can put them in touch with some rocket engineer . . . Suppose the CIA tried to make contact with the engineer and got caught . . . Suppose the KGB wanted to smoke out the CIA, set a trap to put them out of operation? Suppose, suppose . . ."

It was useless. We would never learn the truth and, by now, I didn't even want to know it. The whole affair was a cesspool of intrigue. In the end, all I had to rely on were my instincts: in my opinion, Father Roman Potemkin was a bogus priest on the KGB payroll.

"Maybe the KGB is merely filling up your file," Ruth suggested. "Having failed to dirty you with Goldfarb, they are now trying to lure you into another mess. Probably nothing more will come of it. It's just general harassment. They're trying to scare you, and the worst thing you could do is to look timid. Just forget it. I doubt if anything more will come of it, anyway."

I tried to follow Ruth's advice, and we planned a vacation. On Sunday, June 9, we left by train for a week in Finland. But even in a little house on an island in the Helsinki archipelago I could not escape the KGB's shadow. The following Saturday, I heard on the BBC news that the KGB had detained a U.S. diplomat in Moscow, Paul Stombaugh, on suspicion of espionage.

Though I had never heard of him, I immediately began to wonder if he were in some way connected with Roman. Suppose the CIA had tried to contact Roman and fell into a KGB trap . . . Suppose . . . I listened carefully to the broadcast, hoping my name would not be mentioned. It was not.

Taking the overnight train from Helsinki back to Moscow that night, one thing became clear. I had to get my mind off Roman. I was sick to death of speculating about this so-called priest. I had to put the incident out of my mind before it began interfering with my work. But no sooner did I walk into our apartment on Sunday morning, June 16 than I found a note from our Russian maid, Katya: "Some man by the name of Roman called you urgently on June 14, and he has called several times since. He said it was urgent." I told Zina to say I was out if Roman called again.

On Friday, June 21, just as I was leaving for a noonday reception at the Luxembourg embassy, the phone rang and I picked it up.

"Hello, Nikolai Sergeyevich, it's Roman. I wanted to ask if you could get me another copy of Information Moscow."

"No, I can't give you one." I replied angrily.

"*Obidno.* It's a pity," Roman continued in a plaintive tone. "By the way, I'm leaving for the Baltic states for vacation. I just wanted to know, are there any questions before I go?"

I was fighting mad by then and could hardly control my voice. "Roman," I replied furiously, "I had expected to receive some religious material from you. But I did not. Therefore, I have no questions. Please do not bother me again. Good-bye and good luck." I slammed down the receiver.

Every day for the next few months I scanned the newspapers for articles accusing me of spying. At any moment, I expected to be summoned and expelled by the Foreign Ministry. But nothing happened and time passed. By the end of 1985, I concluded that Roman had disappeared for good; he would remain another mystery I would never solve. By the time I was preparing to leave

Moscow for good, I had forgotten about him. Not until I was arrested did he reappear in my thoughts. All this last week I had been waiting for him to take center stage. Now, as Sergadeyev stared at me, waiting for me to answer, I knew that Father Roman had become a key figure. Nineteen months from the day I met him, the KGB cashed in on its move.

ᔌ ᔌ ᔌ

"So, Nikolai Sergeyevich, you have not answered my question. What did you do with that letter?" he demanded.

At last I answered, "It was addressed to Ambassador Hartman, so I took it to the embassy."

"But whom exactly did you give it to at the embassy?" he snapped.

I hesitated. Giving the KGB names did not sit well with me; I was reluctant to implicate anyone.

"I'd rather not say," I replied, knowing the answer made me look guilty as hell. A vivid image of a Soviet courtroom sprang to mind, the prosecutor pointing at me as he said, "Daniloff admitted he took the letter to the embassy, but like the professional agent he is, he refused to name his CIA contact."

The colonel was not swayed. "It's useless, Nikolai Sergeyevich. You must tell us. We can show you photographs that will make you tell us everything."

Photographs! What photographs? My imagination began running wild. A doctored picture showing me meeting a CIA operative in the embassy courtyard? Something from the banya? Had I drunk too much at a party and been photographed surreptitiously? I tried to remember. Undoubtedly, the threat was intended to make me believe the KGB knew more about me than I knew myself. With all the pressure of the last week, I almost believed they did.

Sergadeyev sat silently, waiting for his answer. I said nothing. He seemed to sense my weakening resolve. "You must tell us,

Nikolai Sergeyevich," he said in a tone that made it clear he had the means of forcing me and would not hesitate to use them. Sergadeyev was implacable, relentless. It was hopeless to hold out. Lowering my voice, I finally gave him his answer: "I gave it to our chief press counselor, Ray Benson." A wave of guilt swept over me. Since embassy officers have diplomatic immunity, no real harm would come to Benson. I might be in danger of going to Siberia, but he was not. Even so, I would have felt happier if I had refused absolutely. Only later was my conscience eased when I learned that the KGB knew a surprising amount about the CIA officers working in the U.S. embassy, whereas I, essentially, knew nothing. Specifically, the KGB knew that Benson was not an intelligence officer.

A look of satisfaction passed over Sergadeyev's face. He had obtained more than just his answer. He had assaulted my self-esteem and won a psychological victory. He knew it, and he knew that I knew he knew it.

After a pause, I broke the silence. "Now this is a purely theoretical question," I began. "Suppose you wanted to mount a provocation against a correspondent, suppose you put incriminating material in his mailbox. What should he do? Burn it? Hand it over to the Foreign Ministry and say, 'This is a KGB dirty trick'?"

Sergadeyev lit a cigarette and pondered my question for a minute. "Neither," he replied thoughtfully. "There is another option. Call up the person who brought the information and tell him to take it away."

In the months since my arrest, I have often reflected on this advice. On balance, I think Sergadeyev had a point. To request the removal of suspicious information is a clear refusal to be drawn into shady dealings. But what if the material is thrust on you anonymously? Once Ruth was sitting in the parked car outside a store when someone dropped a package into her lap through the open window. She immediately threw it out again. Of course,

I could have called Roman and asked him to pick up his material. Meanwhile, the letter would have stayed in the apartment, which the KGB could have searched at any time.

Sergadeyev paused for a minute and offered a further comment: "If you thought provocations were being mounted against you, why didn't you leave Moscow?"

"What, end my assignment prematurely?"

"Exactly."

"Why? I wasn't doing anything wrong. Furthermore, I was learning more and more about my ancestry, which in turn taught me more about the Soviet Union."

"Yes," said the colonel sarcastically, "you certainly did learn something."

I didn't know how to interpret that remark. The clock indicated that it was just after 6:00 P.M. Sergadeyev closed his notepad. The session was over, and I was exhausted and dispirited.

"I would like to call my wife about the indictment," I said.

The colonel motioned indifferently toward the phone. I called the office and Gretchen Trimble answered. Ruth was at the Moscow television studios, doing a Sunday talk show for the United States. "President Reagan has written a letter to Gorbachev, telling him you are not a spy," Gretchen said. That was good news and it cheered me up a little.

I told Gretchen about the indictment, giving her all the details. She sounded alarmed, and I could offer little comfort. "My case is obviously moving into a more serious stage. Charges of espionage put me on a par with another case we know about." For some irrational reason, I didn't want Sergadeyev to know I was discussing Zakharov. "The quickest solution would be if the two cases were viewed on an equal basis. Possibly it will end before being brought to court. But I have the overwhelming sense that they are prepared to pursue the charges of espionage if they want to."

Our conversation foundered. My voice was low from fatigue. Gretchen was silent. I sensed that the news was so depressing, she didn't know what to say. The seriousness of the situation was beyond rational discussion. Hoping to lighten the mood, I switched subjects.

"So, Gretch, what else is new? Tell me something funny!"

"Everything is fine," she replied, groping, "except that Zeus has fleas."

The line instantly went dead. Evidently, KGB monitors cut off the call, believing the reference to our fox terrier's infestation was a coded message. I dialed again, this time getting Jeff. I filled him in on the indictment, and, for the monitors, I repeated that I was not a spy. "What is considered normal journalistic activity in the United States is not seen like that here." I suggested that the Americans and the Soviets might one day want to make some amendments to the Helskinki Final Act to take account of this difference. Jeff, like Gary Lee the day before, noted that I sounded calm but strained.

"I'm calm because I know deep down I'm telling the truth," I said.

Sergadeyev indicated that I should wind up the call. As I said good-bye, I sent love to Ruth and all our friends. A few minutes later the guard returned me to my cell. I pretended to be in normal humor, giving no hint to Stas that I had been indicted. I ate the evening meal in silence. To tell Stas about the formal charges would be to peel away another layer of protection. Besides, I was almost too exhausted to talk.

It had been perhaps the worst day of my life. That night, after the *otboi*, call to turn in, I lay on my cot with my folded handkerchief over my eyes and thought about what would happen next. There was a real chance I would be consigned to the Gulag. I wondered what sort of a sentence they would dream up. A minimum of seven years? A fifteen-year maximum? I never thought they would choose death, however. The Soviet dissident Shcharansky got thirteen years after his phony espionage trial and, taking that as a precedent, I assumed I would be put away for no less than a decade. Since I was fifty-one, that would mean I would reemerge into the world as man of sixty-one. Mandy would be thirty-five, probably married with her own children, and Caleb would be twenty-seven, just a year older than I was when I got my first posting to Moscow. Would he be married? And Ruth. How would she fare in the intervening time? These were ten years I desperately wanted to share with them all.

᪐ *Fifteen*

SLEEP ESCAPED ME that night. The indictment had scared me badly, and I tossed and turned on the thin mattress, my mind in turmoil. The sickening irony of it all! Almost seventy years ago my grandparents and their children had fled Russia to escape repression. That history carried a warning, but did I heed it? No: I brought my wife and children to Moscow, immersed myself in a strange but fascinating society, and ultimately fell victim to the dark machinations of the KGB. Now I lay in a miserable cell, knowing that my Russian heritage was of no help at all; indeed, if anything could save me, it was my blue American passport.

For that I had my father to thank. Serge had paid the price of a lost heritage to give my sister and me U.S. citizenship. He deserved better than to have his son ignore his warnings and end up in Siberia. Then I remembered yet another ironic twist: Serge had also ignored his father's advice. Just recently, I had steamed the back off a photograph of Le Général which had belonged to my father. On it my grandfather had written to Serge in 1924: "Russia and America are two countries that should join happily in your heart. Cherish and preserve everything good which Russia gave you." I suddenly realized that if Serge had listened to his father and not rejected his Russian birthright, I might not have been so driven to find mine.

Listening to Stas's breathing, thinking about the mysterious links that bind and separate fathers and sons, I thought about Frolov. We had been born more than a century apart, yet in a way I was a son of his, too. For five years I had been searching for his story, at first curious about his role in the Decembrist uprising and baffled by his long sentence. Later I had marveled at his strength of character, his ability to survive ten years of hard labor and three different prisons. But in the end I had become completely engaged by the man himself. Who, in fact, was my great-great-grandfather? How had life surprised and changed him as he grew older? The accounts of his prison years began to answer these questions, but Frolov was still only thirty-two when he was released from prison at Petrovsky Zavod; he lived for another forty-nine years. When he died in 1885, who had he become?

Surprisingly, it was the story of these later years that revealed Frolov's character in all its color and complexity. I had first begun to understand this in July 1985, when I unearthed the Manganari manuscript. And my understanding deepened when, a year later, Ruth and I had traveled to the Siberian town of Shushenskoye — formerly called Shusha — to look for traces of Frolov's life. The summer before my arrest, I had continued to turn up pieces of the story, but I never had time to put them together. That, I had told myself, would have to wait until my assignment in Moscow was over.

Now I had plenty of time — too much! The night stretched before me like a wilderness, and once again I turned to Frolov to keep me company. Just as he had knitted and reknitted his socks to preserve his sanity, I would work and rework the pieces of his life to preserve mine. At last I would try to arrive at a truer understanding of his character. But if my research and the Manganari manuscript provided a great deal of information, for the rest I would have to rely on my imagination. As this night wore on, and on succeeding nights, scenes from his life in Siberia and beyond rose before me like pages from an album of old photographs. I ordered and reordered the pictures until they told the whole story, until Alexander Frolov seemed so real that I imagined his release from prison was my own.

Summer 1836: The Mount of Sighs

From the crest of the mountain, Frolov gazed out over the valley of his future exile, which stretched as far as the eye could see. His look swept across the stands of birches and pines that divided the plain. The valley, irrigated by the fast-flowing Yenisei River, was dotted with wild irises, forget-me-nots, and purple lungwort. In the distance stood the snow-capped Sayan Mountains, bordering China to the south.

In June, Frolov had left Petrovsky Zavod to begin his "eternal exile." He traveled with other prisoners as far as Irkutsk, where a Cossack guard, Solovyov, met him and conveyed him to the Minusinsk district of the Krasnoyarsk territory. After spending the night at Minusinsk, on July 14, 1836, the two men headed south on horseback. After hours of hard riding, Solovyov reined in the horses and proceeded up the mountain. It was a tradition for political exiles to stop on these heights, called Dumnaya Gora, and reflect.

The vast territory below filled Frolov with anxiety, and an odd feeling of homesickness for Petrovsky swept over him. He had been glad when Leparsky finally received orders from St. Petersburg to send him to this part of southern Siberia, for he was impatient to start his new life. But leaving the prison stockade for the last time, he had felt a sudden emptiness. Where would he ever find such companionship again? He had made many friends, and he was especially sad about leaving Volf behind. When Frolov embraced the doctor after their farewell feast, he

sensed they would never meet again. (They didn't; Volf died in
Tobolsk in 1854, leaving Frolov 2,000 rubles.)

Frolov glanced down at the two hampers strapped to the pack
horse and wondered if he had the necessary supplies for his new
life in the village of Shusha. Thanks to the Lesser Artel, he carried
carpentry, cobbling, and metalworking tools. His personal effects — all of which would be meticulously entered in the village
records — consisted of a few household goods, one silver spoon,
one blanket, four pillows, sheets and towels, summer and winter
trousers, boots, a fur-lined jacket, two shirts, two handkerchiefs,
and five pairs of underpants.

He already knew something about Shusha from the messages
sent by Lieutenant Colonel Peter Falenberg, a Decembrist who
had been exiled there three years earlier. The village consisted of
sixty households, a mixture of native Khakassians, Kirghiz, and
Russians who scratched a living from the land or shipped wheat,
iron, and gold down the great Yenisei to Minusinsk and Krasnoyarsk. There was an Orthodox church but no school or doctor.
Frolov would be a prisoner of Shusha; he would not be able to
move elsewhere if he could not support himself. And he would
arrive as a known criminal. His Cossack guard carried a letter,
dated July 12, 1836, from the authorities in Minusinsk for the
officials in Shusha. This document, marked SECRET, contained
instructions to keep Frolov under surveillance and to report to
Minusinsk "at the end of each month on his conduct."

As Frolov looked down at the lush grass beneath his feet, his
spirits lifted. The farmer in him responded to the land. Settlers
sometimes described this wilderness valley as "Siberian Italy."
Though the winters were arduous, the territory was not forbidding. The soil was rich and the summers warm.

The guard motioned that it was time to go. Frolov walked
over to his horse and tightened the girth. His eyes took in the
whole valley one last time. He may not have been free, but he
was alive.

Winter 1837: First season of exile

Frolov sat beside his pechka, a wood-fired stove, in the middle of his two-room log house. Wearing a heavy woolen peasant shirt belted over his trousers, he smoked a long-stemmed pipe. Before him was a letter from Colonel Alexander Poggio, a Decembrist of Italian descent. Outside a storm was raging, piling drifts along the ten-foot fence he had built around the cabin to keep the wolves out.

As an exile, Frolov was now free to correspond openly. In the last months, he had received a few remittances. On August 31, a transfer of 240 rubles arrived from some of the wealthier Decembrists — a help, since his annual government subsidy of 114 silver rubles and 28½ kopecks was not enough to subsist on. On November 19, he got another surprise: the arrival of a small crate, carefully secured in gray canvas, containing eight books on farming and forty-seven packages of seeds.

Despite this assistance, the first months in Shusha had been extremely difficult. Frolov was often lonely, and letters from his mother about his father's declining health filled him with remorse. Furthermore, building a new life was not easy, and his isolation was compounded by the hostility of the villagers, who did not welcome another political exile in their midst. A homesteading program had allowed him to claim as much land as he wanted, but he soon discovered that the best parcels were already taken. After trudging around the outskirts of the village for days, he finally staked out a boggy piece of land, covered with reeds and willows, near the Shusha River. But at least he managed to get his cabin built before the first signs of winter, in October. The cabin, with its low ceiling and small windows, had been constructed to withstand the cold, when the thermometer would regularly plunge to minus forty degrees. Looking at the heavy logs caulked against the icy gales, Frolov felt pride in his workmanship.

He shifted closer to the fire and continued reading Poggio's letter, dated January 30, 1837. He was grateful for the promise of seeds for the spring planting. The envelope also contained a note from Princess Volkonskaya, chiding him for thinking that her son Misha had forgotten him. Correspondence with his Decembrist friends invariably increased Frolov's nostalgia for Petrovsky. Peter Falenberg was a good neighbor and had helped him settle in, but the two men were very different. Falenberg was dour and, unlike Frolov, preferred reading to working with his hands.

Frolov was overcome with impatience that first winter. He spent the long evenings turning the pages of the agricultural manuals, planning his crops. It seemed as though spring would never come, for he wanted to start right away; he had to make the earth produce to survive. For him Shusha was a prison; he had nowhere else to go.

Winter 1846: Marriage

Alexander Frolov and Yevdokiya Makarova emerged from the little church in Shusha arm in arm. Frolov was wearing a long sheepskin coat belted at the waist over high black leather boots he had made himself. His head was bare. At forty-two, his chestnut hair was thinning, and his sideburns were flecked with gray. His bride was clad in a dark woolen coat, its hem, cuffs, and collar trimmed with thick brown fur. Her head and shoulders were enveloped in a large shawl, her hands tucked into a fur muff matching the trim on her coat. Twenty years younger than Frolov, she was the daughter of a Cossack chief named Nikolai Makarov from the little village of Kaptyrevo, ten miles south of Shusha. The couple paused for a moment in front of the church, blinking from the glare of the sun on the snow. As they started to walk down the path toward the waiting sleigh, they turned to each other and smiled shyly.

Considering the marriage had been arranged, it was surprising that the couple looked so happy. Frolov had met Yevdokiya several years earlier, when she was a pupil at the Belyayev brothers' school in Minusinsk. Alexander and Peter Belyayev, like many other Decembrist exiles, had devoted themselves to educating the local population. Yevdokiya, who had a good mind, responded so well to her studies that Alexander Belyayev proposed marriage. Although the former naval officer was officially a "state criminal," Yevdokiya's father gave his blessing.

But the marriage never took place. In 1839, news reached Shusha that the czar would allow some political exiles to buy their freedom by serving as ordinary soldiers in the Caucasus. Frolov and the Belyayev brothers immediately applied. "I am waiting with great impatience for permission to go to the Caucasus," Frolov wrote to a friend on February 7, 1840. "You can't imagine how difficult it is to live in exile with three poor wheat harvests and everything here so expensive." To his dismay, Frolov was turned down. Having been in the second category of convicts, he was considered too serious a criminal. Since the Belyayevs had been sentenced in the fourth category, they were accepted. But there was a problem: Alexander Belyayev could not take Yevdokiya with him, and it was unfair to ask her to wait. Yet to back out of marriage with a Cossack's daughter could be even more dangerous than putting down native tribes in the Caucasian Mountains. In the end, Alexander came up with what he considered a brilliant solution: why not offer his fiancée to Frolov, who was despondent after his rejection. A family council — the bride's father, the Belyayev brothers, and Frolov — was convened, and Frolov happily agreed to marry Yevdokiya. He had almost given up the idea of ever having a wife or family. Not only was she attractive, she was also a down-to-earth Siberian girl who was not afraid of hard work.

Yevdokiya was not consulted. "What they talked about I don't know," she told her grandchildren, "but I do remember that to prevent the Belyayevs' work on me from being wasted — they spent two years pounding wisdom into me, teaching me every kind of science, how to comport myself so I would be equal to

them — they came to a decison to give me away to Alexander
Filippovich." In truth, Yevdokiya was secretly relieved to be join-
ing Frolov rather than trying to live up to her teacher's expectations. "The question of protesting never arose, and anyway
there was nothing to protest," she said. "I knew that if I went
with him, I would always be safe."

Spring 1853: The children

Frolov emerged from the stable after feeding the horses. Warmer
weather was coming, and the sun had turned the courtyard into
a morass of mud and melting snow. The two older children —
Nikolai, seven, and Nadejda, four — had followed their father
outside while Yevdokiya stood at the door with six-month-old
Peter on her hip. Frolov leaned on his fork for a moment, watching Nikolai throw a stick for the sheep dog, Kakvaska. Nadejda,
as usual, made straight for the mud. She was a hot-tempered child
and becoming more and more of a tomboy, thought Frolov. She
spent too much time running wild with her reckless older brother
and his friend Fedya Falenberg. The dark-haired girl pretended
not to hear her father's warning as she waited for the mud to
rise over the top of her boots. Frolov shrugged his shoulders and
returned to the stable. Even though they lived in exile, the children
were happy. That was all that mattered, for raising healthy children was not easy. He remembered Aleksei and Vladimir, who
had died in infancy, and how he and Yevdokiya had buried their
tiny bodies under the willows by the river.

Otherwise, the last seven years had been good ones, except for
his father's death in 1848. His marriage to Dusha — they always
called each other Dusha, or Dear Heart — seemed to grow stronger
all the time. And Frolov was no longer lonely: he had a partner
with whom to share everything. Yevdokiya was equally content.
"All day long he was as busy as a bee," she later recalled. "What
couldn't he do — starting by building the house and ending up
making you boots. He made carriages, too, which became known

throughout Siberia as Frolovkas. When I got married, he was the eagle of eagles."

After finding more fertile land on one of the tributaries of the Shusha, Frolov had sold his cabin and built a four-room house on a stone foundation. Little by little, he added outbuildings for cows and horses, planted a kitchen garden, and hired a Kirghiz stablehand called Ahmet. He took great pride in improving his estate and gradually became a valued member of Shusha. He was something of an expert on agriculture. Describing his farming endeavors in Siberia, Frolov once said, "I drew great satisfaction in finding solutions to difficult problems. I would repeat the experiments year after year with cabbages and potatoes. I took a terribly long time with turnips." He also offered herbal remedies and first aid, which he had learned from Volf.

In addition to supporting a growing family, Frolov sent half of his earnings to his mother and sisters in Kerch. To supplement his income and pay for the few essentials like sugar, salt, and kerosene which he could not produce himself, he took on additional work — nothing was too difficult or dangerous. For a while he hauled gold for prospectors to the Kuznetsov works in Minusinsk, an extremely hazardous job because of the escaped convicts lying in wait for the sledges. In one holdup, he would probably have been killed if it hadn't been for his draft horse, Karka Kosmaty. "Karka rose up on his hind legs and knocked one of the robbers off the bridge. How the other horses broke from the sledge I don't know," Frolov told Yevdokiya when he finally stumbled home on foot through the snow. The next day they found one of the bandits, frozen to death at the foot of the bridge.

Winter 1857: Farewell to Siberia

Frolov pulled his heavy sheepskin coat across his chest to shield himself against the icy wind cutting across the wagon. Sitting next to him on the coachman's seat was eleven-year-old Nikolai, bundled to the ears in rugs. As Frolov watched the snow cover the backs of the five horses, he remembered that thirty-one years earlier, almost to the day, he had arrived in Siberia in shackles. Now he was going home.

Every now and then Nikolai would look around to check if he could still see Grandpa Makarov. The old Cossack chief was accompanying the family on horseback to Minusinsk, where the wagon would cross the river and head west toward the Volga, some twenty-five hundred miles away. Kakvaska, the sheep dog, followed at a distance, sensing it was being left behind. Frolov guessed that inside the coach Yevdokiya and the children, Peter, Nadejda, and Fedya, were crying. They were leaving their happy childhood home forever; Nadejda always thought of it as her "golden youth." Fedya Falenberg was accompanying them because Frolov had promised his father to enter the boy in military school with Nikolai. A determined look passed over Frolov's face; he flicked the whip to spur the horses on.

Despite the family's tears, Frolov was convinced he was doing the right thing. Yevdokiya was not so sure. "Why hide it," she once told her children. "I wouldn't have gone, but Dusha insisted." She knew she would never see her parents again. But her husband felt that Siberia was not right for the children. As they had grown older, he began to fret about their education, especially that of the boys. He wanted them to continue the family's military tradition, which he had so rudely interrupted. What he described as his "youthful mistake" should not be allowed to jeopardize their future.

In 1854, Frolov had begun to petition the governor-general of East Siberia for his children to be allowed to attend school in Irkutsk. He wrote urgent letters to his mother in Kerch, asking her to appeal to the czarevitch. In February 1855, Frolov's prayers were answered. Czar Nicholas died suddenly, and the crown passed to Alexander, who as a small boy had watched his father put down the Decembrist uprising. In a gesture of reconciliation, Alexander II decided to grant amnesty to the remaining Decembrists — about thirty-five of the hundred and twenty-one were still alive. The proclamation was not a pardon, however: the Decembrists could return to Russia but not to Moscow or St. Petersburg. And wherever they settled, they had to submit to police surveillance. The amnesty electrified Frolov because of its promise of free education. He was so anxious to return that he abandoned his land and, without waiting for a good price, sold everything that he and Yevdokiya had built up over the years: the house, the outbuildings, the mill, the herd of forty-five cows, the horses, ducks, geese — everything.

Frolov was fifty-three years old. For the third time in his life, he was embarking on a dangerous journey without knowing whether he would reach his destination and, if he did, what he would find. True, the man driving the team of five was more assured than the miserable lieutenant who arrived in Chita in 1827 or even the exile who settled in Shusha a decade later. But Frolov was worried about his family: his mother was blind and ailing, one sister was widowed, the other was a spinster, and he had his own brood.

Now the snow was falling so hard it was almost impossible to see the track. Looking into the sea of whiteness ahead, Frolov made the sign of the cross. If he had made the journey once, he could make it again.

Spring 1858: Across the Volga

As Frolov furiously whipped the horses on, their hooves sank into the slushy river ice. The wagon had to be kept going; if one of the animals fell and the wagon stopped, they would surely crash through the ice. The river was already thawing and cracking. In places the water gushed out of the fissures and poured over the ice, rising up the wagon wheels almost to the portholes. Yevdokiya had begged her *dusha* not to cross the Volga at Kazan at the end of March. But he stubbornly insisted on moving on.

Frolov felt confident that this was the best plan for his family. Although he had sold his home in great haste, he had planned the journey with his usual attention to detail. Shortly after the amnesty, he began building the covered wagon that would carry his family. Not an inch of space was wasted. The passenger compartment, with its tiny windows on either side, resembled the cabin of a sailboat. The seats, upholstered in leather and fastened with copperhead tacks, could be pulled out and turned into bunks at night. A small table stood in the middle of the compartment; there the family took its meals. And all sorts of pots, pans, and dolls hung from hooks in the cross struts.

"That winter journey tired me out unbelievably, and Mother, too," recalled Nadejda, who was nine at the time. "The men supported it far better." Yevdokiya, who had been in poor health for six years, became tired and irritable. She constantly thought of her father, standing on the east bank of the Yenisei, the disconsolate Kakvaska beside him, waving his hat until he dropped from view as the wagon turned around a bend. Nadejda suffered from motion sickness, and every hour or so they were forced to stop to give her fresh air. The coach bucked continuously on the icy track, throwing the passengers against the sides and rattling every item they carried. On several occasions, the wagon tipped over into a snowbank. Sleep was impossible, for Frolov insisted on driving day and night; they would rest only briefly while changing horses at way stations. After all, long stops in the Siberian wastes were dangerous. "Twice a pack of wolves set upon us," Nadejda recalled. "We lit our lanterns, without stopping the wagon, to scare them away. It was terrifying."

As the wagon rolled on, Frolov seemed almost indifferent to his passengers' complaints. He was possessed by one desire: to return to Russia.

Summer 1858: Reunion

His aged mother did not respond when Frolov, accompanied by his two sisters, pushed open the door and entered the room in Yelizabetgrad. She had grown frail in recent years and was now almost blind. Praskovya Frolova had suffered many traumas: the house at Kerch had been razed by the bombardments of the Crimean War, and her other two sons, Nikolai and Peter, had been killed in the fighting with the British and French. Three years earlier, she and her surviving daughters, Claudia and Pelageya, had gathered what they could carry and fled to this southern Ukrainian trading town.

Frolov had not seen his mother in thirty years. He had spent weeks tracking down his two sisters, and now the three of them feared that if he walked through the door after such a long time, it would be too great a shock for the old woman. Pelageya stepped forward and said, "This is the visitor we told you about, the one who met brother Sasha in Siberia."

"Good day," Frolov began as he walked over to his mother, "I have —" Hardly were the words out of his mouth than she recognized his voice. Bursting into tears, she reached out and pulled him toward her, pushing him to his knees before her chair. She ran her hands over his face, along his nose, through his hair, grasping and kissing his callused hands. "My boy, my Sasha . . ."

There had been other tearful reunions as well. Once across the Volga, the family had rested with his old Decembrist friend, Ivan Pushchin, at the estate of Marino. The news of Frolov's return spread, and soon two other friends from Petrovsky, Peter Svistunov and Ivan Annenkov, joined them.

"Lord, what you didn't hear them talking about," Yevdokiya remembered. "They reminisced about their exile in Siberia, about the uprising, how they had been arrested, how the common folk had to live decently, about their hopes for the future political structure of Russia."

Pushchin pressed his friend to stay longer, but Frolov was impatient to continue his journey. He wanted to enroll Fedya and Nikolai in the First Corps of Cadets in St. Petersburg as soon as possible. Then he was anxious to push south and find his family. On April 1, 1858, Frolov and the boys drove off to the capital, leaving Yevdokiya, Nadejda, and Peter behind. Pushchin wrote to Prince Trubetskoi the next day, mentioning his friend's departure and adding that Frolov was "less gauche than he used to be" and that his "Siberian liaison" seemed to have worked out. Yevdokiya, he wrote, is a "wonderful woman." Frolov's passage through St. Petersburg was duly noted by Baron Vladimir Shteingeil, who wrote on April 21 to Maria Bestuzheva that Nikolai had been accepted at the military academy. "Young Frolov is a sharp, handsome boy. I saw them yesterday and said good-bye to Frolov, who is heading back to Pushchin's, where he left his wife."

Many of Frolov's anxieties of the last months fell away after he left Nikolai in St. Petersburg. He thought of his father: he would have been pleased.

Summer 1865: Disasters in the Crimea

As Nadejda ran over the field toward her father, she saw him bent over the wattle fence, his shoulders heaving, his head in his hands. At Frolov's feet lay a dozen dead sheep, their legs in the air. Across the pasture scores of others were spinning in palsied circles or bleating in fright. The dogs, who were almost as frantic as the sheep, were chasing the animals and barking. A dozen neighbors looked on. The peasants shook their heads sadly, and one of the women made the sign of the cross.

"Dear God," Frolov sobbed, "why are you punishing me?" His herd of two thousand sheep, which he had so painfully built up over several years, was rapidly dying from bladderworms, which attack the brain.

"Papa! Papa!" Nadejda shouted, opening her basket. "I've brought a cure. The doctor taught me how to use it. There's nothing to lose, and maybe God will help!"

Frolov wiped a dirty sleeve across his eyes and took the container of disinfectant prepared by the doctor at the Kerch Institute, where Nadejda was studying. For three days and nights, Frolov and his neighbors threw the remaining sheep on their sides, forcing their jaws open and swabbing their mouths with the liquid. Their efforts were almost useless: in the end only fifty sheep survived. The ordeal exhausted Frolov. He was sixty-one, and he no longer had limitless energy.

The decimation of his sheep was not the only disaster Frolov suffered on his return home. After visiting his mother, Frolov bought four pairs of oxen in Yelizabetgrad and set out for the Crimea with the whole family to start a business hauling salt. "We will forge a new life," he told Yevdokiya and the children. His arrival in Kerch in September 1858 did not go unnoticed by the authorities. "State criminal Alexander Frolov has arrived and according to instructions, has been routinely subjected, without his knowledge, to secret police scrutiny," the mayor, Rear Admiral Spitsyn, reported to St. Petersburg.

Since the family cottage was gone, Frolov purchased a small piece of land nearby. With the help of three serfs whose freedom he had purchased, his hauling business thrived. Then, in 1862, disaster hit for the first time. As Frolov was returning home along Lake Sivash one afternoon, a tornado struck. A flash flood swept Frolov, the oxcarts, and the oxen into the water. He was found unconscious the next morning on the shore, clinging to a wooden piling, which had saved him from drowning.

For several days afterward, Frolov was in despair. Then he remembered the lesson of Petrovsky. As long as he was alive, he could work; he could survive. He agreed with Yevdokiya: hauling salt was too hard for a man of fifty-eight. He turned to sheep farming, instead.

Winter 1873: Sasha Manganari

As soon as the old man and the five-year-old boy clinging to his hand entered the basement workshop, the master carver rose from his bench. After greeting Frolov, the artisan picked little Sasha up, threw him in the air, and plunked him on the bed in the corner with the colored quilt. The Safonov Cellar workshop was famous all over Russia for its wooden toys. On display were whittled figures of every description: bears and squirrels; horses hitched to sledges and carts; dolls; soldiers of every nationality, in every imaginable uniform, with rifles, cannons, and all sorts of military paraphernalia.

Frolov's fingers itched to hold a chisel again. The smell of turpentine and wood chips took him back to Petrovsky, to the time when he made toys for the children of his fellow Decembrists. Now that he was retired, some of his happiest hours were spent in this basement with his grandson, to whom he had become a second father. And Sasha was mesmerized by the woodcarvers. "What a magical world opened up," he wrote later. "My sensations were heightened by the idea that it was forbidden and we might get caught." His mother, Nadejda, considered the cellar air unhealthy, but Sasha and his grandpa would slip off to the workshop whenever they could. Sasha credited these visits as the inspiration for his artistic career.

Frolov had continued sheep farming until 1872. But after the sheep epidemic, Nikolai and Peter — who were advancing successfully through the ranks of the military — urged him to move closer to Moscow. Finally, he relented. In 1873, the embarrassed Kerch police sent an urgent message to Moscow to be on the lookout for their "state criminal," who had slipped away without permission. To be near Nikolai, the Frolovs had settled in Sergeyevsky-Posad, a picturesque medieval town fifty miles north of Moscow. Thanks to financial help from other Decembrists, they were able to buy a four-room wooden house. It was surrounded by a garden, and which he was more than happy to work.

The only shadow that passed over Frolov's retirement concerned Nadejda. Her marriage to Viktor Manganari, a naval officer of Greek descent, had broken up and she feared he would return to claim their son. A capable and strong-willed woman, Nadejda wanted to become an actress and occasionally got bit parts with the Maly Theater when it came by on tour. Frolov insisted that she stick to more traditional occupations — midwifery and sewing on her Singer from America. More than once their arguments led to hard feelings.

But Frolov's love for his grandson Sasha grew. With the disappearance of son-in-law Viktor, Frolov turned increasingly to his grandson, until the old man and the young boy became almost inseparable.

Autumn 1881: Zavalishin's broadside

In October 1881, Frolov was dozing in the parlor of Nikolai's house, at 5 Maly Nikolopeskovsky Lane in Moscow, when Yevdokiya announced that Peter Svistunov had arrived to see him. His old Decembrist friend entered the room, clearly upset. "Look at this article by that scoundrel Zavalishin!" Svistunov said, thrusting a copy of the literary magazine *Russkaya Starina* into Frolov's hand. Frolov took the magazine and started to read. As he turned the pages, he became increasingly indignant. Among other things, Zavalishin had accused the Decembrists of homosexuality and inveigling servant girls into their cells at Petrovsky. He also had mean words for Leparsky. And Frolov was cut to the core by his claim that he, not Frolov, had been Dr. Volf's major helper.

Yevdokiya tried to calm her husband down. At seventy-seven, he was frail and easily fatigued; she feared the excitement could bring on a stroke or heart attack. Over tea, Svistunov, who had been singled out in Zavalishin's attack, suggested he help Frolov prepare a rebuttal. Frolov knew that in challenging such a difficult and brilliant man as Zavalishin he risked a vitriolic response. But the attack on the character of the Decembrists had disturbed his image of "the golden cage," and his old fighting spirit was aroused. With Svistunov's help, Frolov composed an answer to Zavalishin which was published in the May 1882 issue of the same journal. On the subject of the doctor, Frolov wrote: "All my comrades know that Dr. Volf was closer to no one than me . . ." As expected, Zavalishin shot back with a personal attack on Frolov,

accusing him of being "ignorant" and "incapable." For Frolov
it was a painful broadside, coming near the end of his life, and
it may have contributed to the stroke he suffered about that time.

Apart from this incident, Frolov's last years were happy ones.
As one of the oldest surviving Decembrists, he had become something of a legend. He was never happier than when he was sitting
around the samovar with old friends, and their children or grandchildren, reminiscing about the uprising. Among the few remaining Decembrists who called on Frolov was Alexander Belyayev,
once Yevdokiya's fiancé. Belyayev would urge his friend to tell
the old stories, and the more he talked, the prouder he became
of being a Decembrist. His eyes filled with tears when the aging
Matvei Muravyov-Apostol asked him to keep the letter that his
younger brother, Sergei, had written before being hanged as one
of the five ringleaders of the uprising.

Frolov also enjoyed the frequent visits from his growing family.
Nikolai had married Elizabeth, the daughter of a high government
official; his sixth child, Gavriil, was born in March 1881. Frolov
was fond of his grandchildren, especially Anna, who, according
to Sasha Manganari, was "a charming, beautiful child, spoiled
by one and all."

For Frolov, his family had been everything. He regarded himself as a simple man. He knew he would not leave any books to
posterity, like Zavalishin or the others, but somehow it didn't
matter as long as he had the love of those around him.

Spring 1885: Final days

Frolov's health had begun to deteriorate almost as soon as he
and Yevdokiya moved to Moscow from Sergeyevsky-Posad in
1879. The dampness of their older son's house opened up the
old sores from his chains. In 1882, Frolov suffered a stroke that
left him partially paralyzed and nearly blind, and he lived increasingly in the past. He would sit, immobile, in his chair in
front of the window and spend hours recalling the many events

of his life. When he thought of his sons — by 1884, both Nicholas and Peter were colonels — he knew his struggles had not been in vain. The boys were carrying on the family tradition, unblemished by his own involvement in the December uprising. His only regret was that his father had not lived to see them.

Toward the end of April 1885, Frolov's condition took a turn for the worse. His windpipe became constricted, and over the next two weeks he had increasing trouble breathing. Yevdokiya and the rest of the family watched Frolov struggle with the paralysis attacking his throat. Nothing seemed to help. His body was racked with convulsions from the choking. Yevdokiya prayed for him to be released from his suffering, but she knew he would not give up easily. This was the old Decembrist's last great battle: he would put up as good a fight with death as he had with life. By the morning of May 6, 1885, he was clearly failing, and friends, too, began to gather.

Frolov lay on the bed in the corner of the room. Yevdokiya, who had not left him in days, was sitting beside him. As she looked at the shrunken form under the blanket, she whispered to Nadejda, who was standing beside sixteen-year-old Sasha, that Dusha weighed less than when he came out of the Peter and Paul Fortress. When Frolov started to choke again, Yevdokiya put her arms under his bony shoulders and raised him. Then she put a glass of water to his lips. He tried to drink, but the coughing overwhelmed him. When the paroxysm subsided he fell back on the pillow, exhausted, and Yevdokiya wiped the sweat from his forehead. He was still conscious and able to mutter a few words. But later that day his heart finally gave out, his breathing stilled, and a look of serenity came over his face. After eighty-one years, he had finally surrendered.

"He had a rebellious soul, my great beautiful falcon," Yevdokiya later told her grandchildren. "As a rebel he lived, and as a rebel he died."

 *Sixteen*

"PODYOM! Podyom!" The six o'clock wake-up call on Monday, September 8, echoed through the corridors as the guards yanked the feed windows open and shut. I rose stiffly, pulled on my trousers, and straightened the bed. The small of my back ached from the hard, springless cot.

"There'll be a surprise inspection during the week, and we've got to make sure the place looks clean," Stas announced as he began bustling around the cell. "Dusting the shelves and the ledge under the window is very important. That's the first place they look. And if they find the crossbars on the beds clean, they'll figure everything else is fine."

His attitude toward regulations was typically Russian: rules exist to be circumvented. Stas wanted to prevent the guards from poking around his bed too much. Beneath his cot, where it was cool, Stas stored five hundred grams of butter in a bowl filled with water, to retard spoilage, and two small boxes of garlic and onions. He also "pressed" his trousers for interrogations by placing them carefully between the cot and the mattress.

He motioned to the cloth lying near the cell door. I picked up the foul-smelling rag and was about to start swishing it around the floor when the *kormushka* flopped open and the face of a guard appeared. He handed in our glasses and a dozen sheets of the coarse, light brown toilet paper. Toilet paper was a privilege, which Soviet jailors frequently withheld to undermine their prisoners. Women were often denied sanitary napkins. Minutes later, the slicer arrived. Stas and I handed out our salami and hard cheese which we kept on our shelves. The guard carefully cleaved a small portion of each one and handed them back. The morning ritual was over. I collapsed onto my bed, hoping to doze until oatmeal gruel at eight o'clock. Suddenly, the metal door swung open and a stocky figure flanked by two guards stepped into the cell.

"*Rukovodstvo,*" Stas whispered. The management. We jumped to attention, hands behind our backs as required by regulations.

Our visitor wished us both good morning. Then, turning to me, he introduced himself as Petrenko, Alexander Mitrofanovich, commandant of Lefortovo prison. "I've just come back from vacation or I would have been to see you sooner," he apologized. "How are you getting on? Do you have any complaints?"

For a moment I didn't know what to make of this older man in a brown trench coat asking, of all questions, if I had any complaints. I looked at him; judging by his expression, he was serious. I decided to take him at face value.

"I could use more exercise," I told him.

"How much?"

"Two hours would be better than one."

"How about three?"

"That would be good, too."

Petrenko turned to one of the guards and commanded, "See that these two men get three hours of exercise today." The guard nodded smartly in acknowledgment.

"Anything else?" Petrenko was addressing me again.

"I have a hemorrhoid that is bothering me."

"I'll see what I can do about it." With that, Petrenko said good-bye and the three visitors left.

What was behind the unexpected concern of the prison brass? Lefortovo's reputation was not one of being solicitous toward inmates. I knew from my reading over the years that during Stalin's time new prisoners were routinely confined in overheated "boxes" too small to sit up straight in. Difficult inmates were subdued by throwing them into cold, unlighted cells, and fed infrequently on bread and water. Others were given salty herring with nothing to drink. Cell 111, which was painted totally black inside, had a particularly nasty reputation.

A few minutes later, the guards arrived and escorted Stas and me up to the dank fifth-floor corridor to "bear cage" number 9. Inside, Stas immediately began his figure eights. I started to pace back and forth — five steps forward, five steps back — like an animal in a zoo. As I paced, I thought about Father Roman and the grueling interrogation of the day before. What next? What other time bombs were waiting to be set off? I knew I should be prepared, so I began recalling everything I could about the KGB's earlier efforts to pin something on me.

During the nine years I had lived and worked in the Soviet Union — four in the 1960s and five in the 1980s — the KGB had paraded a colorful assortment of characters across my path. They had all played different parts in their attempts to influence my reporting, to pressure me, to compromise me. Some of them had played their roles well, others were transparently obvious, and at least two were crazy.

The first KGB presence I remembered was my English-speaking *nyanya*, nanny, from the Novosti Press Agency in the 1960s. The *nyanya* is a classic figure in the KGB arsenal. He — or she — usually operates under the cover of a journalist but reports regularly to the secret police. He invariably speaks good English and moves freely among foreigners, attending diplomatic receptions and other international gatherings. His assignment is to gain your confidence and, gradually, to strengthen the friendship by feeding you "inside information." During this first Moscow tour, my *nyanya* supplied me with much-appreciated scoops, such as the news that the world's first woman cosmonaut, Valentina Tereshkova, had undergone a Ceasarian section and would never fly again.

New correspondents who don't speak Russian are particularly susceptible to the *nyanya*'s services. As I settled in, I began branching out, which displeased my nyanya. If I had any questions, he insisted, I should check only with him; other sources were unreliable. When I returned to Moscow, I was amused to learn that my first *nyanya*, rather than corrupting foreigners, had been seduced by them himself. He had been kicked out of the press agency and dropped by the KGB because of a scam involving the illegal importation of furniture. He was surviving as a hack, writing malicious commentaries on Washington politics for an agricultural newspaper.

When it came to developing an inside informer against me, the KGB employed considerable imagination. Three years into my second tour, the *banya obshestvo* was thrown into turmoil when a KGB officer approached one participant, a party member in good standing, and requested, "Try to get close to Daniloff and develop a relationship with him." The party man, frightened by this assignment, informed Yuri, the *starosta*. When I learned of the KGB's search for an insider, I offered to resign. Instead, the group split in two. Henceforth, only members who wanted to emigrate or who did not have important official jobs would be allowed in my circle.

Almost any Soviet citizen can be suspect. Half the time, it is impossible to recognize a KGB plant for certain. One evening, a regular in our *banya* group brought along a friend of a friend, a gregarious engineer by the name of Valery. After a while, Valery sought me out in the sauna when we were alone. He revealed that he had worked in an institute, developing guidance systems for submarine-launched rockets. I became concerned and told

Yuri about the exchange. For weeks we puzzled over Valery, trying to decide whether he was an inside plant or merely a naive fool trying to impress an American. In the end, we found a way to kick him out of our gatherings.

The KGB is tenacious. Like every other organization in the Soviet Union, its departments have plans to fulfill. If one informer fails to take root, they try another. The "odd ball" appeared in the fall of 1984, while I was doing research for the article on the KGB that convinced Sergadeyev I was a spy. One morning I went down to my car in the courtyard to find a disheveled young man waiting for me. He introduced himself as the nephew of Stanislav Levchenko, a KGB major who had defected to the United States from Tokyo in 1979. The young man claimed that the KGB had put him in a psychiatric hospital and denied him work. He wanted to emigrate but had been refused a visa — and said he had documents to prove his story. The coincidence of meeting the young Levchenko just when I was working on a KGB story was too great, and I tried to put him off. For several days he hounded me, forcing his way into the office. When I finally became angry and said I would call the militia if he didn't leave, he shouted, "You'll never see me again. I'm going to commit suicide!"

I was not totally unsympathetic. The young man was clearly deranged, possibly as a result of KGB harassment. Using someone who is mentally unstable or has a gripe against the Soviet system is not an uncommon KGB ploy. Such a person can sometimes be manipulated by the secret police, who encourage him or her to approach an American correspondent for help. If the relationship develops, the KGB can often influence it to their own advantage.

Finally, of course, there is "the swallow," the professional seductress who seeks out foreign residents and tourists and, when possible, key personnel like U.S. marine guards or the code clerk at the Belgian embassy. During my first tour, I recall working late in the UPI office one night and getting a telephone call from a woman who said plaintively, "Darling, aren't you lonely up there?" I slammed down the receiver. In 1974, when I was visiting Moscow on a trip with Secretary of State Kissinger, at about midnight I got a call in my room at the Hotel Intourist. "This is Olga," cooed the female voice. The next morning, I learned that Olga had telephoned no fewer than six of the journalists in Kissinger's party.

Most reporters put a lot of effort into identifying the hand of the KGB. However, not all danger comes from the Soviet side: Western intelligence officers also pose a danger. Operating under diplomatic cover, CIA agents are as difficult to spot as the KGB. Despite a presidential order banning the use of American journalists as spies, intelligence types view reporters as useful sources of information. They move much more freely in Soviet society than Foreign Service officers, and a correspondent may be passing information directly to the CIA when he thinks he is simply chatting with a diplomat. Committing inadvertent espionage is a particular risk in Moscow, because some information that would be completely open in the United States — photographs of airports or railway stations, for example — are classified in the Soviet Union. I knew a journalist who was invited to step over the line by a friend, a military attaché, before leaving on a trip: "If you happen to be sitting around the airport and see any IL–86s, take a look at the number on the tails." The attaché was hoping to learn where specific aircraft were located so that he could cross-check production rates. Another colleague probably transgressed by giving the embassy a collection of newspapers from a Soviet friend. The newspapers came from a city closed to foreigners and could have contained information the Soviets wanted to keep quiet. Dusko Doder, a *Washington Post* correspondent with lengthy experience in the Soviet Union, made a similar misstep. A Soviet official slipped him a classified document on the Soviet economy which he shared with an embassy friend. This paper almost certainly made its way to the CIA station as well as to the embassy's economic section. "It never occurred to me at that point that I was doing something improper and potentially self-incriminating," Doder wrote in his book, *Shadows and Whispers*.

As I trundled round and round the bear cage, I concluded that Moscow is much more of a minefield than many people believe. Reporters can paralyze themselves with precautions: never open the mailbox; never accept anything from a Soviet citizen; never talk to an embassy official. In the end, such precautions are relatively useless. The day the KGB has a reason to arrest a correspondent or anybody else, they will. Nothing is easier than planting classified documents, drugs, or weapons in a mailbox, in a car, or even in an overcoat. I comforted myself with the thought that if I had refused Misha's package, if I had burned Roman's letter, the KGB would have found some other ploy to incriminate me.

ᔭ ᔭ ᔭ

About fifteen minutes after we returned to the cell, I was summoned for interrogation. After Sunday's indictment, I especially dreaded Monday's questioning. Sergadeyev was waiting for me as usual, sitting behind the desk in his gray cardigan sweater. After greeting me, he announced, "Your wife called about another meeting. We talked about today, but she said she was indisposed and that she might call about a meeting tomorrow."

"Indisposed?" I asked. It was unlike her. I wondered if she was breaking under the strain. "What's the matter?"

"I don't know. She says she is not feeling well."

Was Sergadeyev lying? What sort of game was he playing?

"Now," he continued as he pulled on his cigarette, exhaling the smoke slowly, "I want to know about your relationship with Paul Stombaugh."

"Stombaugh?" I replied. "I don't know anything about him. I never met him." But I did know his name: it was Stombaugh who had been expelled from Moscow while Ruth and I were on vacation in Finland.

"Come on," Sergadeyev goaded me, picking up where he had left off the day before. We were interrupted by the strident ring of one of his four telephones. The colonel snatched the receiver angrily and barked, "Sergadeyev!" He listened for a few minutes, then said sarcastically, "No, we are not there yet. Maybe in America you would be in court at this time. Here we are following our own procedures."

He slammed down the receiver and glowered at me. "Ever since you gave out my telephone number, there have been no end of calls from your friends. I don't know why they find this case of such great interest." He made a visible effort to get his irritation under control, then said, "Now let's get back to Stombaugh."

"Look, I never knew Stombaugh," I repeated. "The first time I ever heard his name was when I was in Finland. I learned about his arrest, and a few months later I read in the paper that he was connected with some Soviet citizen. That's all I know."

"Tolkachov," Sergadeyev said. He stressed the last syllable of the family name and looked at me to note my reaction. "Stombaugh was working Tolkachov."

At the time, I knew no more about Tolkachov than I did about Stombaugh. The only thing I could recall, under Sergadeyev's prodding, was that in September 1985 TASS announced that Tolkachov had been caught passing highly classified information to Stombaugh. TASS described Tolkachov as a research worker in a Moscow aviation institute. That, it turned out, was only a fragment of a much larger story. Later, when I got back to the United States, I discovered that Tolkachov was one of the most important spies the CIA had ever recruited in the Soviet Union.

Far from being a nondescript employee, "Adolf," as he was known to his American handlers, held a very high position in the Soviet defense program responsible for developing avionics, radar avoidance technology, and other electronic countermeasures for aircraft. He is said to have alerted the CIA that the Krasnoyarsk radar station was more than a space tracking center: it was an integral part of the space defense system that was being built in

violation of the SALT II treaty. Tolkachov's first contacts with
Americans began during the Nixon administration. With a min-
iature camera supplied by the CIA, he photographed hundreds,
perhaps thousands, of technical documents until he was arrested
by the KGB. Like Oleg Penkovsky in the sixties, Tolkachov spied
on ideological grounds. Appalled at the aggressive military buildup
in the Soviet Union, he saw the United States as the sole coun-
terbalance to the Kremlin on the world scene and did not want
Washington to be caught unawares. Until his betrayal in September 1984 by Edward Lee Howard, a former CIA deep cover agent
who eventually defected to Moscow, Tolkachov provided a steady
stream of invaluable technological information and saved the
United States billions of dollars.

Even without knowing these details, I could guess where Sergadeyev was heading. The colonel wanted to link me to whatever
espionage activities Stombagh was involved in. Then the Soviet
government could claim that I was part of a major U.S. spy ring,
including Tolkachov, Stombaugh, and whomever else. This tactic
would serve a double purpose: it would give them leverage over
the Zakharov situation while exposing the sins of the CIA in
Moscow at a time when the KGB was under increasing attack in
Washington for economic and industrial espionage.

As the session wore on, Sergadeyev continued to "prove" my
guilt through association. "What other CIA officers besides Natirboff and Stombaugh were you in touch with?" he pressed.

"I wasn't in touch with CIA officers. I didn't know who the
CIA officers were in the embassy."

Sergadeyev grunted disbelievingly and reeled off several names,
including those of Michael Sellers and Erik Sites (two embassy
officials expelled for espionage in 1986), demanding that I identify and describe them. I didn't know any of them and said so.
At one point, hoping to deflect his relentless drilling, I interrupted
him.

"You keep mentioning Natirboff," I said. "Where is he now?"

"Who? Murat?" Sergadeyev smiled.

I nodded. Referring to the CIA station chief by his first name struck me as bizarre. Sergadeyev talked about Natirboff as if they were close friends. In the surrealistic world of spy and counterspy, perhaps the KGB and CIA became so well acquainted that a perverse sort of intimacy developed between them.

"Ah, Murat!" Sergadeyev sighed. "Poor Murat left Moscow about three days after you were arrested." His condescension suggested that he regarded Natirboff as an agreeable enough colleague on the other side but as one who was simply not equal to the wiles of the KGB, which had decimated the CIA's Moscow station.

Follwing this short diversion, Sergadeyev regrouped and began a new assault. "Nikolai Sergeyevich, you say you did not know these CIA officers. Frankly, I don't believe you. Tell me the truth this time. Where did you meet Stombaugh?"

"I never met Stombaugh."

"But we have reason to believe you did." He paused for almost a minute, staring at me with a satisfied smile. "In fact, Nikolai Sergeyevich, we know that Stombaugh telephoned Roman and introduced himself by saying, 'I am a friend of Nikolai's.' How do we know? We recorded the conversation. We have it on tape. It clearly suggests that you were a friend of Stombaugh's and that you worked together. What other explanation is there?"

I was stunned. Could this possibly be true? Stombaugh had called Roman and used my name? No, Sergadeyev had to be lying. It was some sort of trap. But there was worse to come.

"Not only that," he continued. "We intercepted a letter from Stombaugh to Father Roman in which you figure prominently. Let me read you a passage."

He looked through his papers and pulled out a photocopy of a letter, several paragraphs typed on a single sheet of paper. He read with evident delight: "Dear and esteemed friend . . . We would like to assure you that the letter you sent us through the journalist on January 24 reached the destination you indicated. We value your work highly . . ."

My mouth went dry with fear. Not only had the KGB planted secret maps on me, they were inventing phone calls and letters that would surely convict me. The prospect of an infinite prison term had never seemed more real.

"It's authentic enough," Sergadeyev went on. "It even contains spelling mistakes. You Americans seem to have an awful lot of difficulty writing simple Russian. Look at the signature." He chuckled as he handed me the paper. It was typed in Russian and signed Mikhail, Michael. Sure enough, the name was misspelled. It carried the Russian short sign over the second *i*, which meant that it should be pronounced Mikh-*hile* instead of the correct Mikha-*eel*.

"But," I protested, "Stombaugh's first name is Paul, not Michael."

"So, what makes you think he would sign his real name?"

I had no answer.

"And another thing." Sergadeyev's smug expression showed that he felt he was on sure ground. "This letter was typed on your office typewriter."

"It was not!" I snapped back. I took the letter from him, terrified of what I might find. At the top of the copy were several black triangles where the photographic paper had been clamped down during printing. The copy was clear and perfectly in focus; I could make out the typeface easily.

"It was not typed on my typewriter!" I shouted, both relieved and angry. "These letters are smaller, and the type is bolder. I had absolutely nothing to do with this!" I threw the paper back at him. "Anyway, I've told you over and over again, I had no contact with these CIA people."

Hearing the unaccustomed feeling in my voice, Sergadeyev glanced up with a puzzled expression. For a second, it seemed almost as if he believed me. Then he returned to his usual assured look. It suddenly struck me, he was really convinced that I was a spy. He certainly considered the phone call and the letter genuine. To make his job simpler, the Tenth Department of the

Second Chief Directorate, which monitors American journalists, had avoided telling him everything they knew. Undoubtedly, they had explained how the arrest setup would work because he had to handle the prison end of it. But there they stopped. By telling him nothing further — nothing about their agent Roman or how they tried to compromise me over a period of months, and by feeding him false evidence as if it were real — they made it easier for him to act as the determined investigator.

Sergadeyev looked me straight in the eye, then said in a voice laden with sarcasm, "Nikolai Sergeyevich, are you trying to tell me that Murat involved you in the dark?"

"You mean unwittingly?" I replied. "Yes, if I understand the Russian language correctly. If Natirboff and Stombaugh used my name, they did so without my knowledge and without my permission. It was done *v temnuyou*, as you say, in the dark."

ᔕ ᔕ ᔕ

Early the next morning, Tuesday, September 9, as I reviewed the most recent interrogation, my thoughts returned to the letter Sergadeyev claimed that Stombaugh had sent to Father Roman. I was convinced that the Soviet authorities were fabricating evidence; there was no other explanation for the letter. Yet something puzzled me. Why hadn't the KGB done a better job of replicating my stationery and the typeface of my office typewriter? They could have obtained any number of my letters from customs or the Diplomatic Service Bureau. And KGB experts are masters at forgery: Why fabricate a weak piece of evidence instead of a strong one? It did not add up.

My ruminations were interrupted when the cell door swung open and Commandant Petrenko entered, accompanied by his two guards. "Well, now, and how have we spent the night?" he inquired.

"Fine," answered Stas, who was invariably obsequious around authority. "But it's getting a bit cold. The window is slightly open and the air pours in."

"We'll fix that. And how about some better blankets and sheets?" Petrenko asked. He signaled to one of his guards, and moments later an orderly appeared with top sheets and woolen blankets to replace the thin cotton knit covers we'd been using. My cellmate looked impressed. "It really pays to be imprisoned with an American," he said later.

Petrenko turned to me with a frown and announced that he had studied the charges filed against me. "They are serious, no doubt about it," he said. Then, his severity dissipating somewhat, he added, "I only hope you will be able to muddle your way out of this mess." He then went off on a curious tack. "I had a nightmare last night. I dreamt you disappeared . . . You escaped from my prison. You won't do that to me, will you?"

I managed a halfhearted laugh and reassured him that he had little to worry about.

This exchange set the tone for my unusual relationship with the commandant of Lefortovo over the ensuing week. Petrenko was, first and foremost, a KGB professional. He would not have risen so high without possessing that agency's more sinister characteristics. But like Frolov's General Leparsky, he was capable of human decency.

On Petrenko's orders my diet was improved, and I began enjoying two glasses of milk and supplementary meat every day. The change was dictated, the orderlies assured me, by my blood pressure condition. Since milk and meat are not recommended for hypertension, I assumed this was a face-saving explanation and possibly the first real clue that release was in the wind. I tried not to read too much into my new menu, but when medical treatment was turned on with a vengeance over the next days my hopes started to rise.

What an irony. During the next week in prison I received more and better medical care than during all my years in the Soviet Union. I was taken to the medical section of the prison, where a gregarious young doctor named Mikhail Ivanovich insisted on discussing my blood pressure. He summoned an outside specialist,

Nadejda Yepifanovna, for a second opinion. She said that I would never have survived so long without jogging regularly. During another visit Mikhail Ivanovich's *kabinet,* the physician informed me proudly that he had obtained Japanese blood pressure pills to replace the hydrochlorothiazide I would ordinarily take. He insisted that I look at a Soviet medical manual containing a diagram of the chemical composition of the medicine to persuade me that I would not be secretly drugged. Under the circumstances, I thought it unlikely, so I agreed to take the pills in the hopes they would relieve the pressure I could feel in my head. Each day I signed the register in which the dosage was meticulously recorded. I wondered if such sought-after foreign medicine had been purloined from the special supplies of the Kremlin elite. Drugs are so hard to get in the Soviet Union that an ordinary citizen couldn't hope to get Japanese pills.

Having satisfied themselves about my blood pressure, the health authorities focused next on my hemorrhoid. Again, they called in a specialist, who recommended two suppositories a day. I last saw him standing at Mikhail Ivanovich's basin, washing out his yellowing rubber gloves by hand. Like most Soviet doctors, he had no disposable equipment. From then on, I began receiving daily visits in the cell from Sveta, a shy, blond nurse in her early twenties who radiated motherly concern. She took my blood pressure two or three times a day and inserted the suppositories.

The contrast between my medical attention and the way Stas was treated when he complained of a toothache made my special status quite clear. Stas was told that the dentist was on vacation and to return in a month.

のう のう のう

By early Tuesday, my mood had improved considerably. My conversations with Petrenko had provided a welcome relief from both Sergadeyev and Stas. Even more important, his attentiveness suggested that a break in my case might be imminent. How else to explain the sudden concern for my health? Until Monday, they had been indifferent at best. Something good was bound to happen soon — or so I chose to believe.

At the morning's interrogation, Sergadeyev informed me that the meeting with Ruth was definitely scheduled for that afternoon. While waiting, I tried to come up with some kind of diplomatic formula to resolve the Zakharov-Daniloff impasse. For me, the priority was getting out of Lefortovo; for the two superpowers, it was to liquidate the crisis and save face. If Zakharov and I were turned over to the custody of our respective ambassadors, the level of tension would be significantly reduced. Negotiating a political compromise could then follow. I had in mind a precedent, of course, the Enger-Chernyayev-Crawford case. In that affair, the U.S. and Soviet Union negotiated an agreement to release the defendants from jail to their ambassadors.

At about 3:00 P.M., the door of the cell opened; I was escorted to Sergadeyev's office and from there to visitors room. Ruth and Roger Daley had already arrived. Ruth and I embraced, and she quickly filled me in on the latest efforts to bring about my release and the press coverage. "It's the top story in the United States every day," she said.

"And I am told that Mrs. Daniloff has become the number one TV star in America," Sergadeyev interjected sarcastically.

As soon as Ruth and I sat down on the couch, I took out my notes from the last few days. It was my first chance to talk to her directly about the indictment. I held my notebook on my knees and went through the points slowly. As before, Sergadeyev and the interpreter hung on every word. I explained the seriousness of the investigation and indicated that it could go on for several more months, if not longer, before coming to trial before a military tribunal.

"Trial? What trial?" Ruth exploded. "You can't go to trial. You'll get no fair trial . . ." Sergadeyev frowned.

"The Zakharov case and my case are now technically equal," I continued, talking as much to Sergadeyev as to Ruth. "It must be resolved immediately, otherwise it will escalate, jeopardizing

U.S.-Soviet relations." At this point, I began describing my release-into-custody scenario, with U.S.-Soviet negotiations to follow. Sergadeyev scowled and looked up in astonishment, as though some highly classified secret from the Foreign Ministry had seeped through the prison walls into my hands.

"Who told you this?" he shouted, interrupting me in mid-sentence.

"No one told me anything. It is purely my speculation."

Sergadeyev backed off, still looking amazed. Roger Daley broke in and asked the colonel whether an American lawyer could represent me in the event of a trial.

The question infuriated him. "To consult all those American Sovietologists is useless. They don't know anything about our laws. If you want to know about Soviet law, go to a Soviet lawyer. Mr. Daniloff will have the right to a lawyer when the investigation is over, but he will be represented by a Soviet lawyer."

Ruth took advantage of Daley's question to explain to me in a low voice the real reason she had postponed our meeting: she had spent the entire time trying to obtain information from Soviet defense lawyers and dissidents about how to handle a KGB investigation and a possible trial. The American embassy was no help on legal questions about which it seemed to be poorly informed: it did not even possess a copy of the procedural code in its library. Casually, Ruth opened her own notebook on her knees and turned it so that I could read the message: "Under Soviet law, you are not obliged to answer any of the investigator's questions if you don't want to."

I nodded, wishing that I had been told this on the day of my arrest. The choice between answering questions or remaining silent was not easy. To remain silent would require enormous resistance and would have subjected me to even more mental strain than telling the truth. Undoubtedly, the KGB would have used all its ingenuity to break me.

"The magazine has hired Cyrus Vance [a U.S. secretary of state under President Carter] to give advice," Ruth told me, "and they want to send over Leon Lipson, the Yale expert on Soviet law. I told them to wait. We are not dealing with law. We need advice from a lawyer who understands the rules according to the KGB, which is not the same thing as knowing the Soviet criminal code."

I agreed. I suggested she tell the magazine to consult Dina Kaminskaya, a Soviet lawyer who defended many dissidents in Moscow before immigrating to the United States.

In a low whisper, Ruth also said that she had visited Dr. Goldfarb at the Vishnievsky surgical hospital; he had offered to testify on my behalf at a trial. He was too ill to leave the ward, much less testify, but I was very moved by his courage. Also, Alec Goldfarb had called Ruth from New York to give her permission to tell the press about the KGB's efforts in 1984 to make David Goldfarb compromise me. The Soviet authorities, realizing that the story could damage their case against me, moved quickly to isolate the ailing scientist. After Ruth's visit, no Western journalists were allowed to see him, only his wife and daughter, Olga. Nonetheless, two Soviet journalists managed to pass the guards. They tried to make Goldfarb deny that the KGB had involved him in trying to set me up. He refused, but he worried that the Soviet media would twist his words.

"Olga called to tell me about the journalists," Ruth whispered. "David Moiseyevich wanted us to know that he told only the truth and that anything we read in the Soviet press that suggests the opposite is a lie or a distortion."

Ruth also reported that Goldfarb was finally getting decent medical treatment. Ironically, my arrest and imprisonment were responsible: our relationship was receiving a great deal of attention, and his death now would be an enormous embarrassment to the Soviet government. The minister of health had called Dr. Nikolai Kuzin, director of the hospital, who set in motion a frenzy of activity not seen on the trauma wing in years. Orders were issued to paint the walls, scrub the floors, change the sheets, bathe the patients. On September 4, a team of twenty-five specialists arrived to inspect the patient. An outdated Soviet medical device to relieve the pressure on his foot was replaced by a Western model. X-rays were taken which showed a small tumor in his left lung (though nothing was said to Goldfarb about the cancer). The medical team's top priority was to stop the gangrene in the foot and prevent amputation. In the event of Goldfarb's going to New York, they did not want to be accused of negligence. Motivations aside, I was relieved to know that my friend was receiving proper attention.

Sergadeyev broke off his conversation with Daley, clearly annoyed that Ruth and I were whispering again. As soon as I saw him turn toward us, I changed the subject to my improved conditions and described Petrenko's visits in some detail. I knew Ruth would appreciate the parallels with Leparsky. Sergadeyev was not amused, however.

"Why are you spending so much time talking about the commandant? I have asked you not to discuss our internal conditions. Why aren't you discussing your family?"

A few minutes later, while Daley occupied Sergadeyev with questions about another legal matter, Ruth and I resumed our conversation. "The case is becoming very nasty," I told her. "They are going over the whole of my time here."

Ruth saw that I was anxious and tried to comfort me. "That's to be expected, Nick. You should read the article they wrote in *Izvestia*, about how you were skulking in the bushes, suborning innocent Soviet citizens to spy for you. The good thing is that it's all so ludicrous. No one — certainly none of our friends — would ever believe any of it. Many of our Soviet friends are calling and wishing you well. Several said openly over the phone that the accusations are ridiculous. One even volunteered the opinion that the KGB are a bunch of *svolochi,* bastards."

It was hard to believe, and I wondered if Ruth was just trying to cheer me. It was one thing for American friends to call, quite another for people living under the Soviet system to offer support. Their courage and loyalty left me feeling sad: they were such wonderful people, and I would probably never see them again.

The meeting was drawing to an end; we rose to say good-bye. As Daley passed me on his way out the door, I asked him to convey my gratitude to President Reagan and my hope that a diplomatic solution to the crisis could be found quickly.

Sergadeyev and I walked silently back to Room 215. After we took our usual seats, he handed me two items Ruth had brought: the September 7 issue of *U.S. News and World Report,* with an article by Ruth on Soviet archaeology, and a long telex of support from all the magazine's editorial employees. He told me to go ahead and read them while he busied himself with a few administrative chores. Then he leaned back in his chair and fixed me with a withering stare. "I suppose you are going down to your cell now to read those Decembrist memoirs?" His disapproval was palpable.

"And what do you mean by that?" I asked.

Sergadeyev remained silent. He must have realized that I was drawing parallels between my fate and that of the Decembrists. Like most Soviets, Sergadeyev considered the Decembrists' struggle sacred. From his frown, I guessed he was probably cursing himself for allowing me to have the books. Any comparison between today and czarist times infuriates Soviet ideologues, who live with the illusion that 1917 marked a total break with the past. The angry silence seemed to go on and on . . .

ᵔ ᵔ ᵔ

On Wednesday morning, September 10, I received yet another visit from Petrenko. I found it hard to interpret his visits. I hoped his checks on my mood and health were an indication of my imminent release. But maybe, like so many Soviets, he simply liked Americans and was curious. One thing was certain: he enjoyed chatting, especially about the Americans who had passed through his hands. Lefortovo had housed a number of U.S. citizens in recent years, including several drug smugglers and an elderly woman arrested at Moscow's airport with a pistol. She had planned to take revenge on a man in Belorussia who had murdered members of her family during the war.

My ears pricked up when Petrenko mentioned Professor Barghoorn. The Yale scholar, Petrenko said, was a real gentleman, a man of his word. He never talked about his prison experiences when he returned to the United States. Clearly, Petrenko was suggesting that I should do the same if I considered myself a gentleman. I could have told him I was no gentleman, just a journalist. If ever I got out, I would feel obligated to tell the world about his prison in the hope that my words would discourage his bosses from continuing to take political hostages. "If you ever go back to the United States," Petrenko said, "please give the professor my greetings." Later when I visited Barghoorn at Yale, I learned that in 1963, Petrenko had been a KGB lieutenant colonel, in his mid-forties, at Lubyanka prison, and had been the chief of the professor's interrogation team.

Petrenko told me that he had served in the army in World War II, and his unit had joined American troops on the Elbe in April 1945. I understood his visits better then: memories of the war, good and bad, live on in the Russian psyche in ways that Americans find hard to understand. For the Soviet veterans, the meeting on the Elbe has taken on almost mythical dimensions. "Whenever we Russian and American soldiers had a chance to meet," Petrenko recollected, his voice softening with mejory, "we would dig deep into our pockets. Whatever we brought up, we would give to the other fellow without calculating its value. If I had a gold watch, I would give it away just like that, our friendship was that great . . ." His face clouded. "Relations soured when your President Truman issued a nonfraternization order and the Cold War began." He paused for a moment. "Two such nations as ours should have good relations," he reflected. "We saved the world, and today we are responsible for the peace. We must get along; we must coexist. But you Americans should always remember: good relations begin with mutual respect."

After Petrenko's departure, I waited for the call for interrogation. It was not long in coming. When I entered Room 215, I could see by Sergadeyev's smile that he had recovered from his pique over the Decembrists, and I took his mood as a good sign.

"I was quite impressed," he began in a conversational tone, "with what you told your wife yesterday about a solution to your problem. Do you suppose she will know what to do with your suggestion?" Sergadeyev always avoided any acknowledgment that my arrest had anything to do with Zakharov, and he never mentioned his name.

"Of course she will," I said. "But if you want, I'll be happy to call her to reinforce the message."

Sergadeyev gestured, almost benevolently, toward the telephone on the other side of the desk. I walked over and dialed the office number; Ruth answered immediately.

"We're just about to start in on more interrogation, but I'm being allowed to call you. First, how is everything? Are you all right?"

Surprised, Ruth said she was fine. She obviously couldn't understand why I was calling up to pass the time of day. I heard her shout at Jeff to pick up the extension.

"I want you to know that everything I was speculating about yesterday was on track."

"I understand," she replied. "I went to the embassy last night." Ruth made it clear that she had passed on my suggestion, which became known at the embassy as "Nick's proposal." We chatted for a few more minutes about personal matters before I had to hang up.

Naturally, Ruth couldn't give me the details just then, but later I learned that she and Jeff Trimble had been summoned to the embassy after midnight on Tuesday. President Reagan was preparing a negotiating position and had taken the unusual step of soliciting her opinion. One of the elements of the U.S. position was to press for the release of several well-known dissidents in exchange for Zakharov, an initiative suggested by the Enger-

Chernyayev-Crawford precedent. The president's list placed Andrei Sakharov at the top, then his wife, Yelena Bonner, followed by Yuri Orlov, Vladimir Slepak, and Ida Nudel. Ruth and Jeff noted that David Moiseyevich was not named and urged his inclusion high on the list.

Other developments, too, had been quietly taking place since Sunday's indictment. At the same time the formal charges were being made, Gorbachev dispatched a second, personal letter to Reagan, reinforcing the tough Soviet stance: "Daniloff has been involved in impermissible activities since 1982, and there is sufficient strong evidence of this." At the same time, the Soviet embassy in Washington was instructed to take soundings immediately of the Reagan administration's reaction to the formal charges. Moscow rushed through the indictment over a weekend, before Zakharov was arraigned in New York on September 9, to gain the initiative and induce Washington to bargain.

A colleague in Washington, John Wallach of the Hearst newspapers, received a call at home the Sunday of my indictment from a contact at the Soviet embassy. Wallach had been organizing a major Soviet-American people-to-people encounter — the Chautauqua Conference — to begin at Riga, Latvia, on Monday, September 15, and my arrest had thrown the project into question. Wallach played the role of middleman at a time when the U.S. side was refusing to talk directly with the Russians. After reassurance from the State Department, he told the Russians that a Soviet proposal for a dual release into custody would not be rejected out of hand. At the same time, he said that any final resolution would have to emphasize Zakharov's guilt and my innocence.

෧ ෧ ෧

That morning, lying on my cot, I had thought about Sergadeyev's concern at Ruth's passing on the message to the American embassy and sensed that the Soviet Union was casting around for ways to defuse the crisis. To my relief, the interrogation seemed to take on a new focus. What Moscow needed was ammunition to break down Washington's refusal to compromise, so Sergadeyev eased away from his harsh questioning and began eliciting help directly.

"You know, we can proceed in one of two ways," he said. "Either we find a political solution or we go the full course of a trial. Why don't you consider writing a letter to your president, asking for help?" I guessed he was receiving instructions from the Foreign Ministry. On several occasions during our last sessions in Lefortovo, a secretary had brought Sergadeyev large blue envelopes. He would sign for them in a ledger and open them in my presence. The way he folded the documents, I could see the inscription on the title page: "Ministry of Foreign Affairs, USSR — Secret."

At first, I wasn't enthusiastic about writing a letter. Such an appeal would almost certainly be perceived in the United States as being dictated under duress and might be instantly rejected.

"Let me think about it," I replied noncommittally.

Back in my cell that afternoon, I found Stas in an unusually talkative mood. After a lot of chitchat about his years at Moscow University, he came to the point. Soviet prisoners, he said, sometimes maneuver around their interrogator by appealing directly to the procuracy charged with overseeing the administration of justice. Shouldn't I consider drawing up such an appeal? Even better, perhaps I should write directly to my own president. The coincidence persuaded me that Stas was operating under instructions from the KGB; it also suggested that things were moving at last.

Alone in the bear cage that afternoon, I thought further about an appeal. Perhaps, after all, it could help unlock the diplomatic impasse if I could provide the two leaders with an excuse for softening their positions. The trick, I thought, was to address both leaders together. To Reagan, I would stress my innocence and the need to defuse the Soviet-American crisis. To Gorbachev, I would emphasize my health problems and humanitarian concerns in general. The more I thought about it, the more I believed I might actually possess the key to my own release. When the cry *otboi* echoed up and down the basement corridors Wednesday night, I crawled into bed still mulling over the best way to influence Reagan and Gorbachev.

✐ Seventeen

WHEN I AWOKE the next morning, Thursday, September 11, my thoughts returned to the letter to Gorbachev and Reagan. What had seemed like a good idea looked more dubious after a night's sleep. When I was called for interrogation that morning, I still hadn't decided what to do, and as I walked down the corridor to Room 215, I braced myself for pressure from Sergadeyev.

The colonel was waiting for me with a pile of typed protocols on his desk. With no mention of the letter, he asked me to go over my testimony. As I read and reread the questions and answers, he grew impatient. "You don't have to worry about my questions," he said, "just your answers."

"But I do worry about your questions," I replied, "because they're phrased in such a way as to make me look guilty even before I've answered them."

Sergadeyev looked at me with annoyance. "If you feel I am not being objective, you can request another interrogator. You know I am not the only one involved in this case. We are a team of three — myself, Major Cheredilov, and Captain Ivanov."

I did not particularly want to change interrogators in midstream. Better the devil you know . . . "I understand my right to change interrogators," I replied, "and I'll exercise it if I feel it's necessary."

We returned to the transcripts, and I persuaded Sergadeyev to rephrase one of his more egregious leading questions. As it was being retyped, we both signed the other pages. When we finished, Sergadeyev indicated that that would be all for the morning. "By the way," he asked casually as I was getting up to leave, "how are you progressing with the letter to your president?"

"I'm still thinking about it," I answered. I continued to ruminate about the letter, especially when I went out for a two-hour walk alone in the bear cage. That evening, when Stas and I had finished our supper, I decided, at last, to rough out a draft along the lines I had been thinking.

On Friday morning, I took my English version to the interrogation. Sergadeyev insisted that I translate it for him immediately. As I read it, I could see him scowl, and he began to twiddle his pencil.

"It's no good," he declared when I was done. His reaction disappointed me. I had hoped that he would forward the letter to the two leaders and it would improve my chances for release.

"How would you recommend I adjust it?" I asked.

"In the first place, eliminate all references to the general secretary," Sergadeyev snapped. "Second, stop calling it the so-called Daniloff affair."

He handed me some sheets of paper; I was being given a second chance. Sitting at the table, I contemplated my next step. It seemed clear that Sergadeyev would refuse to send any letter addressed to Gorbachev, so I had to decide whether to appeal to Reagan alone. I knew that many of his right-wing critics were urging him not to compromise. If I appealed to him, it would have to be very carefully composed so that it would strengthen his political hand at home.

I started to write, but the ball-point pen refused to work on the hard surface of the desk. Sergadeyev noted my difficulty and

handed me a soft file folder to press on. As I put it underneath
the paper, I noticed a handwritten note at the upper right-hand
corner which stopped me cold. It was the Russian family name
Suslov. Several months earlier, the Soviet press had carried a short
report about Ilya Suslov, a television commentator who had been
arrested and tried by a military court for passing secrets about
the space program to West German diplomats. Was Sergadeyev
trying to link me to a West German spy operation as well as an
American one? I tried to stop my imagination from running wild.
A totally meaningless action can sometimes cause a sudden rush
of panic in a prisoner. My mind was constantly running, desperately trying to stay a step ahead of my inquisitor, knowing
full well that the odds were stacked against me.

Forcing my voice to sound calm, I said, "I assume this folder
has nothing to do with me."

"Nothing to do with you," the colonel answered, expressionless.

Again, I tried to fucus on the letter. I finally decided to keep
it simple: to state my innocence and ask the president to help
resolve my case for the sake of Soviet-American relations. I skipped
over the dual release scenario that Sergadeyev was pressing; it
had been sufficiently promoted by Ruth. The more I thought
about the letter, the less I liked it.

As I passed the new draft to Sergadeyev, I told him it would
be a mistake to publish it. If he insisted on using it, I said, it
should go through diplomatic channels to Washington.

"Yes, you may be right." Sergadeyev seemed to agree. He laid
the paper on his desk and glanced up at the clock between the
windows. Several hours had gone by, and it was nearing lunch-
time.

"I'll see you later this afternoon," he said as I walked out the
door with the guard.

I spent all that Friday afternoon alone in the cell. Stas was
called away for an interrogation, which he predicted would be
his last. I sat on my cot in a state of high expectation, but my

summons never came. The hours ticked away, minute by minute. To help pass the time, I read, then paced. When the supper trolley trundled down the corridor, I knew it was about 5:00 P.M.

I had no idea why Sergadeyev had not called me, but I tried to be optimistic: either I was to be released or events were moving in that direction. To avoid becoming too hopeful, I told myself that I would probably spend a quiet weekend in Lefortovo; I tried to look forward to the Saturday shower. Then, after supper, I was unexpectedly dispatched to the bear cage.

వు వు వు

I was returned to the cell shortly before seven o'clock. A few minutes later, the *kormushka* snapped open; a guard pointed at me and growled, "Danilov, *na vyzov!*" Interrogation in the evening? What would force such a change in the routine?

As I marched to Room 215, I steeled myself. But no sooner did I enter the room than I realized there must have been a break in the case. The colonel was not alone. He had a guest, a stocky, middle-aged man with white hair, clearly some high official. This stranger motioned for me to sit down behind the tiny desk at which I had been indicted. I became tense and tried to anticipate my fate from the man's expression. Although he wore a dark suit, he did not appear forbidding; in fact, he seemed relaxed and in good humor.

"Gospodin Danilov," the stranger began formally, "at three o'clock this afternoon a political agreement was reached under which you will be released into the custody of your embassy. I would ask you to call the chargé d'affaires of your embassy, Mr. Combs, for details."

Outwardly, I hardly reacted. As before, I did not want to display emotion in front of my jailors. But inside my muscles suddenly unknotted and a flood of relief swept over me. Hoping that my voice was steady, I addressed the anonymous official in Soviet bureaucratese: "May I know with whom I have the honor of speaking?"

"It doesn't matter," he replied curtly, displaying that penchant for secrecy so deeply ingrained in Soviet officialdom.

I dialed the embassy: the line was busy. After a few more tries, I finally got through. Combs's secretary put me on hold; for a horrible moment, I thought he wasn't there. Finally, he came on the line and greeted me almost humorously, as though he got calls from Lefortovo every day. Without wasting time, he told me that the release was scheduled for eight o'clock that evening. Timing in diplomatic accords is as important as in a Bach fugue. I was to be released at the same moment that Zakharov was to be handed over to Soviet diplomats in New York. Combs then explained the conditions: I would be in his personal custody. My passport would be handed over to the Soviet authorities, and I could not leave the Soviet Union until both the Zakharov and Daniloff cases were resolved. Each day I would be obliged to call Sergadeyev to see if he needed me. I could live anywhere in Moscow and travel freely within a forty-kilometer radius of the center. "See you soon," Combs said as we hung up.

Turning to Sergadeyev, I said, "I have two requests. I would like to return to my cell to pick up my personal effects, and I would also like to say good-bye to the commandant."

"You will be allowed to do that," he said, "but I would ask you to give me your notebook and empty your pockets first." I laughed to myself at the thought of what he would find. I pulled out a dirty handkerchief from one pocket and a piece of crumpled toilet paper from the other — the same scrap on which Stas had explained integral calculus. Sergadeyev glanced at me suspiciously, then picked it up. He scrutinized the graph and curve carefully, as if hoping I had wheedled an important state secret out of Stas. A smile of triumph flashed across his face; he stepped over to the iron safe, unlocked it, and thrust the toilet paper and notebook into the files.

It was now about seven-thirty; there was plenty of time to return to the cell. I looked over at Sergadeyev for a signal, but neither he nor the other official moved. The three of us just sat there in awkward silence. I wondered why I had not been permitted to have a shave or shower. Allowing me to leave the prison unkempt and smelling terrible was a public relations snafu. Someone would be reprimanded, no doubt. But all I cared about was that I got out.

It was hard to believe. Was I really about to walk out of prison after fourteen days? I looked across at Sergadeyev. He sat there, smoking, his immobile face staring out the widow. I would have given anything to see inside his head. How was he going to describe his encounter with "the American spy" to his family and friends?

Just before eight, Sergadeyev looked at his watch and got up. "It's time to leave," he said, stubbing out his cigarette. The three of us walked to the door, turned right, and proceeded to the visitors room. Shortly after we arrived, Dick Combs and Ruth entered, smiling broadly. Ruth ran over to me, waving her arms victoriously above her head. "We've done it!" she shouted, ignoring Sergadeyev and the nameless official.

Sergadeyev shook hands with Combs stiffly. Combs handed over my blue U.S. passport and a letter outlining the conditions of my release. They exchanged a few polite words. Then the colonel motioned me to follow the guard to pick up my things. To my surprise, he did not take me back to my cell. Instead, he led me down a flight of stairs to a small cubicle, where I found Petrenko and a second guard waiting. All my belongings had been assembled and spread on a table. Each item — the four Decembrist books, my wallet, the severed shoelaces, my belt and watch, and pieces of salami, bread, and cheese — was checked off. To my delight, the guards ahd overlooked some notes I had hidden between the pages of the books.

"Please write on this paper," said one of the guards with exquisite courtesy: " 'I have received all my possessions and I have no complaints.' "

Everything seemed to be there; it wasn't until a few days later that I realized Sergadeyev had confiscated the slip of paper with the telephone number of my Russian friend (who subsequently emigrated). It was another instance of bureaucratic carelessness or deceit which I had not been sharp enough to catch at the time.

I looked up at Petrenko. "Alexander Mitrofanovich," I said, "I have forty-three rubles in my wallet. Why don't you take them and buy some more books for the prison library?"

He seemed rather pleased, and for a moment he looked as if he would accept.

"Go on," I urged him. "Take the money. Other prisoners will appreciate the books it will buy."

Petrenko wavered, then firmly said, "No." I understood. He could not accept a gift from an "American spy," especially not in front of two guards.

"Well, at least give my food to my cellmate," I said. "He will be able to use it."

"Yes," Petrenko replied, "that is the custom. The departing prisoner leaves his food behind for the others."

I held out my hand to Petrenko, and he extended his. Suddenly I was filled with warm feelings for this man who had brought welcome relief into my prison existence. In a strange way, he personified both the good and bad in the Russian character which Baboota had talked about so often. As he took my hand, I remembered his words about the Elbe and turned the handshake into a Russian bear hug. Psychologists may claim I was succumbing to Stockholm syndrome, but I was not embracing my jailor so much as the kindly veteran of World War II with a fondness for Americans.

The guard and I turned and walked out the door; we marched silently back to the visitors room, where Ruth, Combs, Sergadeyev and the nameless official were waiting. After the colonel explained when I should call him every morning, we all shook hands stiffly. Then I picked up my things and we walked out the door, accompanied by a guard. We proceeded along the corridor, descended the stairs to the glassed-in booth guarding the gate. I could feel the surge of freedom taking over. My spirits began to soar.

"You're only half free," Ruth whispered to me, sensing I might succumb to euphoria. "Now the really hard part begins. Never forget you were kidnapped and you're still a hostage."

As we stepped over the prison threshold into the cool night air, several KGB photographers in the courtyard began taking pictures. I thought at first they were the American press, but Ruth pulled me back; she knew that Soviet policemen had barricaded the street to prevent the press from getting near the prison. She slipped a camera out of her purse and shot back, blinding the KGB photographers momentarily with her flash. Not wanting any trouble, Combs hustled us into his sleek black Cadillac. As the chauffeur started the engine, I stole a look at my watch. It was 8:47 P.M.

෴ ෴ ෴

The tension of two weeks dropped away; the lethargy that had dogged me in prison evaporated. I was ready to jump out of the car and celebrate with the American and West European press corps gathered at the end of the street. I owed them an enormous debt. They had kept the story alive, they had supported Ruth, and it was largely thanks to them that I was out of Lefortovo.

The reporters let out a roar as the limousine, with an American flag fluttering on its right fender, reached the spot where they had been ordered to wait. Several Soviet policemen and plainclothesmen were watching from the side. As the car drew to a halt, I jumped out, still rallying my thoughts. I explained — first in English, then in French for a TV correspondent from Paris — the terms of the release, thanking both Gorbachev and Reagan for their good sense. I also noted that I was not yet completely free: "I've changed one hotel for a better hotel . . ."

During the ride to the embassy, Ruth speculated about options for resolving the affair. But I was so relieved to be out of prison,

I did not want to focus on political reality. "Being a prisoner in the U.S. embassy is fine," I quipped. "I can easily stay here till Christmas, doing research on my book about Frolov and the Decembrists." Combs and Ruth looked shocked. They understood better than I did at that moment how important it was to keep political pressure on the two superpowers.

Both Ruth and I wanted to return to our apartment on Leninsky Prospekt and have dinner with the Trimbles and Hank Trewhitt, my foreign editor and an old friend who had flown in a few hours earlier to argue for my release. But Combs talked us out of it: the press would be clamoring for interviews. At first I resisted, for I didn't want to hold out on my colleagues. Still, we all understood the need for a low profile while Moscow and Washington worked out a solution. Combs offered us a guest room for the night, and in the end we accepted.

Almost as soon as we entered the embassy, Combs said he wanted to talk to us in "the bubble." Ruth and I followed him and sat down around the oblong table. He asked me to describe the interrogation, particularly the sequence concerning Father Roman. I was about to recount Sergadeyev's outlandish claims — his assertion that Stombaugh telephoned Roman, the phony letter from Stombaugh — when Ruth interrupted, her voice shaking with anger. "Don't tell him anything, Nick!" she shouted. "You know where he is going to send it and why he wants it. Believe me, those people have done you enough harm already. You don't have to tell them anything!"

I did not understand what she was talking about or why she was so upset.

Then Ruth dropped the shocker: the Stombaugh letter was real. Real! Not a forgery at all! Stombaugh had really telephoned Roman, had said he was a friend of mine, even though we had never met. The CIA station had shamelessly used me without my knowledge. The embassy had admitted everything to Ruth, but she had never breathed a word of it to me in prison for fear of undermining my morale.

My head reeled. I could hardly believe what I was hearing. After my warnings to Benson and Kamman, how could the CIA have walked straight into an obvious trap? How could they have dragged me in? I had brought Roman's letter to the embassy, suspecting it was a provocation and wanting to protect myself. What a fool I had been not to burn it. I struggled to put the whole disastrous affair in perspective. I was arrested because the KGB needed a hostage, and the CIA played straight into their hands.

I stumbled out of "the bubble" in a daze and followed Combs back to his office. He sat me down in a leather chair and handed me a beer. Then he placed several calls to the United States, and I spoke at length with Dave Gergen and Mort Zuckerman at the magazine. We tried to get through to President Reagan, but he was en route by helicopter to Camp David.

Before the eveing was over, there was one more bizarre twist — this one a crazy connection with Frolov. Before going to bed, I thought I should check in with the embassy doctors, so I asked Combs for his name.

"Why, Dr. Wolfe, of course," he said. "Dr. Stanley Wolfe." It was the Anglicized surname of Frolov's prison mentor, Dr. Volf.

That night I went to bed in my prison underwear because Ruth had forgotten to bring my pajamas. She complained that I reeked of Lefortovo even inside the embassy, a reminder that my fate was not yet settled. I slept much worse that first night in the embassy than the last night in prison. The CIA revelations kept jangling about in my head.

෨ ෨ ෨

I never thought I would like living inside the U.S. embassy compound. During my years covering the Soviet Union, I had largely avoided this "little America" on the other side of the iron gates on Tchaikovsky Boulevard. In many ways, it was a small, incestuous community that sought refuge from Soviet reality in its cocktail parties, marine dances and broom ball games. But for the next seventeen days, I found comfort in listening to the American voices in the courtyard, sipping coffee in the snack bar, and having a drink with diplomatic friends. I left the compound occasionally to go jogging or visit the *U.S. News* office across town. As a precaution, Dick Combs or another diplomat would usually accompany me. The one time I drove to the office by myself I got caught in a traffic jam, causing people at both ends to think the KGB was harassing me.

I was still a hostage, however, and I was reminded of my status every morning at ten, when I called Sergadeyev. At first our conversations were rather stilted, but as the days went by he seemed to relax a bit. He asked how I was occupying myself, whether I was jogging regularly. He even joked that he was relieved I had not departed "independently." He never did call me back for more questioning. If he had, the FBI would have summoned Zakharov immediately, and the Soviets wanted to avoid that.

But the KGB was not yet through with me, and during my stay at the embassy, I had a sense of being under constant attack, as false accusations continued to appear in the Soviet press. What a way to end an assignment! I had spent so much of my professional life covering Soviet-American affairs, and now it was unlikely that I would be able to continue. I was particularly sickened by the claim of a Foreign Ministry spokesman, Gennadi Gerasimov, that a trip I had made to a Soviet nuclear power station at Novo-Voronezh in June 1983 had been a spying expedition. Fortunately, Dick Combs's attitude, a mixture of humor and combativeness, helped to put these lies and innuendoes in a more balanced light. "Never forget," he would say, "this is a political case, not a legal one."

Within a few days of my release from Lefortovo, it became clear that a battle was raging in Washington. The hard-liners in Congress and the Justice Department were eager to try Zakharov; the pragmatists in the State Department and the National Security

Council wanted some kind of political compromise along the lines of the Enger-Chernyayev-Crawford case. This precedent worried me in one respect: Crawford had been placed on trial in Moscow and found guilty. That was something I was determined to resist, especially since the CIA had handed the Soviets evidence on a plate. I was innocent and wanted the charges dropped unconditionally. Combs and I made this clear to the State Department in a classified cable sent on Monday, September 15, in which we also urged that Goldfarb be part of any deal.

Ruth and I decided that if there was a trial, we would do everything in our power to turn it into a farce. We marshaled material to rebut Soviet allegations and wrote a press statement, to be released later, denouncing the proceedings. We decided that I would refuse point blank to go to any courthouse, even if it meant being arrested by the embassy marines and handed over bodily to the KGB. I announced that decision "to the walls" and spoke about it over international phone lines, which the Soviets could monitor.

It soon became apparent that Washington would insist on some form of trial for Zakharov. On September 9, he had been indicted on espionage charges, and American legal procedure required that the process be concluded. This determination to try Zakharov was confirmed the evening of September 16, at a dinner party at Dick Combs's apartment in honor of a visiting White House official. Combs had invited half a dozen other embassy officers, mostly from the political section. After chatting for a while, the subject of my case was raised. "What do you care if you are put through a trial in a Mickey Mouse court in Moscow as long as you are released later?" the White House official said. It was a flip comment that ignored the implications to me personally and to U.S.-Soviet relations in general. I did not want to live the rest of my life with the stigma of a spy conviction, even from a court in Moscow. His remark irritated me, but I held my tongue.

After we moved to the dining room and sat down, someone

mentioned the CIA's letter to Father Roman. This time I could not contain my anger. "I want you all to know," I broke in heatedly, "that I consider the dragging of my name into this operation to have been amateurish and unconscionable. When I return to Washington, I am going to dig into this opration and get to the bottom of it!"

A stunned silence fell over the dinner table.

"You are absolutely right," the White House visitor finally conceded.

ഗ ഗ ഗ

Meanwhile, every morning we listened anxiously to the BBC, and every afternoon we scanned the news reports for evidence from Washington that progress was being made in solving the Zakharov-Daniloff case. The signs were contradictory. On September 18, during a walkabout in a provincial town, Gorbachev claimed that I was "a spy caught red-handed." It sounded ominous, but I interpreted it as another political tit for tat: on September 8, in Denver, President Reagan had called Zakharov "a spy caught red-handed."

The Reagan administration saw the affair as an excellent excuse to decapitate the KGB's operations in the United States. In recent years, Soviet spying activities had climbed to massive proportions in America and seemed totally independent from diplomatic efforts to improve relations. In March 1986, Washington had ordered Moscow to reduce its mission at the United Nations, which was a major center for espionage. The confrontation over the issue had been growing increasingly tense. On September 12, the Soviet ambassador, Sergei Belogonov, declared the cuts illegal and said he would not make them, further infuriating the White House.

I waited nervously for the meeting between Secretary Shultz and Foreign Minister Shevardnadze, which was scheduled for September 18. If they failed to unravel my case, I feared a breakdown in Soviet-American relations, which could result in my being tried and sent back to prison. The day began ominously. As Shevardnadze flew from New York to Washington, the Reagan administration ordered the expulsion of twenty-five Soviets from the country — just the beginning of an aggressive house cleaning that would continue in stages until April 1988. The administration supplied the Russians with the names of the Soviet personnel being ordered to leave. They included intelligence chiefs in Washington, New York, and San Francisco, their deputies, counterintelligence officers, communications experts, cipher clerks — and eventually the list mounted to eighty key agents in all.

Shevardnadze learned of the expulsions shortly after his plane landed and was visibly irritated when he reached Shultz's office. Shultz spirited him off to the White House so that he could see for himself how angry Reagan was. Negotiations came to an impasse almost immediately. Shevardnadze had come with very limited instructions. If the United States would not agree to swapping Daniloff for Zakharov, he was authorized to say that the next step should be a trial. Then negotiations could continue for a one-for-one swap. But the expulsions made it clear that Reagan was unwilling to accept a straight swap. Shevardnadze was forced to cable Moscow for further instructions.

A major problem was the Zakharov trial. Reagan, unlike Gorbachev, does not have the authority to interfere in the judicial process once it has begun, so he could not turn it off. The logjam began to break when someone on the American side — a number of people claimed credit for the idea — came up with a legal facesaver: Zakharov could change his plea from "not guilty" to "nolo contendere"; in other words, a plea that does not dispute the charges but avoids the words "guilty." A nolo plea would give the federal court in New York the chance to subject Zakharov to a brief nonjury trial, find him guilty, and expel him. The compromise would satisfy Justice and FBI officials, who had sufficient evidence to convict him. But the Soviets were not familiar with the nolo plea, which does not exist in Soviet law.

The State Department's legal adviser, Abraham Sofaer, tried to explain the plea to Soviet diplomats in Washington. At the same time Armand Hammer, on his own initiative, flew from Los Angeles to Moscow to explain the option. He arrived late on the afternoon of September 23 and rushed immediately to Communist Party headquarters. Anatoly Dobrynin received him and insisted strongly that White House ideologues had manipulated and misled the president. Daniloff was a spy, he said, and the Soviet authorities had more than enough evidence to prove it. Hammer stated his conviction that I was not engaged in espionage and assured Dobrynin that an arrangement could be worked out to satisfy both sides. Since Dobrynin, too, was unfamiliar with the nolo plea, Hammer offered to write to Gorbachev personally.

The next afternoon, at about four o'clock, Hammer received a call from Dobrynin. "Mission accomplished," said the party secretary. "You can go home. The general secretary has only one question: 'Where does Dr. Hammer get his energy?' " Hammer was back in the United States only thirty-nine hours after leaving California, confident that my case would be resolved.

Meanwhile, Shultz and Shevardnadze continued their meetings, moving the venue from Washington to New York where the annual meeting of the U.N. General Assembly was in session. The radio reports we received in Moscow were cryptic, suggesting that progress, if any, was slow in coming. We crossed our fingers and hoped. Finally, late Sunday night, September 28, Shultz and Shevardnadze agreed on the final terms.

I would be released unconditionally: the Soviets would drop the charges; there would be no trial; my valid multiple-entry visa would be returned; no protocol banning my return to the Soviet Union would be drawn up. After I left Moscow, Zakharov would plead nolo contendere before the U.S. District Court for the Eastern District of New York, which could be expected to find him guilty. In addition, the Soviets agreed to pay a premium by releasing Yuri Orlov, the former leader of the Helsinki Watch Committee who had been imprisoned for seven years, and by allowing

Goldfarb and about ten other Soviet citizens suffering from serious illness to seek treatment in the West.

And there was a final bit of high politics: the Iceland summit. Throughout 1986, Gorbachev had urged Reagan to agree to a small-scale summit about a ban on nuclear tests. Reagan had held out for a full-fledged meeting in Washington. Now, to wash away the bad publicity, both sides agreed to the smaller meeting in ten days' time. The two superpowers had stepped back from an ugly confrontation in hopes of making a breakthrough in relations.

I did not hear of the agreement until many hours later, but the BBC broadcasts over the weekend and that Monday morning had put me in an expectant mood. The tone of my conversations with Sergadeyev seemed to confirm my optimism. I kept notes of our last conversations. On one day, he had volunteered, "Your affairs are moving right along . . . *Vashi dela idut, idut.*" Then, to my amazement, on September 26 he asked me for the latest copy of *U.S. News and World Report,* "the one devoted to our common problem." I told him that if he really needed it for his work, he should contact the Foreign Ministry. I suspected what he really wanted was a souvenir of our encounter.

"Well, all right, if it's not possible . . . *Yesli ne vozmozhno, nu ladno,*" he replied. I could feel the disappointment in his voice.

On the morning of September 29, I called Sergadeyev for what turned out to be the last time. Once again, he said he would not be needing me that day. "I'll call you again tomorrow," I replied. Those were my final words to him.

Sensing that a resolution could come at any moment, I began winding up the details of our Moscow stay. I paid my outstanding Soviet income taxes (3151.57 rubles; about $4,400) at a savings bank and received a written receipt, duly stamped, in return. In the end I decided against paying a surprise call on my Soviet cousin, Svetlana Algazina, who I knew had a weak heart. To be confronted by a cousin who had been denounced by the Soviet press as a CIA spy might cause her to have a heart attack.

I also decided to make one last visit to Frolov's grave that

Monday forenoon. The day was bleak and raw; winter was already approaching, and yellow leaves were swirling around the graves. I bought some chrysanthemums from a sidewalk vendor and walked slowly down the tree-lined alley. I realized it was now my turn to be exiled, to say farewell to Frolov and all of Russia. It was like saying good-bye to a member of the family I would never see again, like Grandpa Makarov's salute to the Frolov wagon as it turned around the bend and left Siberia forever. The bones had become flesh and blood for me. I had the KGB to thank for allowing me to appreciate Frolov's life fully. After being in prison, I understood his struggles in ways I had never dreamed of when I stood at the grave listening to Svyatoslav Alexandrovich recite his verse. And I saw ever more clearly the links that chained his life to mine. If Frolov had not been a Decembrist, I would never have become fascinated by his story; if I had not extended my search for him, I would not have been arrested and imprisoned. If Frolov had overcome Siberia, I would not be standing in Vagankovskoye Cemetery on this day. Two lives, I mused as I placed the flowers on his grave, but only one Russia; one Russia, cruel and generous ...

I was back at the embassy by one o'clock and half an hour later received a call from Dick Combs. The deal was cut: we were to leave in three hours, taking the evening plane to West Germany, spending the night in Frankfurt, and flying to Washington on September 30. I tried to extract the terms of the agreement from Combs, but he refused to tell me. Our departure was to be a secret so that President Reagan, campaigning for Republicans in the congressional elections, could make the dramatic announcement at a stop in Kansas.

The journalist in me balked at keeping the news from my Moscow colleagues. Suspecting that something was about to break, they kept bombarding the embassy with calls. Ruth said it was unfair not to tell them when we were leaving. I agreed; I also wanted the press at the airport to record my final statement to the government that had caused me so much agony over the past month. As soon as we learned the time of our departure, Ruth arranged a leak, though she needn't have bothered. TV crews were staking out the embassy, and at about four-thirty, as the portcullis of the auto exit went up to let our van out, I saw a group of correspondents outside on the sidewalk, waving us on our way.

It was dusk. A light snow was falling and turning to slush on the potholed streets. The passersby were bundled up, looking as sour as ever, as they jostled each other on the slippery sidewalks. Seeing Moscow at its worst reminded me of a comment Serge Schmemann of the *New York Times* had made after we had seen a brilliant one-man show by the actor Alexander Philippenko several months earlier. "When you see something as good as that," said Serge, who, like me, was coming to the end of his assignment, "it almost makes you wish they would pull something nasty against you to make it easier to leave." They had pulled something nasty, but I still had mixed feelings about leaving. There were so many things I would miss.

We arrived at the airport, and a crowd of colleagues surrounded Ruth and me on the sidewalk. I expressed my thanks for all their concern and said I was leaving more in sorrow than in anger. Then I pulled out a famous poem by Mikhail Lermontov. It was written in exile, and every Soviet schoolchild learns it and associates it with tyranny:

> Farewell unwashed Russia,
> Land of slaves, land of lords,
> And you, blue police uniforms,
> And you, the people bound to them.
> Perhaps behind the ridge of the Caucasus
> I will be able to hide from your pashas,

> From their all-seeing eyes,
> From their all-hearing ears.

I handed the poem to Gary Lee of the *Washington Post* and asked him to share it with the Moscow press corps. Then I took Ruth's hand, and together we walked toward the gate.

✍ Afterword

Two years have passed since my arrest by the KGB. Looking back at the international uproar, I have concluded that I was the victim not only of KGB banditry but of blunders in Washington as well. For the Soviet Union to take a hostage to obtain the release of one of its citizens is a violation of international law and civilized behavior. However, for the United States to arrest a minor Soviet spy at a crucial moment in Soviet-American relations is diplomatic myopia. After returning to the States, I tried to find answers to some of the questions that had troubled me in Lefortovo and afterward.

Why did the FBI arrest Gennadi Zakharov, a Soviet physicist assigned to the U.N. secretariat, just weeks before an expected summit? From the FBI's point of view, the arrest was justifiable. Since his arrival in New York in 1982, Zakharov had aggressively sought out students, traveled to campuses, developed friendships, and urged his contacts to seek careers in the U.S. defense industry. He recruited and ran four student agents, including Leakh Bhoge from Guyana. One student quit after the Soviet Union shot down

KAL's Flight 007, but Bhoge agreed to become an FBI double agent.

By actually running agents, Zakharov stepped over an invisible line. Usually, Soviet agents without diplomatic immunity do not undertake such active intelligence operations. Instead, they conduct lesser activities like "spotting," identifying Americans who could be developed into Soviet agents.

"Zakharov was a hustler, more interested in quantity than quality," one Justice Department official told me. Zakharov met with Bhoge thirty-five times over three years; paid him a total of $6,000 for increasingly sensitive information (he was carrying a receipt for $1,000 signed by Bhoge when he was arrested); had Bhoge write out an espionage contract by hand on May 10, 1986, promising to obtain classified information for the Soviet Union during a ten-year period.

Apart from wanting to teach the KGB a lesson, the FBI was also anxious to make a political point in the United States. The American intelligence community had been smarting over a series of disasters that became known in 1985 — the leak of highly secret information from the National Security Agency to the Soviet Union through Ronald Pelton; the John Walker–Jerry Whitworth spy ring in the U.S. Navy which was finally busted after seventeen years of operation, and the devastating defection to Moscow of a deep cover CIA operative, Edward Lee Howard. Well before the first Reagan-Gorbachev meeting in Geneva in November 1985, the president made it clear that he wanted the KGB cut down to size.

When President Reagan left Washington for a West Coast holiday in August 1986, the FBI was hardly operating out of control, as some people have speculated. The Bureau contacted the relevant government agencies, including the White House, State Department, CIA, Defense Department, with requests for approval to detain Zakharov. Perhaps the FBI exaggerated Zakharov's importance; it would be difficult for any government agency to second-guess the FBI on such a matter. In any event, the State Department reported to the Justice Department on August 21, 1986, "There is no foreign policy objection" to the proposed arrest.

Here the judgment of foreign policy professionals can be faulted. Although officials realized that the Zakharov arrest might precipitate retaliation in Moscow, they assumed it would be aimed at an American businessman and could be worked out without too much bother. They failed to consider that the Soviet Union was courting U.S. businessmen and in mid-August adopted new rules on joint ventures with overseas investors. No one apparently foresaw that a journalist might be arrested. In retrospect, it might have been more sensible to string Zakharov along a bit longer or ask the Soviet ambassador to have him removed. On August 22, 1986, the FBI laid out its case before a U.S. magistrate in Brooklyn and obtained search and arrest warrants. The next day, two FBI agents, posing as lovers, pounced on Zakharov on a New York subway platform after Bhoge gave him the Soviet classified documents supplied by the FBI. During his initial interrogation, Zakharov broke down, fearing that the FBI would arrest his wife, Tatyana, and his daughter, Irina, who were expected from Moscow the next day. He tried to get out of his predicament by offering to be a double agent in Moscow. The FBI refused, and he was confined in New York's Metropolitan Correctional Center.

The superpower confrontation might still have been averted if the Soviet embassy had not slipped up when Zakharov's American lawyers tried to get their client released to the custody of the Soviet ambassador. Ambassador Yuri Dubinin, who had only recently taken up his post in Washington, failed to elicit State Department support for the custody request. Without such official U.S. backing, the New York court was unwilling to let Zakharov out of jail.

The incentive for Moscow to retaliate was now very great. The KGB was concerned that Zakharov might betray operational secrets to the FBI and that his physical safety in the MCC, where several prominent underworld characters were being held, might be in danger.

Who gave the order for my arrest, Gorbachev or a lesser official? My information is that Anatoly Dobrynin and Alexander Yakovlev, high party officials and foreign policy advisers to Gorbachev, approved retaliation; the choice of the target was up to the KGB. Regardless, the KGB, like the FBI, received political approval before acting. Gorbachev, who was on vacation, was informed and did not dissent. This followed the pattern of the Barghoorn case, in which Leonid Brezhnev, the number two man, endorsed the professor's arrest in the absence of Khrushchev, then informed the party leader, who was on vacation.

I believe that Gorbachev saw Zakharov's arrest as one more American provocation and wanted to strike back hard. The KGB used every opportunity to make my situation appear the mirror image of Zakharov's. The method of my arrest was probably designed to imitate Zakharov's. To reinforce its credibility, the KGB argued that my arrest had nothing to do with Zakharov and was ordered on its merits. If they could sustain that argument, they figured they had a good chance of negotiating a one-for-one swap, as in the Sjeklocha case of 1972. Here, of course, sloppy CIA work with "Father Roman" played into their hands.

Why did the CIA's Moscow station make contact with Roman when evidence indicated that he was a KGB provocateur? I believe the answer lies in the pressure the CIA director, William Casey, was putting on his station chiefs in the Soviet Union and Eastern Europe to sign up new agents. The Casey policy followed the deemphasis on human intelligence which occurred during the Carter administration. "Father Roman" offered an opening: he had transmitted a letter, whose handwriting was identical to that of a dissident scientist who had communicated with the CIA "over the transom" several years earlier. That first letter contained diagrams and a handwritten account of new Soviet rocket technology, a subject of constant interest to U.S. intelligence. According to Washington officials, this first letter led to a few furtive contacts in Moscow between CIA operatives and the scientist's courier. The author of the letter was never precisely identified and eventually dropped out of sight. It seems likely to me that the initial letter was also a KGB scheme, designed to flush out the CIA in Moscow. Or, if the first letter was genuine, it is probable that the author was uncovered by the KGB, which forced him to work under their control.

Undoubtedly, the CIA's Moscow station knew that the contact with Roman was risky. However, if the dissident scientist turned out to be genuine, the payoff could be another Colonel Penkovsky or Adolf Tolkachov. If the contact failed, nothing much was lost. The worst that could happen was that the CIA agent making the contact might be caught and expelled, which indeed did happen.

Why Natirboff and Stombaugh used my name when they contacted Roman will probably never be satisfactorily answered. It was unnecessary. Various U.S. officials with whom I have spoken, including Secretary of State Shultz, agreed the CIA was sloppy. Stombaugh, a former FBI employee who transferred to the CIA, had only slight experience in Moscow. Natirboff, an experienced professional, should have known better.

A CIA weakness in Moscow is its use of obscure junior personnel in high-risk operations who are no match for the KGB. The idea behind this ploy is that these junior officers are hard for the KGB to identify because they do not have a long working history. This policy really backfired in assigning Edward Lee Howard, a mentally unstable sometime drug abuser, to go to Moscow to handle Tolkachov, one of the most important agents the CIA ever had in Moscow.

By comparison, the Soviet secret police, operating on home ground, is highly skilled. The KGB has had considerable success in penetrating NATO embassies in Moscow over the years. Between 1981 and 1986, the KGB bugged the electric typewriters in the American embassy; seduced at least one U.S. Marine; traced the movements of other American officials with "spy dust," and planted bugs in the structural materials of the new U.S. Embassy building. Its attack on other Western embassies was no less impressive: KGB counterintelligence taped into the communications equipment at the French embassy and seduced the code clerk at the Belgian embassy.

Will the Soviets make any more retaliatory arrests? After the propaganda fallout of the last one, I believe they will think twice before taking another hostage. However, there is no guarantee against its happening again as long as Soviet judicial organs can be manipulated by the KGB or the Kremlin. True, Mikhail Gorbachev is turning his attention to reforming the Soviet legal system and making it more fair. The criminal and procedural codes are currently being revised. And there is talk about allowing defendants to have access to legal counsel once an indictment has been handed down (but not from the moment of arrest). What is lacking is a strong commitment to make the Soviet judiciary truly independent. The Communist Party wishes to remain the leading force in Soviet society and does not contemplate sharing its power with other independent branches of government.

I also believe that a retaliatory arrest could occur again because of the continuing pressure on the KGB to conduct major industrial and technological espionage in the United States. Despite Gorbachev's reforms, the Soviet economy will lag behind the postindustrial West for the foreseeable future. In sum, Soviet espionage in America will continue, and more spies will be caught by the FBI.

Observers should ask whether the policy of arresting a spy without diplomatic immunity and insisting on prosecution is sensible in a period of improving relations with the Soviet Union. Under the Nixon administration, such cases were often handled discretely. But beginning with Ford, and especially under Carter, the decision was made to take strong legal action. Much will depend on whether Soviet espionage eases off or remains at today's levels.

Many people have asked how could my arrest occur under

glasnost? The question itself betrays a semantic misunderstanding. *Glasnost* is not a political reform policy, nor does it provide a guarantee against arbitrary arrest. *Glasnost* is a media management policy; it is permission for journalists and the public to speak more honestly about troublesome issues. Nonetheless, *glasnost* did play a small, and welcome, role in my story. The Soviets were anxious to show the world, especially in the second week of my detention, that they were treating me well. I had three meetings with Ruth, one with Mort Zuckerman, and several phone calls — much more outside contact than a Soviet prisoner would be accorded. When Professor Barghoorn was arrested in 1963, he was thrown into solitary and held incommunicado; the American embassy was not even informed of his arrest. Undoubtedly, Zakharov's prison conditions in New York played a role, too. The Soviets were not anxious for Lefortovo to be compared unfavorably with the MCC in New York.

Not only could Zakharov telephone out at will, he received visits from his lawyers before and after his indictment. His meetings were not monitored by the prison authorities; he was not interrogated by the FBI after the initial questioning; he was informed fully of his legal rights under the *Miranda* rule. He could fraternize with fellow prisoners in the lounge or exercise center; he could inform himself of the legalities of his case by consulting the law library on his floor. He had continual access to television and newspapers and was well aware of the worldwide attention focused on the Zakharov-Daniloff case. He was allowed to shower and shave every day and could choose from five different menus — mainline, vegetarian, low-sodium, diabetic, and bland.

What counsel can I offer reporters going to Moscow? I hesitate to offer advice; a long list of dos and don't would only serve to intimidate new correspondents and play into the hands of the KGB. For reporters working in Moscow, the KGB is a fact of life which will continue as long as superpower adversity exists. Unfortunately, American correspondents must cope with the KGB in the same way that Soviet correspondents must deal with the FBI. The major difference is that the FBI is ultimately constrained by law; the same cannot yet be said of the KGB.

Of course, correspondents going to Moscow should be aware of the dangers just as they should if they were going to the Middle East. Preparation for the assignment should include a greater familiarity with the Soviet criminal and procedural codes than I had. The main thing to remember is: you are not obliged by Soviet law to answer questions (Article 46) nor are you obliged to sign documents (142). Not that a knowledge of Soviet law is any real protection, but the familiarity will serve as helpful reinforcement in intimidating situations. The American embassy, too, should improve its acquaintance with Soviet law, making sure it has a copy of the RSFSR procedural code in its library the next time an American citizen is arrested.

As for myself, my Lefortovo experience has not changed my views of the Soviet Union. The Soviet people are generous and talented and deserve a more responsive government than the one they have. I personally wish Mikhail Gorbachev success with his reforms. He is by far the most interesting leader to appear in Russia since the 1920s. Of course, I would like to see him turn his attention to reforming the KGB, as Nikita Khrushchev did. But I doubt he will do it soon, since he depends on this powerful agency for support. With its vast network of informers and military forces, greater than the U.S. Marine Corps, the KGB represents a repressive and divisive force in Soviet life.

What has happened to the major actors on the Moscow end of the Zakharov-Daniloff affair? I can report the following from sources in Moscow:

• Misha Luzin dropped out of sight entirely. When I got back to the United States, I compared notes with an American diplomat about a Misha Kuznetsov whom he and his daughter met in the Ala-Too Hotel in Frunze in July 1980. Misha Kuznetsov's physical description and initial pitch were similar to Misha Luzin's, which leaves me with the suspicion they were one and the same.

All I can say is that if Misha Luzin was a KGB plant from the beginning, he deserves the promotion he has undoubtedly received.

• Stas Zenin. I have no idea what happened to him. I shall continue to believe he was a real prisoner, acting on KGB instructions in jail, until I meet an authority who can demonstrate otherwise.

• Father Roman, or at least a man who identified himself as Father Roman, reappeared in December 1986, after I had left Moscow. He called the Associated Press bureau, asking if he could examine the news reports that cited his name. The bureau chief, Andrew Rosenthal, refused. This curious episode clearly suggests that Roman faced no trial for treason; there was no reason why he should.

• Colonel Sergadeyev did not immediately end the investigation into my case, despite the Soviet-American agreement resolving the Zakharov-Daniloff crisis. He continued to interview witnesses, largely, I believe, to gather material for a counterpunch if I should come out with an "anti-Soviet" book. I learned that Sergadeyev bluffed to one witness that there was "an understanding with the United States" that I would be sent back to the Soviet Union one day to be tried and sentenced. Following that report, I wrote to Procurator-General Alexander Rekunkov of the USSR in October 1987, asking whether the case was still active. The Soviet Foreign Ministry informed me orally, in November 1987, that the case was closed; they reconfirmed this in writing to the State Department in March 1988. So far I have not received the closing document in accordance with Article 209 of the procedural code.

• Paul Stombaugh was promoted from Class 4 Foreign Service officer to Class 3 in October 1986, apparently in recognition of his willingness to risk arrest in case the Roman contact failed.

• Murat Natirboff was brought back to Washington under a cloud and given a job on the staff of the director for central intelligence, coordinating activities throughout the U.S. intelligence community. His long experience in Eastern Europe and the Soviet Union is said to be appreciated.

• The Soviet Union announced on October 22, 1987, that Adolf Tolkachov had been executed for high treason.

∽ ∽ ∽

Looking back at my experience, I continue to feel more sorrow than anger. It seems unlikely that I will be able to return to Moscow to complete my search for Frolov's descendants. However, there have been so many unexpected changes under Gorbachev that one can never be sure. Despite my hasty departure, I have been able to tie up a few loose ends of family history.

Frolov's older son, Nikolai, was promoted to major general in 1901 and commanded the artillery arsenals of the Moscow, Odessa, and later the Amur district. At some time — records and memories are unclear — he abandoned Baboota's mother and fathered an illegitimate child. He retired in 1907 but returned to active service in World War I; he died of typhoid fever in about 1920. His two legitimate sons, Alexander and Gavriil, both served in the military briefly but finally broke with tradition and went into the theater. Alexander, who died in 1942, was associated with the Bolshoi Theater as a set designer; Gavriil was a member of the Moscow Art Theater and other troupes; he died in 1947.

Peter Frolov's military career was the family's most impressive. He was promoted to major general in 1894 and served as acting chief of the Kiev military district before being named a member of the national military council in St. Petersburg. In 1915, he was appointed commander of the St. Petersburg military district; in 1916, he became an aide to War Minister Vladimir Soukhomlinov, and in 1917 he was named to the State Council, the upper house of the Russian parliament. General Frolov retired after forty-nine years of active service in 1918. Lenin allowed him, as the son of a Decembrist, to retain the family *dacha* at Issar, south of Yalta, for his lifetime. Peter lived there with Nadejda and Sasha

Manganari until unknown assailants stabbed him to death in October 1919.

Nadejda continued to live at the Ben-Djanym estate until she broke her hip and died in about 1930. She was buried on the grounds, next to her favorite brother, Peter, of whom she used to say "We are two birch trees growing from a single root." According to a note I found in the archives, the estate was taken over by the Soviet airlines sanatorium, and in 1950 a neighbor saw a bulldozer level the two Frolov graves to make space for a football field.

As for Sasha, he almost vanished, too. At the Decembrist exhibition at the Pushkin Museum in December 1985, I discovered that Baboota's brother Alexander had a stepson still living in Moscow. I visited this gentleman, a literary critic, who showed me a folder of drawings, including some of Manganari's engravings, which he had rescued after the war from a steamer trunk. "I remember him," he told me. "He often came to dinner. He wore his hair long, and we used to call him Karl Marx. He was a curious person, distinctive because he limped so badly."

Sasha's own end remains mysterious. One version claims that he was arrested for killing his mother and died in prison. Another, that he took ill on a train returning to the Crimea in 1932. He was taken off the carriage, died nearby, and was buried in an unmarked grave like so many other figures in this family history. Whatever the truth, I will always be in his debt.

I never did track down the coffer of medals that Baboota promised was waiting for me in Moscow. I did find a consolation prize, however, in Le Général's military service record, which is preserved in the military-historical archives. In it were listed all the decorations he received from the Russian government as well as from Britain, France, China, Bulgaria, Montenegro, and Bokhara.

Perhaps my greatest discovery was one I made only very recently: my Russian friends, in my absence, go regularly to Vagankovskoye Cemetery to palce flowers on Frolov's grave.

A Note on Sources
&
Appendices

✍ A Note on Sources

One peculiarity of a centralized government with a highly developed bureacuracy is that it generates many documents, especially about individuals who fall into trouble with the authorities. I was amazed to discover how much material is available on the Decembrist uprising, its prelude and aftermath. These materials include Nicholas I's recollections of his questioning of suspects; his remarks as recorded by contemporaries, such as the historian N. K. Shilder and the French observer the Marquis de Custine; interrogatories of the Commission of Inquiry and reports of the czar's Third Department (secret police); correspondence of various prison commandants; and, of course, the copious memoirs of the Decembrists themselves, published at the turn of the century. The East Siberian Book Publishers at Irkurtsk are currently bringing out out an important set of Decembrist recollections, the Polar Star series.

To describe Frolov's encounter with Czar Nicholas, I drew on five separate descriptions: the account in P. M. Golovachev's *Dekabristy, 86 Portretov* (Moscow, 1906); my father's version, published in the *Open Road* magazine (Boston, Mass., 1924); Alexander Manganari's handwritten narrative of November 1925; an unsigned typewritten account in the Frolov file in the Central State Archives of Art and Literature in Moscow (File 2560); and an oral rendition by my uncle Michael Daniloff in March 1981. All these reports are substantially the same, evidently because they emanated from Frolov himself. Czar Nicholas made no reference to Frolov in his recollections, which were published in *Krasnyi Archiv*, Vol. 6 (Moscow, 1924), and his only reaction of which I am aware is the paper with his instructions: "Imprison and hold under severe conditions."

The Manganari manuscript is the key to understanding Frolov the man. His grandson's invaluable gift provides a generous insight into the Frolov clan, complete with quotations from family conversations, which reproduce Yevdokiya's vernacular speech and offer other colorful descriptions. The vast majority of quotations attributed to Frolov in this book come from Manganari. Yet the manuscript must be used with caution. Manganari had far less access than I did to primary and secondary sources, and he made innumerable mistakes. Consequently, I have tried to corroborate his assertions and dates with other sources whereever possible.

Information on Alexander Frolov can be found in the multivolume series *Vosstaniye Dekabristov (The Decembrist Uprising)*, published by the Soviet Academy of Sciences from 1925 through the present day. The original documents of this series are held in the Central State Archives of the October Revolution, and Frolov's papers are in File 48. The Central State military-Historical Archives in Moscow houses the documents relating to Frolov's incarceration in the Peter and Paul Fortress, his dispatch to Siberia, his arrival at Chita and, later, at Petrovsky Zavod. The Central State Archives of Literature and Art preserves the Frolov file, which contains the manganari manuscript and various assorted papers, including a family tree and photographs that I contributed. The Martyanov Museum in Minusinsk and the Minusinsk archives contain papers about Frolov's exile in Shusha, including the list of items he carried with him. The archives in Krasnoyarsk preserves court documents relating to the disposition of Frolov's land, which he abandoned when he returned to Russia, as well as references to the death of his two infant sons. I presume that archives in Kiev, the Crimea, and Irkutsk would yield more information, but I was not able to reach them. The museums at Chita and Petrovsky Zavod have few materials relating to my ancestor. I was pleased to hear, however, that the museum at Petrovsky has planted individual fir trees to commemorate each Decembrist held there, including Alexander Frolov.

In transliterating Russian names into English, my editors and I have adhered to the principle of accessibility to the general reader rather than any academic system of rendering Russian names. I note, too, that in the nineteenth century, Russia still adhered to the Julian calendar, which had fallen thirteen days behind the Western Gregorian calendar. Therefore, all dates before the Russian Revolution are given in the old, Julian style.

I would like to add a word about the way I approached the reconstruction of the Zakharov-Daniloff affair. Naturally, I collected and studied the numerous written and televised media reports from August 30 through September 30, 1986. In addition, *U.S. News and World Report* gave me complete access to its raw files for this period, which contain Ruth's unedited "Diary of Anguish" and numerous messages between the Moscow bureau and Washington as well as related reporting generated in Washington.

At Lefortovo, I kept notes on the interrogation in the green notebook that Colonel Sergadeyev gave me; although I had to relinquish this record on leaving prison, the exercise helped fix events in my mind. When I was released, I immediately made sketches of my cell and Sergadeyev's office; outlined a chronology, and drew up a list of every statement, important or unimportant, which I could recall from Sergadeyev, Commandant Petrenko, Stas Zenin, and others. In the following weeks, I tried to place each of these quotes in an expanded chronology, which guided me in drawing up the outline for this book and to which I frequently referred while writing. I supplemented my memory by interviewing in Washington many of the American officials involved in unraveling the affair from their posts in Washington and Moscow.